BACKGROUNDS TO AUGUSTAN POETRY: GALLUS, ELEGY AND ROME

BACKGROUNDS TO AUGUSTAN POETRY: GALLUS ELEGY AND ROME

DAVID O. ROSS, Jr
Associate Professor of Classics
University of Michigan

CAMBRIDGE UNIVERSITY PRESS

CAMBRIDGE

LONDON · NEW YORK · MELBOURNE

Published by the Syndics of the Cambridge University Press
The Pitt Building, Trumpington Street, Cambridge CB2 1RP
Bentley House, 200 Euston Road, London NW1 2DB
32 East 57th Street, New York, NY 10022, USA
296 Beaconsfield Parade, Middle Park, Melbourne 3206, Australia

Library of Congress Catalogue Card Number: 74-31782

ISBN: 0 521 20704 5

First published 1975

Printed in Great Britain
by W & J Mackay Limited, Chatham

Contents

GENITORIBUS MEIS

Preface

The arguments and conclusions in this book are intended for scholars, but I have tried to present the material in such a way as to be intelligible and even helpful to graduate students and, perhaps, undergraduates. I hope that serious students of Latin poetry accept with patience the pages in each chapter that are a general introduction or summary, and that other classical readers will find their way as easily as they can through the discussions of details on which my generalities are based.

The troublesome question of reference to the work of other scholars is related. As a general rule, I have tried to cite either the first substantive discussion of any particular relevant question or a recent discussion from which a student can find his way back through the previous literature: on very few points have I tried to present anything like a full introductory bibliography. There is much work of real worth that unfortunately I have not been able to cite, and conversely I have referred to some work (representing the *communis opinio*) I consider of little value, but I hope the balance and economy so achieved outweighs both these faults. Finally, of course, I cannot pretend to have read more than a fraction of what has been written on Augustan poetry and its antecedents.

A large part of this book was written during the academic year 1970–71: I am indebted to the Committee for the Morse Fellowships in the Humanities, Yale University, for a grant making that year's uninterrupted work possible.

Many friends, colleagues, and students have helped me shape my ideas. R. O. A. M. Lyne and J. Bramble shared with me their own enthusiasm for Gallus at a particularly crucial time; their conversation encouraged me to think that even if my conclusions were wrong, my questions were not irrelevant. H. D. Jocelyn read a draft of this book with his usual care, learning, and perceptiveness. Mistakes of all sorts necessarily remain, but at least I have made a fair number of them knowingly. Finally, my thanks are due to Janalyn Gibb for her expert preparation of the manuscript; and to the Syndics and staff of the Cambridge University Press.

Ann Arbor, Michigan   D.O.R.
October 1974

I

Introduction:
from Catullus to Gallus

This book is a somewhat specialized history of Augustan poetry. It is specialized in that it does not attempt to cover or present a synopsis of the most important questions concerning the poets of the period or to provide a comprehensive guide to the interpretation of their poetry; only a few questions are discussed, and only a few works are considered, with the result, inevitably, that the argument may seem to some one-sided or even distorted.[1] Yet it is a history in that it presents a literary background for the Augustan poets. Attempts to write biography, both in antiquity and by modern scholars, by abstracting biographical information from the poems themselves, are now generally considered dangerous and futile; this book is essentially an attempt to write poetic biography and, while there is nothing new in its method or approach, may be considered equally futile on similar grounds. It can be argued, however, that the Augustan poets were not primarily concerned with presenting autobiographical details in their work (the opposite, in fact, is more often clear – that they purposely constructed poetic *personae* having no relation to their real lives), but that they *were* concerned in what they wrote with the work of previous poets and of their contemporaries. Augustan poetry, like Alexandrian, was intensely self-conscious.

There are three major concerns in these pages. The first is the figure of Cornelius Gallus, an important poet in his own right and time and still important now: he alone supplies us with the transition from the generation of Catullus to the Augustans, a necessary link lost with his poetry. He stands as the first Latin elegist, without whose four books of *Amores* we are at a serious disadvantage when we read the elegists who wrote as they did largely because he had written as he had. He had been as well a friend of Virgil, with whom, as a reading of Eclogues VI and X suggests, he had discussed and shaped many of the ideas that were to set the course of subsequent poetry. I have assumed for Gallus, therefore, an importance

[1] For instance, Virgil's *Georgics*, perhaps the most Augustan poem of all, is referred to only in passing in these pages, and Ovid's *Amores* likewise plays a very small part in my discussions of elegy; but I hope my view of such poems will be apparent from the passages and works treated in more detail.

far greater than that indicated by most of our literary histories and have tried to find traces of and clues about him where they are most likely to exist – admittedly a hazardous occupation – and then from such evidence to reconstruct in outline not so much *what* he wrote, but *why* he wrote. Again, I have not tried to include here all that might be said or imagined about Gallus' poetry, but rather only that which contributes with some degree of probability to an understanding of extant Latin poetry.

My second concern has been with the origin and development of elegy, a question debated and discussed largely with the same assumptions and on the same terms for over three-quarters of a century. My assumptions about Gallus' poetry have provided certain premises for thinking about Propertius' start and development as an elegist, and for questioning the validity of considering elegy essentially as love poetry, in which subjectivity is the necessary ingredient. The origin of Latin elegy is of far more than scholarly or historical interest, for on our view of the question depends our approach to and reading of Propertius, Tibullus, and Ovid.

My third concern has been to sketch a historical unity that I have come to see in Augustan poetry. There is an opposition or conflict between the professed poetics of the Augustan poets and what most of them (at least) came eventually to write about. In the case of their forerunner Catullus this opposition (now, perhaps, largely resolved) has been seen as that between the learned Alexandrian poet and the poet of passionate personal experience. Virgil began his career as a 'neoteric' but finally produced the national epic. Propertius wrote at first as the subjective lover moved to personal expression but ended as the *Romanus Callimachus* writing on patriotic themes; what then of Horace, who rejected neoteric nonsense (we are led to understand) and became Augustus' poet laureate? From Catullus on, poets professed themselves on artistic grounds unable or unwilling to sing of *reges et proelia*; and modern readers have seen a similar conflict between love and art. Much of what follows here is an attempt to sort out the real from the illusory in such oppositions, to observe the inevitable but unintended contradictions that appear when inherited poetic creeds are used for new purposes.

This book views Augustan poetry as a natural growth in the soil prepared by Catullus. We need, I think, a clearer conception of 'neoteric' poetry, what the term (or the idea, as he may never have heard the term) meant to Catullus, what the poetry and poetic ideals of Catullus, Calvus, and Cinna meant to Gallus and Virgil in, say, 45 B.C. and again to Virgil and Horace twenty years later. We need to consider carefully the development of poetry in a period when so much was happening so rapidly and in which poets were so aware of the innovations of their immediate predecessors and knew the work of their contemporaries so intimately. These poets saw themselves not as isolated innovators, but as the latest representatives of a purposefully selected succession of antecedents, giving new life and purpose to an established inheritance. It is with this genealogy that we are primarily concerned.

The question 'Who were the neoterics?' naturally demands an answer, but none can be given. It was Cicero who supplied the name 'new poets', but what poets he may have had in mind cannot be known.[1] With the exception of Catullus, no poet of the period is represented by more than a handful of fragments that afford little idea of the nature of their work,[2] and if there was some sort of school centered around Valerius Cato, there is no good indication that Catullus was any part of it.[3] Only one thing is clear, that Catullus, Calvus, and Cinna were poets of importance, knew each other well, and read each other's work – not necessarily a school, but certainly a group of friends sharing interests and the excitement of discovery. Rather than to speculate further on the relationships of other names we happen to know, it is more productive to assess the nature and purpose of this new movement, to which the term 'neoteric' will be applied largely as a convenience to designate what we can know of the new poetry from Catullus.

Certain characteristics of the new poetry have been singled out but often are misleadingly applied to poets who had no real share in the new

[1] In 50 B.C. he concocted a one-line parody, a spondaic and learned hexameter, for the amusement of Atticus, granting him permission to sell it as his own 'si cui voles τῶν νεωτέρων' (*Ad Att.* 7.2.1); in 46 B.C. (*Orat.* 161) he mentioned that the '*poetae novi*' regard suppression of final *-s* as inelegant (*subrusticum*); and in the next year (*Tusc.* 3.45) he defended Ennius against the scorn of the '*cantores Euphorionis*'. It seems to me likely that the term 'neoterics' is Cicero's own: the context of the letter to Atticus, with its Greek, suggests a man pleased with his own verbal cleverness rather than one using an accepted designation for a new school of poets, nor need his other two remarks suggest the existence of any school.

[2] See the useful collection of A. Traglia, *Poetae Novi*, Poetarum Latinorum Reliquiae vol. 8 (Rome, 1962), with basic bibliography for each poet and a balanced introduction.

[3] The assumption of a school rests with the figure of Valerius Cato, whom Furius Bibaculus (probably, at least – see Traglia, *Poetae Novi*, 64–5) referred to as *Cato grammaticus, Latina Siren,* | *qui solus legit ac facit poetas*, and again as . . . *unicum magistrum,* | *summum grammaticum, optimum poetam.* (Cf. Suet. *De Gramm.* 11.2, *docuit multos et nobiles visusque est peridoneus praeceptor maxime ad poeticam tendentibus, ut quidem apparere vel his versiculis potest*, citing then the lines quoted here first; but Suetonius' tentative deduction – indicated as such by the phrases *visusque est* and *ut quidem apparere vel his versiculis potest* – is obviously of little value.) Inevitably Catullus has been sent to Cato's school, but all (including the identity of the Cato in poem 56) is pure speculation.

movement:[1] characteristics of meter, language and diction, form, and content are illuminating but generally can be used only to exclude, when they are absent, a poem or poet from a movement, group, or tradition. Consideration of external characteristics has often led scholars to consider Laevius, for instance, as an important forerunner of the neoterics, or even as a neoteric.[2] Laevius experimented with language and meter, wrote with erudition, seems to have been concerned with the psychology of his heroines, and used a number of novel shorter forms of verse; and even Cicero – and not just in his translation of Aratus – can be shown to have qualified as a neoteric as early as 86 B.C. according to definitions of neoteric meter, language, forms, and content. Then, too, the variety of Catullus' poetry presents us with such a diversity of such characteristics as to make strict definition impossible or valueless. Catullus and almost certainly Calvus and Cinna were not altogether innovative, but they did put recent innovations to new purposes that were to lead directly to the achievement of the Augustans. Their real contribution cannot perhaps be defined, but it can be described.

What the neoterics discovered was the poet's place in poetry. There are two aspects of this discovery: the individuality of the poet in his own poems, and his place in the poetry of the past. In the one case the poet was now audible in his own poetry; I do not mean simply that Catullus discovered subjective love poetry, but rather that the personality of the poet finds expression in, or is an important part of, whatever he writes. The epigrams of Aeditus, Licinus, or Catulus could have been written by anyone; a poem of Catullus can be the work of no one else. On a different but related level, the neoterics saw in an entirely new light the position of the poet in relation to the poetry of the past. The Roman poet was no longer a translator or an imitator, but a new, and again individual, voice within an established succession.[3]

[1] C. J. Fordyce, for instance, in his article 'Alexandrianism, Latin' in the recent revision of the *Oxford Classical Dictionary* (1970), lists four 'outstanding characteristics' of neoteric verse: '(1) the development of new genres, especially "epyllion", elegy, and epigram, all miniature forms replacing the large-scale epic and drama; (2) a regard for form, for concinnity and symmetry in language and metre...; (3) the cult of erudition, seen in the vogue of didactic verse, in wealth of mythological allusion, and in the search for novelty in story-telling; (4) the emergence of a subjective and personal way of writing – in elegiac and lyric a new individualism, in narrative a sentimental treatment and a psychological interest.'

[2] E.g. most recently, J. Granarolo, *D'Ennius à Catulle* (Paris, 1971). I have argued against such a view in *Style and Tradition in Catullus* (Cambridge, Mass., 1969), 155–60. This first chapter is based for the most part on arguments and evidence presented in my monograph, to which, in fact, it might stand as a conclusion.

[3] Ennius, for example, saw himself in his *Annales* as a second Homer, a view reflected in every detail of his verse; the neoterics, however, and later the Augustan poets, never

4

What this two-fold discovery meant can be seen better by looking at three reasons for it. First, of course, is the matter of individual genius, the sudden appearance of poets capable of poetry and not merely of verse. Second, the neoterics saw in Alexandrian poetry, and especially in Calli-machus, what had not been seen before – not simply form or content to be reproduced or imitated, but rather the expression of certain poetic principles that were strikingly relevant and applicable. Finally, these poets had at their disposal, for the first time, a poetic technique which they could adapt and develop further to turn the resources of Latin to new ends. We should go further into these reasons before turning to the results of the discovery.

The first poets at Rome were in effect professional writers – Livius Andronicus, Naevius, Ennius, the dramatists – and professionals con-tinued to find support in the first century B.C. (Archias is a good example). Paid writers may or may not be men of genius (Ennius was), but they are always subject to the demands of their audience and to the necessity of selling what they produce: what this must have meant for the beginnings of Latin literature can be gathered by comparing Terence's audience with that which attended the productions at the festival of Dionysus at Athens or listened to Pindar's Odes; and the difficulties which patronage often brings with it can be seen from the career of Naevius. At the end of the second century we find another recognizable group of poets – amateurs, such as Lutatius Catulus, consul with Marius in 102 B.C., who not only supported professional writers but dabbled in verse themselves. Roman society was changing rapidly, and it is partly due to social change that an entirely different sort of poet emerged toward the middle of the first century. Catullus was a full-time poet of independent means: it is highly unlikely that even a few decades earlier a man of good social standing and ambition would have come to Rome with any intention other than to enter upon the legal and military ladder to political prominence; yet Catullus, as far as we know, never argued a case in a court of law, never ran for office, and only half-heartedly joined the retinue of a provincial governor. It had become possible for such a man to consider poetry a career. Others who had more of a stake in public life, such as Calvus and perhaps Cinna, could also regard poetry as something more than an

imagined themselves becoming their exemplars, but rather were independent individuals following in a tradition established by their models. Ennius was engaged in the same task as Homer had been, and in this respect can be said to be an imitator; but Propertius, for instance, even as the *Romanus Callimachus*, never saw his relation to Callimachus in such a way. The implications of this essential difference between the neoterics and their Roman predecessors (one which they perhaps never formulated, but which the Augus-tans did) will I hope become clearer in what follows.

evening's entertainment. When Catullus came to Rome, poetry was no longer the preserve of the professional and could be viewed by anyone of inclination, talent, and means as a serious calling.

A change in social conditions and expectations, however, will not in itself explain the emergence of the new poets: something not available before provided a definite reason why men like Catullus and Calvus could devote themselves seriously to poetry and regard composition as more than a pastime. Callimachus, suddenly appreciated and understood as he had not been previously at Rome, supplied that reason.[1] Parallels can be seen between the circumstances of Callimachus and the Alexandrians and the situation of the neoterics: what had led Callimachus to formulate poetic principles describing and governing the work of a small group of Alexandrian poets was precisely what appealed to Catullus and others. Alexandrian poetry rediscovered human scale: Hesiod replaced Homer as a model, shorter forms of verse replaced epic. We are inclined to misunderstand Callimachus' scholarship and even to resent his learning, but what is significant about it is that in such a way the poet assumed complete control of his poetry, receiving the past not with passive awe but actively manipulating his inheritance so as to make it his own. The Alexandrian poet thus found his identity, both within a literary tradition and in his own poetry: no longer a faceless producer of endless imitative lines, he became the initiated priest of Apollo, proud of his own personality, fully in control of his own work, a small craftsman rather than a laborer in a machine shop. The significance of such a poet was suddenly recognized at Rome, and so apt were the terms Callimachus had devised that many of them could be taken over with little change. But there is one striking aspect of the neoteric discovery of Callimachus that supplies the key to his sudden and lasting importance at Rome and which has not, I think, been recognized clearly enough. Actual parallels to Callimachus (lines or passages closely imitated or even translated, forms copied, poems adapted) are surprisingly few in the Latin poets. Catullus, for instance, refers to Callimachus as *Battiades* twice (65.16, 116.2), with a similar suggestion in poem 7 (*et Batti veteris sacrum sepulcrum*, 6), translates the *Lock of Berenice* (poem 66), and refers to a Callimachean poetic topic in poem 95 (with 95[b]): otherwise there are only scattered suggestions of Callimachus.[2] Similarly, the Augustan

---

[1] On Callimachus and the *poetae novi*, and on the role Parthenius must have played after 73–65 B.C., see W. V. Clausen, 'Callimachus and Latin Poetry', *GRBS* 5 (1964), 181–96.

[2] Cf. for instance Cat. 80 and Call. *Epigram* 30 (Pfeiffer), or Cat. 70 and Call. *Epigram* 25; in both examples it is important to note that Catullus is making free use of, rather than translating or even imitating, the Callimachean epigrams.

poets make use of a strictly limited number of Callimachean passages in their own poetry, mostly those of a programmatic content. What is surprising and novel is that a model no longer meant imitation but rather was a justification of individual and personal expression: the importance of Callimachus for the neoterics lies in the fact that he supplied a set of precepts that not only allowed but demanded such expression.

A third fundamental reason for the sudden emergence of the new poetry is the discovery of a style capable of the range of expression required by the new poets, and here again Callimachus' precedent must have seemed singularly appropriate and fortunate. Modern criticism has been too ready to regard certain stylistic innovations in Catullus merely as affected mannerisms, but consideration of different aspects of Catullus' style soon leads to the conclusion that he had a clear idea of what he wanted to achieve and how best he could do it. Callimachus had available the infinitely rich resources of Greek poetry, upon which he drew with the interests of a scholar: the natural evolution of the Greek literary language from Homer to his own contemporaries, the diversity of poetic dialects, the variety of myth and allusion developed during a long literary history, furnished him in a retrospective age with the raw material for the density and intricacy of his poetry. No such background was available to the neoterics, who had to supply what was lacking. Ennius had shown in his exuberant way how the language and meter of Homer could be reproduced in Latin, and such experiments in various genres continued, reaching a particular peak of frenzy with Laevius' attempts to reproduce certain trends in Hellenistic poetry. But it was the task of the neoteric poets, as we can see from Catullus, to refine and purify previous excesses, to shape and form existing poetic diction while adding new elements as appropriate: for instance, urbane Latin was eminently suited to the subjects and tone of Catullus' polymetrics, just as in his formal epyllion (64) certain Alexandrian features of language and meter were exploited so as to fit neatly into the modified structure of Latin hexameter verse devised originally by Ennius. What made this process something new, and what gave it a significance that was to continue in importance far beyond this first generation of new poets, was the fact that it supplied what Callimachus had inherited, a rich diversity of poetic expression. Suddenly Latin poets had learned how to write whatever they wanted to express.

The common element in these three reasons is the individuality of the poet, how he appeared at Rome, what model showed him the place and function of an individual within an inherited literary tradition, and how individual expression was possible. The discovery of the neoterics – the poet's place in poetry – involves far more than the discovery of subjective love poetry on the one hand, or on the other the awareness of, and the ability to recreate, abstract and artificial poetic conventions. As an illustration of what the discovery meant, I would like now to discuss briefly Catullus' Lesbia.

There has been universal agreement concerning one point about Lesbia: she did exist, whoever she may have been.[1] I see no reason to question this assumption, or that Catullus had an affair with her, but I do wonder whether she is fairly represented in his poems, whether he wrote his love poems simply about his own experiences, and even whether he always wrote love poems about love. Our concern with the actual identity of Lesbia is similar to the attention that has been devoted to unraveling the strands of autobiography which we imagine make up the fabric of Catullus' poetry. A good case can be presented that Lesbia is a poetic fiction, and though I cannot argue it in detail here, I would like to suggest at least that we have been missing a great deal by reading the Lesbia poems simply as the record of an affair.[2]

If we think for a moment of the Lesbia of the polymetrics, we think first perhaps of her incomparable sophistication and wit: the girl of the reprobate of Formiae cannot be compared with her, at least by anyone with taste and discrimination: ... *decoctoris amica Formiani.* | *ten provincia narrat esse bellam?* | *tecum Lesbia nostra comparatur?* | *o saeclum insapiens et infacetum!* (43.5–8). The Lesbia of the sparrow poems, the recipient of the *basiationes* of poems 5 and 7 who is so pointed a contrast to the *senes severiores,* or the object of the elaborate literary joke of poem 36, this Lesbia seems to us so real and immediate a figure of fashionable Rome that it is something of a surprise, when we begin to look for specific characteristics, physical or otherwise, to find actually very little. We know, for instance, that the *decoctoris amica Formiani* had a big nose, ugly feet, eyes that were not black, squat fingers, wet lips, and a coarse tongue, but we have no descriptive physical details of Lesbia. I do not mean to imply, of course, that we can therefore conclude that Lesbia is an entirely

[1] For the latest review of Lesbia's identity, see T. P. Wiseman, *Catullan Questions* (Leicester, 1969), who after sensible discussion ultimately suspends judgement.
[2] The following pages are based mainly on two sections of my monograph *Style and Tradition,* 'Urbanitas and the Vocabulary of the Polymetrics', 104–12, and 'Lesbia and the Vocabulary of Political Alliance', 80–95, to which the reader is referred for particulars, background, and references to scholarly discussion of the topics.

fictional character – fictional characters need, and are normally granted, considerable characterizing detail, whereas figures of personal biography may neither require nor allow such description, particularly if they are publicly well-known.

My point is simply that our picture of the Lesbia of the polymetrics seems the consummation of a style, the representation of an idea rather than of an individual. What this idea was is not hard to discover, for the provenance of those terms with which Lesbia *is* characterized (though often by implication rather than directly) is clear. In the poems I have just referred to she is a representation of *urbanitas*, that quality Catullus valued so highly in his friends, in life, and in poetry. So pervasively do the characteristics of *urbanitas* color the world of the polymetrics that it is impossible to distinguish any sphere to which the terms naturally belong from any other to which they are applied metaphorically. We know from Cicero, for instance, that Clodia's smart set did consider themselves *faceti*, *delicati*, *dicaces*, *venusti*, just as the same set appears in Catullus; but much of the actual language of the polymetrics is demonstrably that of the new circle of bright young men, and Catullus characterizes his *nugae* (meaning his polymetrics) in the same way. We have only to think of poem 50, which equates the writing of this poetry with the sensations and mental state of being in love, to realize how thoroughly the values of this new circle of society pervade all aspects of Catullus' world. When we read of Lesbia in these poems, then, we may not be reading about an individual, nor necessarily of personal experiences which led immediately to the expression of the poems, but rather of yet another figure, and yet another situation, exemplifying the ideal of *urbanitas*.

The diversity of Catullus' character, both as poet and person, has long impressed critics and scholars. Sophistication and wit, as he found them in society and expressed them in his poetry, may have fascinated his poetic imagination, but he was no intellectual playboy, by nature or circumstances, and we can see another very different side of his genius – more serious, traditional, and Roman. Here too Lesbia plays an important role.

In the epigrams 69–116 Catullus uses a very different set of terms to present his relation with Lesbia – the terminology of political alliance. That this is so should immediately alert us to an intriguing possibility. If the polymetrics 1–60 and the epigrams belong, as I believe, to two very different poetic traditions and are distinct in tone, expression, and purpose, then the different Lesbias presented in each group of poems may suggest that the poetic conception of his mistress preceded and controlled

9

any real experience Catullus may have lived through with the real Lesbia; and if this suggestion can plausibly be entertained, we may get a somewhat better idea of what his poetry was really about. To do this a quick review of the *amicitia* metaphor in the Lesbia epigrams is necessary.

It is difficult to know to what extent we are at liberty to recreate the affair chronologically, as has been done for so long as a matter of course and with such varying results. We are confronted with a series of poems on the affair, not as we have them arranged by Catullus as a cycle, but obviously representing different stages of a single experience: we may, then, describe the changing function of this particular terminology at such different stages without implying that any cycle or story was intended by the poet.

In poem 109 Catullus clearly presents his relationship with Lesbia in terms of a Roman *amicitia* – that is, a political alliance between equals: *ut liceat nobis tota perducere vita | aeternum hoc sanctae foedus amicitiae* (5–6). But here his doubts about the practicality of such an arrangement are all too evident: *di magni, facite ut vere promittere possit | atque id sincere dicat et ex animo...* (3–4). In a political alliance, a Roman statesman would have admitted, expediency is the most powerful element, that and cold obligation: sincerity has no place. Poem 87 too presents the metaphor: 'No woman can say that she is loved as much as is my Lesbia,' says Catullus simply in the first couplet, but in the second he substitutes for *amor* the terms of an *amicitia*: *nulla fides ullo fuit umquam foedere tanta* (3). The metaphor is both novel and real: the terms so common in an actual *amicitia* – *fides, officium, benevolentia, gratia* – seem eminently applicable and, on a certain level, expressive, when applied to an idealized relationship between lovers.

The metaphor, so apt at first, assumes, at a later stage, an aspect of impossibility. *Odi et amo: quare id faciam, fortasse requiris? | nescio, sed fieri sentio et excrucior* (85.1–2). When one party in a political *amicitia* had done dirt to another, had committed an *iniuria* – when, that is, political necessities had changed and it became expedient to sever the connection – nothing was easier than to break it off, more often than not coolly and with perfect composure. Lesbia's *iniuria*, her *culpa*, whatever it may have been, did not lead to any similar painless solution: the flaw in the metaphor of *amor* as an *amicitia* suddenly becomes all too apparent.

> nunc te cognovi: quare etsi impensius uror,
>   multo mi tamen es vilior et levior.
> qui potis est, inquis? quod amantem iniuria talis
>   cogit amare magis, sed bene velle minus.
>
>   (72.5–8)

Poems 72, 75, 76, and 85 (and probably 73 as well)[1] are all concerned with this paradox.

The impossibility in Catullus' simultaneous loving and loathing (the loving being his continuing *amor*, the loathing the result of the shattered *amicitia*) is, of course, inexplicable and paradoxical only on one level – that of the fictional situation. The rhetorical questions that point up the impossibility – *qui potis est, inquis?* or *quare id faciam, fortasse requiris* – are dramatically fitting and proper. Poetically, however, there is nothing unreal or difficult whatsoever. The *amicitia* metaphor continues in this later stage to be effective poetically precisely because it is ineffective to the point of impossibility in the imagined dramatic situation. So effective is the metaphor, in fact, and so much attention does Catullus give to working out all possible permutations of the theme at this stage, that I feel sure it was conceived with this very end in mind: that is, Catullus did not write 87 and 109 (the two epigrams which simply set forth his relationship with Lesbia as an *amicitia*) and then find, as the affair reached its unhappy climax, that he had ready to hand a means of expressing his inevitable and human feelings of simultaneous love and disgust, but rather he must have had both stages of his affair in mind when the *amicitia* metaphor first occurred to him.

Two simple inferences are possible at this point. First, that Catullus wrote all these poems (and perhaps others) about Lesbia after the affair had turned sour: the poems are not a day to day account of a love that never did run smooth, but a later reconstruction. Such an inference denies us any right to view the poems, strictly speaking, as autobiography: we must read them only as the recreation of states of mind and emotions, and we may well suspect that the situation presented in the poems is one we may therefore properly call fiction. The second possible inference is more interesting, and is the one I would like to follow up more closely: if we can say that the *amicitia* metaphor influenced and controlled the composition of this group of poems, then it may be that the entire dramatic situation presented by the poems is to some extent simply a fictional context allowing the metaphor a means of expression.

The terminology of an *amicitia* occurs, of course, in other poems than the Lesbia epigrams, and not so metaphorically. In poem 30 Alfenus is accused of having violated the sacred trust inherent in an *amicitia*:

---

[1] O. Skutsch (*BICS* 16 (1969), 41–3) has proposed reading *quae* (=Lesbia) for V's *qui* at 73.6, an emendation made previously by Birt (*Philol.* 63 (1904), 469); it is, I think, almost certainly correct (the sequence 72, 73, 75, 76 may indicate that the editor of the book read *quae*) and would set the poem among those to which it properly belongs.

Alfene immemor atque unanimis false sodalibus, | *...iam me prodere, iam non dubitas fallere, perfide?* | *nec facta impia fallacum hominum caelicolis placent* (1, 3–4). But the gods, and *Fides*, will take notice and cause the offender to repent. Alfenus was not the only friend to have betrayed Catullus. Rufus is so accused in 77: *Rufe mihi frustra ac nequiquam credite amice* | *...heu heu nostrae pestis amicitiae* (1, 6); and a Quintius seems likely to act in a similar fashion in poem 82. The infamous Gellius is attacked in poem 91 for his betrayal and violation of *Fides*: *Non ideo, Gelli, sperabam te mihi fidum* | *in misero hoc nostro, hoc perdito amore fore...* (1–2). On the positive side, Caelius is supported in poem 100 precisely because he had passed the test of loyalty (*nam tua nobis* | *perspecta est igni tum unica amicitia*, 5–6): in the working of a political alliance, one *beneficium* deserves another, mutual support is expected and required. Likewise in poem 102 Cornelius can expect Catullus' loyalty: *Si quicquam tacito commissum est fido ab amico,* | *cuius sit penitus nota fides animi...* (1–2).

Quite clearly, then, one of Catullus' chief concerns was the working of that formal and typically Roman code of behavior that governed and made possible everyday relationships between men. Trust and betrayal are extremely important to him, and any violation of the code moves him to the verge of anger and despair. But something far larger than personal hurt was involved in Catullus' sense of betrayal. It is easy to forget that Catullus was a Roman of the late Republic: his modernity and apparent immediacy of feeling and emotion are seductive. We view the elder Cato's morality as a quaint source of anecdote and consider it miles removed from Catullus' directness and passion, but the Roman concern with social morality was very much a part of the poet's intellectual and emotional character. For some years before Catullus wrote, Romans had been wondering, with their own peculiar cast of thought so un-Hellenic, what had happened to the *mos maiorum*: it was obvious to all who thought about it – and most, it would seem, did – that not only had the national character changed, but that social and political institutions were not functioning as they once had in an often imaginary past. Sallust made a system of the terms Romans like Cato had been using for some time, and perhaps a great part even of his system was not of his own devising.[1]

In Catullus we can often see the contemporary Roman's preoccupation with a pristine past. For instance, in poem 34, the hymn to Diana, the final stanza invokes the goddess' protection of Romulus' people, as it

[1] See, for instance, D. C. Earl, *The Political Thought of Sallust* (Cambridge, 1961).

was of old: *sis quocumque tibi placet | sancta nomine, Romulique, | antique ut solita es, bona | sospites ope gentem* (21–4). Any mention of Romulus or Remus was bound to conjure up thoughts of lost innocence, of Rome whose strength was as the strength of ten because her heart was then pure, and any suggestion of that day would lead just as inexorably to the decadent present.[1] In poem 28 Memmius is told to be off to his *nobiles amicos*, the *opprobria Romuli Remique*. In poem 29 the effete Mamurra devours Gaul and Britain: *cinaede Romule, haec videbis et feres?* asks Catullus twice (5, 9), the implication being that Romulus does see and does put up with it, and thus is no better now than Mamurra himself. In poem 58 the mocking irony of the heroic *magnanimi Remi nepotes* is perfectly clear. And finally, from these contexts it should be plain that the address to Cicero in poem 49, *disertissime Romuli nepotum*, can only be sarcastic.

Another, far more suggestive, indication of Catullus' natural acceptance of Roman morality can be had from a glance at that most characteristic word, *virtus*. It occurs only in the epyllion 64 (5 times) and in poem 68 (once). The word occurs first in the lines (50–1) introducing the Theseus and Ariadne story: *haec vestis priscis hominum variata figuris | heroum mira virtutes indicat arte*. The coverlet is embroidered with the figures of the past (*priscis figuris*) and depicts the *virtutes* of the heroes with wonderful art. But what these *virtutes* are soon becomes clear: desertion, loss and betrayal, love and devotion scorned; as has become clear, Ariadne's story is Catullus' own.[2] Theseus' father reminds us of his son's *fervida virtus* later in the first lines of his speech (218), a *virtus* soon to lead to Aegeus' death. At the very beginning of the Fates' song in the second half of the poem, we meet with *virtutes* again (line 323), *o decus eximium magnis virtutibus augens...*, and twice subsequently, as events are played out in the prophecy, we realize what was meant, as the word recurs in connection with Achilles' deeds of blood and violence (lines 348 and 357). One could say that the subject of the epyllion is, in fact, *virtus*, that the poem illustrates the concept in Catullus' own life and times. From Achilles' Troy to the contemporary site is no long journey through time in the poet's mind: in the lines in poem 68 which make the transition from the mythical Troy of Protesilaus to the site of his brother's death, *virtus* is again prominent: *Troia (nefas!) commune sepulcrum Asiae Europaeque, | Troia virum et virtutum omnium acerba cinis* (89–90). In his

---

[1] I have found no trace at this time or before of the Romulus who will appear in Augustan poetry: the fratricide whose crime led to civil war, the source of a curse upon Rome.

[2] See M. C. J. Putnam, 'The Art of Catullus 64', *HSCP* 65 (1961), 165–205, and D. F. S. Thomson, 'Aspects of Unity in Catullus 64', *CJ* 57 (1961), 49–57.

epyllion Catullus sketches the outlines of the heroic past, a time when *virtus* was, or should have been, splendid and pure; but the details of his canvas are those of his own day and of his own experience.

Likewise, I think, we ignore a great deal if we regard the Lesbia epigrams simply as expressions of personal experience, for by employing the terminology of *amicitia*, Catullus extended the scope and significance of these poems just as surely as he did when he filled in the heroic outlines of his epyllion with contemporary and personal concerns. Just as desertion and betrayal, violence and slaughter, have become *virtutes*, so in these epigrams personal injury is constantly expressed in the terms of the code that made Rome's social and political life what it once was. *Fides, foedus, officium, benevolentia, gratia*, all suggest Rome's past just as splendidly as the Greek poetic past is recreated (to be redefined) in poem 64.

Roman piety (*pietas*) was essentially concerned with human, not divine, affairs: Roman religion did not explore celestial spheres but was concerned, typically, with the here and now, with the efficient and orderly functioning of the everyday world. Catullus so defines *pietas* in the first lines of poem 76:

> Siqua recordanti benefacta priora voluptas
>   est homini, cum se cogitat esse pium,
> nec sanctam violasse fidem, nec foedere nullo
>   divum ad fallendos numine abusum homines,
> multa parata manent in longa aetate, Catulle,
>   ex hoc ingrato gaudia amore tibi.
>
> (1–6)

The divine is only a function of the human: *fides* is called 'holy', *sancta*, and the divine will of the gods is provoked or respected only to the extent that a *foedus* between men is violated or observed. Catullus' regard for the sanctity of personal relationships is both thoroughly Roman and thoroughly personal, and as such is perhaps his single most important concern. Poem 76 may be read as the voice of one crying in the wilderness of his own day, when the structures of the past have fallen, when every law of the universe has suddenly been revealed as meaningless. But what 76 is *not* is good love poetry, unless, of course, one defines love poetry as that which allows affairs of the heart so secondary a place that they are almost forgotten. Lesbia, who is not named in the poem, has become only a shadow representing the iniquities of the present, and the affair itself is now a moving and affective synonym for betrayal of trust, for a general dissolution of human values. It has always been a vexing question, how Catullus was able to love his Lesbia 'as a father cherishes his sons and sons-in-law': *dilexi tum te non tantum ut vulgus amicam,* | *sed pater ut gnatos diligit et generos* (72.3–4); and I consider equally valid the question why a love-poet should imagine piety in the observation of his relationships with other men as any sort of qualification for fair treatment at the hands of his mistress. But if we can allow ourselves to be equally unromantic, we may understand that Catullus' unhappy affair becomes at times, though not always, a stage on which characters of far different dimensions, attributes, and relevance move and speak.

We have suggested, then, two aspects of Lesbia, each of which seems to be a coherent part of that group of poems in which it appears. In the polymetrics Lesbia is a figure representing and illustrating the new ideal of *urbanitas*; in the epigrams she has a different role, as an antagonist in a drama in which personal betrayal and loss are only a part of a larger scheme of political and social disintegration. I should say again that I see no reason to doubt that behind the Lesbia poems lies a real experience: my point is simply that these poems are not entirely the autobiography of an unhappy affair, but rather the expression of more universal, more characteristically Roman concerns. The idea of *amicitia* was of great importance to Catullus, though it was only one manifestation of a world gone wrong: the *amicitia* metaphor governed and shaped the Lesbia epigrams from the very beginning – to such an extent, I think, that Lesbia and the affair became secondary, as the finest of these poems, 76, shows clearly. Much of Catullus' love poetry (though not all of it) goes far beyond immediate experience, and this, perhaps, explains its lasting appeal and significance.

What is clear, I hope, from this discussion of Catullus' Lesbia is how, for the first time in Latin poetry, the deepest concerns of the individual poet have found complete and unified expression. Love poetry previously existed only as epigram molded on Hellenistic precedent, the work of amateurs such as Catulus, cold, flat, derivative, and hardly a personal expression of even the one emotion it pretended to convey. History and the Roman past had been the sphere of epic, and while continuing to provide subjects for opportunists such as Archias and the despised Volusius, had found more suitable expression in prose. Laevius' efforts were perhaps little more than impersonal word games, even when ample allowance is made for the particular interests of the sources for our knowledge of his verse. If any individual before Catullus had written about himself and his world, it was Lucilius in his satires, which, indicatively, owed the least of any genre practised at Rome to Greek precedent.

What the neoterics discovered is thus all the more impressive, and its importance for Augustan poetry cannot be underestimated.

As a group Catullus' epigrams 69–116, of all his poetry, have the closest ties with previous Latin verse, and it is worth reflection then that in many ways (in characteristic diction, in metrical practice, as well as in tone and content) these poems had the least importance for and influence on subsequent poetry. They can be characterized as direct and emotional in a manner that will not be found again. The next generation of poets was too fascinated with the possibilities of the new poetry to consider what Catullus' epigrams with their Roman inheritance had to offer, and when the Augustan poets became again concerned with Roman topics, it was no longer possible, and barely even conceivable, to write in such a direct and relatively unsophisticated way. That Latin poetry eventually became a sterile wasteland was due as much to the discoveries made by the neoterics as was the brilliance of Augustan poetry.

The possibilities for a thorough break with previous poetry, both in its substance and in its values, are most apparent in Catullus' polymetric poems 1–60. There is an obvious delight in language, reminding the reader of the delight of first discovery so remarkable in Ennius and Plautus; most characteristic of this language is its urbanity – the vocabulary, syntax, and undoubtedly the rhythms of the speech of the new generation of sophisticates. The precise wit of these poems contrasts sharply with the direct invective – often blatantly coarse – of the epigrams. It should not be forgotten that the new language in these poems is that of the poets themselves, and that the characteristic wit comes directly from their own conversations: almost every polymetric is, in fact, addressed to one of Catullus' friends or enemies – they are indeed *sermones*. But what forms the language and wit and makes the poems more than well-phrased anecdotes is the new impulse received from Callimachus, without which the taste and literary wit of the new poets would have been mere preciosity.

Catullus' longer poems 61–68 are the supreme achievement of the neoteric poet, the blending of contemporary idiom and individual expression with the Alexandrian example. The translation of the Lock of Berenice (66) is a demonstration that the new poetry can match effectively the range of subtlety of Callimachean verse. The two marriage poems (61 and 62) combine Greek and Roman elements at every level, in diction and meters as well as in content. 67 is more Roman and closer in content and style to the epigrams, and yet it too could not have been written without Catullus' polymetric experiments. The *Attis* (63) is in many ways the most Alexandrian of these poems: its subject (erotic psychology at its most unnatural) and presentation (the long speeches of the hero, connected by brief narrative passages) are reflected in the novelty of diction and meter. But two poems, 64 and 68, made most vividly clear what the new poetry offered.

We should remind ourselves again that subjective expression had no place in the higher genres of Greek poetry. In addition to the many other ways in which the epyllion conformed to and represented the canons of Alexandrian art and learning, not least important is its literary objectivity. We have no idea of the real nature of the epyllia composed by such as Calvus, Cinna, or Caecilius, and it may well be that the identity of the poet was entirely obscured in those works; but what is clear from Catullus' epyllion is that the abstract form itself allowed him a depth of expression possible in no other type of poetry. Poems 64 and 68 present more than ideas or generalized human emotions; the figures from myth in these poems respond to the emotions and conflicts of the poet himself. The epigrams are clearly the work of the individual, but their range of expression is limited; in the polymetrics the range of expression is extended in direct relation to the degree they make use of literary conventions, topics, suggestions, or whatever; but in the longer poems, and especially those in which art dominates, Catullus represents himself most truly. Lesbia and his brother's death are both the subjects of 68, and in his epyllion, as we have suggested above, love and loss are but aspects of themes far more universal and significant.

We need not expand upon and illustrate further this remarkable innovation, showing as well how style and technique contribute to personal expression, how neoteric interest in and awareness of the expressive possibilities of features of Greek and previous Latin poetry provided the means of reflecting accurately and subtly a range of literary emotions and allusions. The discovery of the poet's individuality was indeed something new in ancient literature – and something perhaps particularly Roman – not because poets had not spoken before of their own experiences, but because of the manner and form this new expression found. We must turn now to the figure of Cornelius Gallus with this background clearly in mind, trying to see who he was and what he wrote as an intermediary between Catullus and the poetry and poetics of the Augustans.

2

The Sixth Eclogue:
Virgil's poetic genealogy

By the time Virgil published his *Eclogues* – in 35 B.C., as now seems likely[1] – the course that Latin poetry was to follow for the next century had been firmly set. When Catullus died in 54 B.C. there were still a number of possibilities open: the first generation of new poets had broadened poetic horizons by their discoveries and experiments – in technique, in verse forms, and in subjects. It is hard to imagine what Latin poetry, even in the next generation, would have been like without their experiments and innovations; yet the very diversity of the new poetry makes it equally hard to predict a future course. But after 35 B.C. there remained only one way a poet could write, only one direction in which he could set out. Instead of a number of possibilities open to the poet, there was only one narrow road: the future of poetry suddenly became clear and definite, so much so that it soon was to cease to exist as a future at all.

Latin poetry matured almost overnight, and its brief maturity produced great achievement from men of genius and splendid poetry from good poets. The pages to follow will deal with two basic aspects of the achievement of the Augustan poets, how the sudden definition of poetry came about, and how it led easily and naturally to the expression of the deepest concerns of the time. The peace that came after September of 31 B.C. to a vast empire had been bought at tremendous cost, of which the last and largest payment had just been made; over the next few years it became more and more likely that stability and order had returned to stay, that the recent domination of fear and chaos was past for good. There have been few such times in Western history, and even fewer in which poets have been able to voice with complete conviction the profound relief and pride of achievement felt by the people. That Augustan poets were able to do so when the time came was the unlikely result of the discovery of Callimachus' narrow road some years before.

It may seem a paradox that the greatness of Augustan poetry was a

[1] See G. W. Bowersock, 'A Date in the *Eighth Eclogue*', *HSCP* 75 (1971), 73–80, and W. V. Clausen, 'On the Date of the *First Eclogue*', *HSCP* 76 (1972), 201–5.

direct result of a narrowing of poetic horizons, and even more a paradox that the poets who spoke for the national experience in the decade or so following the battle of Actium were able to do so only because in the preceding decade poetry had become private, personal, and esoteric. The previous chapter was a summary of what Catullus had accomplished, the discovery of the poet's place in poetry – the ability to write as an individual in both direct and (what was more important) abstract forms of verse, and the realization of a poetic history that included a role for the poet of the present. This realization, however, remained without clear definition or formulation until Virgil and Gallus in the next generation. From Catullus we look forward, and from the *Eclogues* back, to the process that set the course, and consequently we can see its evolution only dimly; but following the publication of Gallus' *Amores* and the completion of the *Eclogues*, there was only one position a serious poet could assume: how this single tradition was specified and what it meant for the poets who followed is the subject of this chapter.

It should be obvious that the Sixth Eclogue is largely concerned with poetry,[1] but it is far from obvious just what sort of poetry Virgil intends, and even less clear what he is saying about it. The twelve-line introduction takes the form of a *recusatio* (the refusal to write epic, *reges et proelia*, 3; *tristia bella*, 7) and includes three lines (3–5) translated directly from Callimachus' prologue to the *Aetia* – this, in fact, the first formal, fully-developed *recusatio* in Latin poetry. As a Callimachean statement it includes words denoting elegance and refinement (*deductum. . . carmen*, 5; *tenui. . . harundine*, 8) and neoteric lightness opposed to gravity (*ludere* vs *cum canerem*, 1 and 3). At the same time the poetry is to be pastoral (*Syracosio. . . versu*, 1; *silvas*, 2; *agrestem Musam*, 8; *myricae* and *nemus*, 10–11), obvious enough, perhaps, in a book of pastoral poetry, but emphasized by Virgil in the one important departure he has made from the Callimachean original: instead of Apollo's address to the poet concerning the fat sacrificial victim (as Callimachus had put it, 'ἀοιδέ, τὸ μὲν θύος ὅττι πάχιστον | θρέψαι', fr. 1.23–4 Pf.), Virgil's Apollo tells the shepherd to fatten his flock ('*pastorem, Tityre, pinguis | pascere oportet ovis*', 4–5).[2]

---

[1] For scholarly discussions and opinions concerning the questions raised here, see the bibliographical notes to the following: K. Büchner, *RE* 8.A.1 (1955), 1219–24; Z. Stewart, 'The Song of Silenus', *HSCP* 64 (1959), 179–205; W. Wimmel, *Kallimachos in Rom*, Hermes Einzelschriften 16 (1960), 132–47; J. P. Elder, '*Non iniussa cano*', *HSCP* 65 (1961), 109–25.

[2] R. Pfeiffer, 'Ein Neues Altersgedicht des Kallimachos', *Hermes* 63 (1928), 322.

The setting of what follows (Silenus' capture) is indeed pastoral, but the subject is not: Silenus is a seer, and reveals his secrets only after ritual binding.[1] The song itself, though containing enough pastoral suggestions and motifs to have led some critics to stress this aspect of it,[2] seems to have eluded all scholars in their attempts to discover its unity: cosmogony, psychotic love, and metamorphoses are hardly the most convenient and conventional subjects for pastoral. Yet here too poetry itself is obviously prominent:[3] it is stressed in the introductory scene (*carminis*, 18; *carmina...carmina*, 25; *canebat*, 31); the whole song is at its conclusion associated with Apollo (*quae Phoebo...meditante...ille canit*, 82–4); and central and prominent in the song is the ritual initiation of the poet Gallus:

> tum canit errantem Permessi ad flumina Gallum
> Aonas in montis ut duxerit una sororum,
> utque viro Phoebi chorus adsurrexerit omnis;
> ut Linus haec illi divino carmine pastor
> floribus atque apio crinis ornatus amaro
> dixerit: 'hos tibi dant calamos, en accipe, Musae,
> Ascraeo quos ante seni, quibus ille solebat
> cantando rigidas deducere montibus ornos.
> his tibi Grynei nemoris dicatur origo,
> ne quis sit lucus quo se plus iactet Apollo.'
>
> (64–73)

Much of the extensive literature on the Sixth Eclogue that deals with the unity of the themes of Silenus' song fails to find a satisfactory explanation for the intrusion of these lines, and conversely scholars primarily concerned with Gallus seldom deal in any detail with the context surrounding what is, with the Tenth Eclogue, our most important, and elusive, source for the poetry of Virgil's friend and contemporary.[4]

Few, I think, would not grant that there must be some reason behind the diversity of theme and subject in Silenus' song, and if we may also be allowed the assumption that poetry of some sort is a primary concern in

[1] See F. Klingner's clear recapitulation, *Virgil* (Zürich, 1967), 106.
[2] Elder, for instance, 'the poem may contain a brief...for his own kind of Latin pastoral' (p. 121); cf. his discussion of the pastoral motifs, HSCP 65 (1961), 116–20.
[3] Büchner stresses poetry as the central theme of the Eclogue ('Das Gedicht zeigt die Macht, Fülle, Verzauberung des Gesanges', p. 1223); cf. C. Becker, 'Virgils Eklogenbuch', *Hermes* 83 (1955), 317–18.
[4] The striking exception is F. Skutsch, *Aus Vergils Frühzeit* (Leipzig, 1901) and *Gallus und Vergil* (Leipzig, 1906). It may be fairly said that Skutsch is the only scholar to have dealt properly with both Gallus and the other themes of Silenus' song, and to have realized fully the importance of *Ecl.* 6 and 10 as a source for Gallus' poetry: his extreme and unwarranted inferences and conclusions, however, effectively scared subsequent scholars away from profitable inquiry along similar lines.

this Eclogue, then we may with equal validity expect a unity in Virgil's conception of poetry: it may be possible to find some thread to follow from the pastoral and the neoteric to poetry as revelation, to cosmogony and science, to the strange and unnatural. We may begin conveniently at the center, with the details of Gallus' initiation.

Gallus, wandering by the river Permessus, was led by one of the Muses to the Aonian mountains, where the whole chorus of the Muses (*Phoebi . . . chorus omnis*, 66) rose in greeting and Linus, with a speech, presented him with the pipes of Hesiod, on which he was to sing of the Grynean Grove. Why should Linus be given a role of such importance? Who is he, and what does he have to do with Apollo and the Muses, with the pipes of Hesiod, and particularly with Gallus? Modern commentators are of little or no help with such questions: 'There seems no evidence that Linus was supposed ever to have been a shepherd, but it was natural for a pastoral poet to conceive of him as such.'[1]

It was not natural at all. Linus, at different places and at different times, had assumed several forms: as poet and musician (commonly the son of Apollo and sometimes of a Muse) he had come to be associated with the dirge, credited with the invention of certain instruments and even of the hexameter, and often appears as a semi-divine singer much like Musaeus or Orpheus. Linus' role as mythical singer could be taken for granted by Virgil, as in the Fourth Eclogue:

> non me carminibus vincet nec Thracius Orpheus,
> nec Linus, huic mater quamvis atque huic pater adsit,
> Orphei Calliopea, Lino formosus Apollo.
>
> (55-7)

But only here in the Sixth Eclogue does Linus appear as a shepherd: if we can see why and how Virgil has created this new role for Linus, presumably we will be closer to understanding why he acts as spokesman for the Muses at Gallus' initiation.

In Theocritus (24.105-6) Linus had made a brief appearance as teacher 'of letters' to the young Heracles:

---

[1] J. Conington *ad loc.* On the Linus figure in Greek religion and myth, see the articles by Abert and Kroll, *RE* 13.1 (1926), 715-17. Stewart notes Linus' associations with the lament and suggests (*HSCP* 64 (1959), 193) that 'it would be not unreasonable to assume that Linus is meant to represent the earlier and simpler form of elegy, that which was later combined with a Hesiodic tradition to produce, in Hellenistic times, the kind of poem which Gallus is urged to write.' But the parsley crown need not be a symbol of mourning, and there is no particular reason to see in Virgil's Linus the inventor of the dirge which then becomes real elegy.

γράμματα μὲν τὸν παῖδα γέρων Λίνος ἐξεδίδαξεν,
υἱὸς Ἀπόλλωνος μελεδωνεὺς ἄγρυπνος ἥρως.

This too is an odd role for Linus:[1] he has, in fact, become an Alexandrian singer, literate and learned. The epithet ἄγρυπνος indicates the labored polish demanded of the new poets of Alexandria, a title of distinction.[2] μελεδωνεύς, 'guardian', remains unexplained in this context: perhaps it contains a pun on μέλος, referring to the usual tradition where Linus is indeed a musician; if so, it would be a characteristic Alexandrian touch.

More to the point, though, is the Linus Virgil found in the first book of Callimachus' Aetia (fr. 26–8 Pf.).[3] The mythographer Conon, in his Diageseis (published between 36 B.C. and A.D. 17), gives us a full account which must depend on Callimachus: Linus, son of Apollo and the Argive princess Psamathe, daughter of Crotopus, was raised by a shepherd and torn apart by the shepherd's dogs one day; a plague sent by Apollo led to the propitiation of Psamathe and Linus by the festival Arneis (the lamb festival), to the naming of the month Arneus ('because Linus had been reared amongst lambs'), and to the dirge.[4] Here was an easy aetiological explanation not only for the dirge, but also for the custom of killing stray dogs on the day of the festival: the names Arneis and Arneus were more troublesome, but finally yielded when Linus, the bastard exposed as an infant, was found to have been brought up by a convenient shepherd.

It is a pity we have so little of Callimachus' version of this story. One couplet, though, is eloquent:

ἄρνες τοι, φίλε κοῦρε, συνήλικες, ἄρνες ἑταῖροι
ἔσκον, ἐνιαυθμοὶ δ' αὔλια καὶ βοτάναι.

(fr.27 Pf.)

On this couplet Pfeiffer observes, 'in anaphora post diaeresin bucolicam "pastorale" quiddam inest cf. Theocr. 1.64 et passim': it may be that Callimachus has used this device purposely to mark the bucolic nature of the passage.[5] We may suppose that Callimachus developed the pas-

---

[1] See A. S. F. Gow's comment *ad loc.* Theocritus is here unusual in that Linus teaches γράμματα to Heracles (also reported by 'Suidas', s.v. Λίνος); Eumolpus becomes the music master.

[2] Cf. below, p. 29 n. 2.

[3] See the convenient summary of the story given by C. A. Trypanis in the Loeb *Callimachus*, 24–6; and Wilamowitz, *Sitzungsber. der Berl. Akad.* 1925, 230–4.

[4] See Pfeiffer's note to *Aetia* fr. 26.1, citing Conon fr. 19 (Jacoby *FGH* vol. 1, pp. 195–6), μῆνά τε ὠνόμασαν Ἀρνεῖον, ὅτι ἀρνάσι Λίνος συνανετράφη· καὶ θυσίαν ἄγουσι καὶ ἑορτὴν Ἀρνίδα . . .

[5] Pfeiffer's Index Rerum Notabilium (*Callimachus* vol. 2, p. 127, s.v. anaphora 'bucolica')

toral character of Linus at some length and, with characteristic wit, gave the young Linus a new literary occupation, that of shepherd.

Virgil's Linus, though, is neither the mythical *Ursänger*, nor the somewhat mock-heroic poet-scholar-teacher suggested by Theocritus, nor the pastoral figure we can imagine in Callimachus, but rather all three at once, something new and undoubtedly more significant than the prototypes: *divino carmine pastor*. Whether Virgil himself was responsible for this transformation, or to what extent, is a question to be asked shortly.

Such is the Linus, then, who acts as spokesman for Apollo and the Muses in handing on Hesiod's pipes to Gallus:

> 'hos tibi dant calamos, en accipe, Musae
> Ascraeo quos ante seni, quibus ille solebat
> cantando rigidas deducere montibus ornos.'

Once again, in these lines, there is something new, as Heyne noted in a comment repeated by most subsequent editors: 'Novum vero hoc, quod nunc Hesiodo tribuitur, id quod de Orpheo sollenne est, silvas eius cantum esse sequutas.' The attribution to Hesiod of the Orphic ability to charm forests would indeed be unusual, especially as Virgil in an earlier Eclogue had specifically given Orpheus what was rightfully his (*Orpheaque in medio posuit silvasque sequentis*, 3.46). But there is no need to disfigure Hesiod in such a way. The two relative clauses (*quos...quibus...*) can be taken separately, and *ille*, in the second, can be understood in its common Latin function as indicating a change of subject: '...which before they gave to Hesiod, on which that (other well-known singer, Orpheus) used to play to charm the ash trees down from the mountains.'

The ambiguity was undoubtedly intentional, for Hesiod does, by implication, receive a share in Orpheus' powers and is brought into the same line of poetic descent, but Virgil had a further purpose. The second relative clause is, in effect, a riddle, a poetic elegance used to avoid the obvious.[1] A similar 'riddle' occurs in *Ecl.* 3.40–2, when Menalcas puts up his wager, the cups, *caelatum divini opus Alcimedontis*:

lists *Epigram* 22.3 as the only other occurrence of this anaphora in Callimachus, in which 'pastorale quiddam' should also be noted:

> Ἀστακίδην τὸν Κρῆτα τὸν αἰπόλον ἥρπασε Νύμφη
> ἐξ ὄρεος, καὶ νῦν ἱερὸς Ἀστακίδης.
> οὐκέτι Δικταίῃσιν ὑπὸ δρυσίν, οὐκέτι Δάφνιν
> ποιμένες, Ἀστακίδην δ' αἰὲν ἀεισόμεθα.

[1] The proper riddles of *Ecl.* 3.104–7 remain unsolved. Silenus' first words in *Ecl.* 6 are

23

> in medio duo signa, Conon, et – quis fuit alter,
> descripsit radio totum qui gentibus orbem,
> tempora quae messor, quae curvus arator haberet?

The answer, Aratus, needed no gloss for Virgil's readers.[1] The chief function of Menalcas' forgetfulness here seems almost to be a preparation for the riddle at *Ecl.* 6.70–1; the Alexandrian scientist and scientist-poet are in fact balanced by Orpheus himself, whom Alcimedon has set in the cup Damoetas offers as his stake:

> Orpheaque in medio posuit silvasque sequentis.

> (3.46)

It is no mere coincidence (as I hope to make clear) that in the Third Eclogue Conon and Aratus appear with Orpheus, who is identified by the magic power of his song over nature. There should be no difficulty in granting Orpheus his own proper magic in a similar (riddling) context in the Sixth Eclogue and allowing him to appear with Hesiod.

We have met Orpheus already in following various other questions involving these lines, not perhaps by accident: Orpheus and Linus appear together at *Ecl.* 4.55–7, and Orpheus with Conon and Aratus at 3.40–6; at *Ecl.* 8.55–6 Orpheus occurs again as a singer, *in silvis*, and with Arion (*certent et cycnis ululae, sit Tityrus Orpheus,* | *Orpheus in silvis, inter delphinas Arion*). But it is in the Sixth Eclogue that the most important appearance occurs. When Silenus begins his song,

> tum vero in numerum Faunosque ferasque videres
> ludere, tum rigidas motare cacumina quercus;
> nec tantum Phoebo gaudet Parnasia rupes,
> nec tantum Rhodope miratur et Ismarus Orphea.

> (6.27–30)

The proemium to Silenus' song ends with Orpheus, and in the preceding parallel line stands Apollo. Silenus' song thus is clearly associated in this introduction with both Apollo and Orpheus, an association expanded by Virgil in the language of lines 27–8. First, *Faunosque ferasque*. The use of *-que -que* connecting two items is archaic-epic (that is, solemn, ritualistic, and ancient), and is naturally infrequent in the Eclogues.[2] The appear-

---

worth noting in this connection: '*quo vincula nectitis?*' *inquit.* | '*solvite me, pueri...*' (23–4); *solvere* can be used in Latin of 'solving' a riddle (Petron. 58.8, '*qui de nobis longe venio, late venio? solve me*' – though *solve* here of course involves a further pun).

[1] There is no real reason why Eudoxos of Cnidos, the astronomer whose writings Aratus versified, should be assumed here rather than, or to the exclusion of, Aratus himself, who has ample reason to appear.

[2] On *-que -que* connecting two items see Schmalz–Hofmann–Szantyr, *Lateinische Syntax und Stilistik* (Munich, 1965), 515, with refs. (esp. for the poets, E. Norden, *Aeneis Buch VI*

ance of the Fauni cannot be set down simply to their being pastoral creatures, as they occur nowhere else in the *Eclogues*; rude deities of ancient Latium, who spoke in Saturnians,[1] they were banished by Ennius, along with the older poets: *versibus quos olim Fauni vatesque canebant.*[2] Secondly, *ludere*, repeated from the first line of the Eclogue, carries not only its pastoral associations there, but a certain neoteric connotation as well:[3] the magic of Silenus' song brings about a union of the old and the new, the old Fauns return to participate in the new poetry. Thirdly, *rigidas* (*quercus*) anticipates *rigidas* (*ornos*) of line 71. Here again is the magic power of Orphic song, associated with Silenus and Apollo, just as later (70–1) it is extended to Hesiod and so to Gallus. A poetic unity is beginning to appear, with Orpheus providing a focus.

In this setting, then, Silenus begins his song. The cosmogony with which it opens has too often been associated by modern scholars simply with Lucretius. The language, at least in some details, is indeed Lucretian, but it would have been difficult and odd for Virgil or any poet of his time to write on such a theme without a certain Lucretian flavor.[4] We should not be misled by this general poetic flavor to see in the passage a compliment to Lucretius and no more, or to consider him the sole 'source' for the lines. Not only are the lines not entirely Epicurean, but the language itself immediately points to other sources.[5] In the first book of Apollonius' *Argonautica*, Orpheus sings for the heroes a song which begins with a very similar cosmogony (496–502); Silenus' Creation is in fact framed by lines closely corresponding to the first and last lines of Orpheus':

(Stuttgart, 1957), 228, and H. Christensen, *ALL* 15 (1907), 165–211). Elsewhere in the *Eclogues* -*que* -*que* appears only at 8.22 (again in a line suggestive of the magic of poetry over nature, *Maenalus argutumque nemus pinusque loquentis | semper habet...*) and in 10.23 and 65–6.

[1] Varro, *LL* 7.36 (*Fauni* < *fari*), commenting on Ennius' line.

[2] Ennius, *Ann.* 214: see O. Skutsch, *Studia Enniana* (London, 1968), 31–4 and 119–29.

[3] Cf. *ludere* in Catullus, and on the 'Ludus Poeticus' in general, H. Wagenvoort, *Studies in Roman Literature, Culture and Religion* (Leiden, 1956), 30–42.

[4] See G. Jachmann, 'Vergils Sechste Ekloge', *Hermes* 58 (1923), 290: 'Das [dass Vergil sich in der Diktion an Lukrez angeschlossen hat] ist aber so gut wie selbstverständlich, für diese Dinge war damals Lukrez in Rom eben das grosse Muster. Der Inhalt entspricht dem durchaus nicht.'

[5] Stewart (*HSCP* 64 (1959)) has a fine summary of the work done to establish the eclectic nature of these lines: for Empedoclean elements see nn. 25–30 (pp. 200–1), with related text (184–5); for correspondences with Apollonius, p. 186 and n. 35, pointing out as well 'Stoic and Neo-Pythagorean' elements; Stewart (p. 201 n. 36) also notes that 'Orpheus' song in Apollonius appears to imitate what must have been a prominent passage in Parmenides: ... πῶς γαῖα καὶ ἥλιος ἠδὲ σελήνη, etc.' But that *Ecl.* 6.31–40 is eclectic and goes beyond Lucretius and Epicurean doctrine is by no means generally accepted: see, most recently and with extensive bibliography, W. Spoerri, 'Zur Kosmogonie in Vergils 6. Ekloge', *Mus. Helv.* 27 (1970), 144–63.

ἤειδεν δ' ὡς γαῖα καὶ οὐρανὸς ἠδὲ θάλασσα (496) =
namque canebat uti magnum per inane coacta
semina terrarumque animaeque marisque fuissent (31–2)[1]

οὐρεά θ' ὡς ἀνέτειλε, καὶ ὡς ποταμοὶ κελάδοντες
αὐτῇσιν νύμφῃσι καὶ ἑρπετὰ πάντ' ἐγένοντο (501–2) =
incipiant silvae cum primum surgere, cumque
rara per ignaros errent animalia montis (39–40)

Within this Orphic framework a rich suggestion of various philosophical doctrines points to Virgil's purpose: a poetry of 'science', rather than of a particular school or sect, is suggested. The power of the mythical Orpheus – his ability to charm all nature – takes on a real poetic form in these lines, and the reference to Apollonius' Orpheus suggests the continuation and transformation of this poetic magic from the distant past to Alexandria; once again, old and new are united.

We may return now to lines 70–1 (... *quibus ille solebat | cantando rigidas deducere montibus ornos*), which I feel certain are to be understood as a direct reference to Orpheus, not as an Orphic characteristic attributed to Hesiod (though this, of course, is implied as well).[2] One word, by its position at the center of the line, demands attention: *deducere*. We have noted that the neoteric *ludere* of the first line is repeated as Silenus begins to sing, suggesting the neoteric quality of Silenus' song, and by extension in the context, attributing this quality to Apollo and Orpheus as well. *Deducere*, similarly, must suggest *deductum* in line 5. This is no chance recall, nor one to be explained by the mystical workings of the poetic subconscious. In the three lines of the opening *recusatio* translated directly from Callimachus, *deductum carmen* reproduces τὴν Μοῦσαν λεπταλέην, and has been thoroughly studied in the context of neoteric terminology.[3] We have, in fact, become so accustomed to the term that we need to be reminded of its boldness in Latin: unlike *tenuis*, or even *gracilis*, it is

---

[1] Virgil has added a fourth element in the following line (*et liquidi simul ignis*), as if emphasizing the addition. That the language of these lines is not simply Lucretian has been clearly indicated by Virgil by the Grecism *-que -que -que* (*et*). Only once elsewhere in the *Eclogues* does *-que* occur three times in one line: *terrasque tractusque maris caelumque profundum* (4.51).

[2] Propertius (2.13.3–8, discussed below) has reassembled Hesiod, Orpheus, and Linus, surely with *Ecl.* 6.67–71 in mind. Propertius' clear suggestion of Orpheus (*aut possim Ismaria ducere valle feras*, in which *Ismaria valle* corresponds to *miratur et Ismarus Orphea*, *Ecl.* 6.30) is the best commentary on the identification of *ille* in *Ecl.* 6.70–1, though the authority of E. Reitzenstein in his influential article 'Zur Stiltheorie des Kallimachos' (*Festschrift Richard Reitzenstein* (Leipzig/Berlin, 1931), 49–51) has perhaps caused hesitation in many minds: he refers Prop. 2.13.5–6 to Hesiod (as well as *Ecl.* 6.70–1).

[3] First and most thoroughly by E. Reitzenstein (pp. 25–40); cf. Wimmel, *Kallimachos in Rom*, Stichwortindex s.v. λεπτός, and *passim*.

anything but an obvious translation for the idea of λεπτός.[1] It is impossible to imagine that Virgil was unaware of the prominence he gave *deducere* in its context at line 71: the result again is that Orpheus and the new poetry are associated.

These observations on Linus and Orpheus have, perhaps, done little more than lead up to (and I hope elaborate and support) J. P. Elder's illuminating discussion of the Sixth Eclogue.[2] Elder finds that Virgil's intention was 'to associate himself with the company of other inspired poets in the great tradition – with Apollo, Linus, Orpheus, Hesiod, Silenus, and Gallus,' though only indirectly, because 'His is usually a connotative world, in which things are not "spelled out"; that is the business of prose.'[3] He then marks 'the chief points of interconnection' between these inspired singers, in more detail than can be repeated here,[4] and shows 'how subtly Virgil has used these associations, one by one, to build up throughout the poem his House of Inspiration, and delicately to include himself within the edifice.'

I would substitute for Elder's 'House of Inspiration' the term 'poetic genealogy' (the descent of the pipes that Gallus finally receives might almost be diagrammed in a stemma). The founder of the line is, of course, Apollo, and with Apollo stand the Muses (*Phoebi... chorus omnis*).[5] In

---

[1] *Deducere* in the sense of 'spinning a fine thread': here, at least, the poet of the *Culex* knew what he was doing when he wrote, after Virgil, *Lusimus, Octavi, gracili modulante Thalia,* | *atque ut araneoli tenuem formavimus orsum.* | *Lusimus...* (1–3). Note *gracili* and *tenuem* (=λεπτός), that the idea of *deducere* is conveyed by the spider and the web, and that *Thalia* and *lusimus* are repeated from the opening lines of *Ecl.* 6. In this connection, the terms used by the poets of the spider's spinning are not generally noted: cf. Cat. 68.49 (*nec tenuem texens sublimis aranea telam*), Ovid, *Am.* 1.14.7 (*vel pede quod gracili deducit aranea filum*).

[2] See also O. Skutsch, 'Zu Vergils Eklogen', *RhM* 99 (1956), 193–201.

[3] P. 114.

[4] I have touched upon most of Elder's points above, but should add here a few more of his observations (*HSCP* 65 (1961), 115–16). 'Virgil's song of Silenus' was originally Apollo's song. '...the phrase *Linus divino carmine pastor* (line 67) brings divinity and the bucolic together (cf. *E.* 10.17 where Gallus is hailed as *divine poeta*)' – and where, I might add, divinity and the bucolic are again associated: *stant et oves circum* (*nostri nec paenitet illas,* | *nec te paeniteat pecoris, divine poeta*). Line 8 (*agrestem tenui meditabor harundine Musam*) is recalled at the end of the poem, *omnia, quae Phoebo quondam meditante beatus* | *audiit Eurotas* (82–3): 'The succession, via Silenus, is from Apollo to Virgil, and both "meditate" it; *now* at least it is a pastoral song (*agrestem Musam*) and in the Alexandrian style (*tenui harundine*).' Elder finds in uses of *canere* (*cantare*) throughout the Eclogue 'the obvious verb employed as a kind of formalizing link between Silenus, Hesiod, and Virgil, with Apollo in the background' (at 71 *cantando* I would see Orpheus instead of Hesiod).

[5] It is strange that we do not have a good study devoted to Apollo in Latin poetry. (J. Gagé, *Apollon Romain* (Paris, 1955) has little to say of the Callimachean Apollo who merged so opportunely with the Actian Apollo.) The Callimachean Apollo (of the *Aetia* prologue and *Hymn* 2, esp. lines 105–12; cf. on the 'Museum' at Alexandria, its

the next generation appear Linus and Orpheus, the mythical, semi-divine singers (together in *Ecl.* 4.55–7, where Apollo is Linus' father and Calliope Orpheus' mother, permitting us to speak properly of a generation). Then Hesiod, the inheritor of Orpheus' pipes (as we have read the lines), which represent what may be considered 'scientific poetry' – poetry as the power over, and understanding of, nature. All these figures have participated directly in Gallus' initiation, but we may add a further poetic generation present in the scene by implication and specified elsewhere in the *Eclogues*, the Alexandrians: Callimachus (*Ecl.* 6.3–5), Aratus[1] (with Conon, and associated with Orpheus, in *Ecl.* 3.40–6), Theocritus of course, Apollonius (here through his Orpheus, just as Virgil through his Silenus), then (as discussed below) Euphorion and Parthenius. Finally, as the last representative, Gallus receives from Linus the pipes on which Orpheus and Hesiod had played. Silenus, who tells of the scene as one of his *carmina*, seems both to represent and to be an integral part of this poetic genealogy.[2] We may perhaps begin to understand now why Virgil presents Silenus in a pastoral setting, but as a seer who must be ritually bound, a figure foreign to pastoral: in Silenus the pastoral and the 'scientific' are united, just as they are in the Orphic-Hesiodic pipes which Gallus receives through the *pastor* Linus.

We must, for a moment, expand somewhat and attempt to clarify this idea of scientific poetry, though our discussion must necessarily be very incomplete. Some apology must be made for the term 'scientific' itself, both because it reproduces nothing in Latin and because it is far from apt to our ears (though unfortunately the best single term I found): in what follows, then, it must be understood to have a special sense and significance, which did exist for Virgil. For us, science and poetry are incompatible, and the appeal of Aratus' *Phaenomena* to the Hellenistic and Roman worlds remains something of a mystery.[3] Virgil's own debt to Aratus was acknowledged in a characteristic way. When in the first book of the *Georgics* Virgil comes to the weather signs given by the moon,

religious character, and the poets as ἱερεῖς, R. Pfeiffer, *History of Classical Scholarship* (Oxford, 1968), 96–9) comes to Rome first with the *recusatio* in *Ecl.* 6: there is no such Apollo in Catullus – Virgil was definitely aware of the literary origin of his innovation.

[1] Though Aratus, of course, never lived and worked at Alexandria, he may be considered an Alexandrian poetically.

[2] O. Skutsch (*RhM* 99 (1956), 193–4) acutely observes, 'Die leicht begreifliche Umgestaltung Silens von Verkünder der Weisheit zum Vertreter der wahren Poesie ist Alexandrinisch', a remark noted by Elder.

[3] The *Phaenomena* was graced with at least 27 commentaries, and was translated at Rome by Varro Atacinus, Cicero, Germanicus, and Avienus. Cicero, for instance, praises Aratus for his *ornatissimis atque optimis versibus*, though conceding that the poet was *ignarum astrologiae* (*De Or.* 1.69).

he translates the corresponding passage of Aratus unusually closely. In this passage Aratus had set an acrostic in a period of five lines, beginning with the line (783) *ΛΕΠΤΗ* μὲν καθαρή τε περὶ τρίτον ἦμαρ ἐοῦσα, and continuing so that the first letters of each line in the period spell *ΛΕΠΤΗ*. Virgil, also within five lines (*Geo.* 1.429–33), has signed his passage in a somewhat different way: 429 *MA*ximus, 431 *VE*ntus, 433 *PU*ra; that is, in reverse order, *PU*blius *VE*rgilius *MA*ro.[1] By this device Virgil may be pointing particularly to the key word (almost a stylistic *terminus technicus* for the new poets) λεπτή. Aratus' acrostic was recognized by Callimachus; a reference to it may conclude his epigram (27 Pf.) on the *Phaenomena* (beginning 'Ἡσιόδου τό τ' ἄεισμα καὶ ὁ τρόπος): χαίρετε λεπταί | ῥήσιες, Ἀρήτου σύμβολον ἀγρυπνίης.[2] 'Hesiod's is the content and the manner': how Hesiod came to replace Homer as the poetic exemplar for the Alexandrians need not be recited here, but for Virgil the 'manner', or style, of scientific poetry had already been defined, and acclaimed, by Callimachus, and Aratus' direct succession in the line of Hesiod clearly established.

Virgil's singular contribution, however, seems to be Orpheus, and Orpheus stands for something far greater than 'manner'. Orpheus has the power to charm nature, and, as it develops, the knowledge and understanding of it. The poetry Orpheus represents can thus properly be called scientific. Virgil has described such poetry most fully and evocatively in the famous passage at the end of the second book of the *Georgics* (475–94), introducing the lines with a suggestion of himself as priest of the Muses[3] (*me vero primum dulces ante omnia Musae,* | *quarum sacra fero ingenti percussus amore,* | *accipiant...*), but with the request that they *receive* him and *teach* him 'science' (*... caelique vias et sidera monstrent,* | *defectus solis varios lunaeque labores...*). The power of such knowledge extends over the underworld itself (*felix qui potuit rerum cognoscere causas,* | *atque metus omnis et inexorabile fatum* | *subiecit pedibus strepitumque Acherontis avari,* 490–2). Here too it is still generally assumed that in the entire passage Virgil had Lucretius in mind, and that Lucretius is referred

---

[1] See J.-M. Jacques, 'Sur un acrostiche d'Aratos', *REA* 62 (1960), 48–61, with a good review of the significance of λεπτός following Aratus; and E. L. Brown, *Numeri Vergiliani*, Coll. Latomus 63 (1963), 96–105. Though I cannot follow Brown in all his observations, I find it difficult not to believe in his discovery of Virgil's 'acrostic' signature. Note also, in Aratus, καθαρή (783) = *pura* in Virgil (433): it became another key term in Callimachus (*Hymn* 2.111) and was taken over by the Latin poets (e.g., to be discussed below, Prop. 2.13.12).

[2] σύμβολον, an emendation by Ruhnken accepted by Pfeiffer, may thus be confirmed and explained ('λεπταί' is the σφραγίς = σύμβολον of Aratus). Note also ἀγρυπνίης, and cf. above on Linus (Theocr. 24.106) as ἄγρυπνος ἥρως, Alexandrian singer (cf. Cinna's epigram (*FPL*, p. 89 Morel) with the words *Arateis multum invigilata lucernis carmina*).

[3] Cf. above p. 27 n. 5.

to directly in lines 490–2,[1] but here again the associations extend farther and Virgil's reference should not be limited to a particular individual or philosophical sect. It is Orpheus who, in the corresponding section of Book Four, can exert power, through his poetry, over the underworld,[2] and it would seem to be the whole tradition of 'Orphic' poetry (as we have attempted to outline it) that is suggested here. Moreover, lines 477–8 are an allusion to Aratus;[3] Stewart has discussed this passage in emphasizing most usefully the eclectic nature of Virgil's conception of scientific poetry in *Ecl.* 6.31–40.[4]

The most striking aspect of *Geo.* 2.475–94 is the opposition of the scientific and the pastoral. (Here again I must ask for the reader's temporary indulgence, this time for taking liberties with the term 'pastoral'.) Lines 475–82 (scientific poetry) are followed by the pastoral alternative (483–9); the balance is repeated immediately by the opposition in lines 490–4 (*felix qui potuit rerum cognoscere causas... fortunatus et ille deos qui novit agrestis | Panaque Silvanumque senem Nymphasque sorores*). The whole passage seems to be a comment on (and a revision of) the poetic genealogy represented in Gallus' initiation in the Sixth Eclogue. One difficulty one would have in drawing a proper stemma of the genealogy would be that Linus and Orpheus cannot be related linearly, one descended from the other – both are, as it were, 'brothers' by separate parents.[5] Such an oversimplification undoubtedly never occurred to Virgil, but it suggests nonetheless what does seem to have been Virgil's purpose, that Linus

---

1 That the *felix qui potuit...* is a *macarismos* is a fact too often overlooked or ignored: the convention is necessarily a generality – Lucretius may be *suggested* by the lines, but he cannot be referred to *directly*. That Virgil is not referring specifically to Lucretius here is made clear by the parallel *fortunatus et ille*: whom does Virgil have in mind there?

2 Orpheus, with his divine power, can achieve what mortality cannot (*...manisque adiit regemque tremendum | nesciaque humanis precibus mansuescere corda. | at cantu...*, *Geo.* 4.469–71); it is particularly Virgilian, however, that it is his 'humanity' that causes the final loss of Eurydice.

3 See the discussion by E. Paratore, 'Spunti Lucreziani nelle "Georgiche"', *Atene e Roma* 7 (1939), 180 n. 6; Paratore sees the lines immediately following, however, as simply Lucretian. We should note that Aratus is adapted again by Virgil in the first couplet of the singing context in *Ecl.* 3.60–1, after the wager of the cups with representations of Conon, Aratus, and Orpheus: *Ab Iove principium musae: Iovis omnia plena* = Ἐκ Διὸς ἀρχώμεσθα . . . μεσταὶ δὲ Διὸς πᾶσαι μὲν ἀγυιαί κ.τ.λ., *Phaen.* 1–4.

4 Stewart, *HSCP* 64 (1959), 185, concludes on *Ecl.* 6.31–40: 'By taking traits from different, partly opposed, doctrines Virgil has made a new formulation which represents "scientific" poetry in general, not one school or one work.' He supports his conclusion with a discussion of *Geo.* 2.475–92, pointing to elements of Lucretius, Empedocles, and Aratus.

5 Cf. again *Ecl.* 4.55–7; that Orpheus and Linus are brothers is reported (for what it is worth) by Apollodorus, 1.3.2. Those who have noted that Linus was Orpheus' teacher (T. E. Page in his comment on *Ecl.* 6.67; Elder, *HSCP* 65 (1961), 115) seem to be repeating not Virgil but a worthless remark in 'Suidas' (s.v. Ὀρφεύς), καί φασι μαθητὴν γενέσθαι αὐτὸν Λίνου: cf. also Apollodorus, 2.4.9.

and Orpheus each represent, on the same level, different aspects of poetry.[1] Virgil's poetic genealogy is an attempt to relate, and unify, a poetic diversity: Gallus' inheritance becomes that of a single tradition.

Gallus was wandering by the Permessus (*errantem Permessi ad flumina Gallum*); one of the Muses led him to the Aonian mountains where Linus gave him the pipes with instructions that with them he sing the *aetion* (*origo*) of Apollo's Grynean Grove. Here is a further unifying point in the tradition, and one of great importance. We are reliably informed by Servius (on line 72), 'hoc autem Euphorionis continent carmina quae Gallus transtulit in sermonem Latinum,' and Gallus' interest in Euphorion is confirmed by Virgil himself when in the Tenth Eclogue Gallus says, 'ibo et Chalcidico quae sunt mihi condita versu | carmina pastoris Siculi meditabor avena' (50–1). We can also be certain about the reason for Gallus' interest in Euphorion and in the Grynean Grove: Stephanus of Byzantium gives us the information that the ethnic form Γρύνειος – the form used by Virgil here, *Grynei nemoris* – occurred in Parthenius' poem *Delos* (λέγεται καὶ Γρύνειος Ἀπόλλων ὡς Παρθένιος Δήλῳ).[2] Virgil has extended his poetic genealogy to include Euphorion and Gallus' friend and poetic mentor Parthenius, for there can be little doubt now that it was Parthenius who was largely responsible not only for the general direction of Gallus' poetic career, but for the specific subject of the Grynean Grove. The impression is conveyed that Parthenius, as much as Linus, stands as the Muses' surrogate in presenting Gallus with the pipes.

We now come to a crucial point in our discussion, one which concerns the actual poetic production of Gallus, the author of four books of elegies (only so much can be said with any certainty). Are we to understand from the scene of his initiation that he is leaving elegy and is henceforth to write a new and different sort of poetry such as is suggested by the Grynean Grove – Alexandrian aetiology, in whatever form? This is what scholars have generally concluded from the passage, and the only question remaining, it seems, is whether Virgil is urging this as a change for his friend or is reporting a new course already taken. Almost all the details of Gallus' poetic career are open to debate, but all are crucial for an understanding of the development of Augustan poetry. We must

[1] But not that noted by Servius on *Ecl.* 4.58: *PAN ETIAM* redit ad rustica numina: nam satis excesserat dicendo Linum poetam, Orphea theologum.
[2] For this point, and for Parthenius' relationship to Gallus, see the decisive remarks by W. V. Clausen, *GRBS* 5 (1964), 191–3: Clausen's demonstration (pp. 188–91) of the importance of Parthenius for Cinna's *Zmyrna* and Catullus (esp. c.95) should be kept in mind.

therefore discuss certain details of Gallus' initiation again, to see what assumptions we may or may not make and to place the scene in the context of Virgil's poetic genealogy as we have developed it thus far.

First, the river Permessus. The identification of it as 'the stream of elegy', and hence the conclusion that Gallus leaves elegy for another sort of poetry (represented by the Aonian mountains, or Helicon), are based entirely on a couplet of Propertius:

> nondum etiam Ascraeos norunt mea carmina fontis,
> sed modo Permessi flumine lavit Amor.
>
> (2.10.25–6)

Here, at the very end of a *recusatio* (*aetas prima canat Veneres, extrema tumultus:* | *bella canam, quando scripta puella mea est*, 7–8), Propertius can only mean, we are told, that he cannot yet write epic (*Ascraeos fontis*) because his whole poetic experience has been of elegy (*Permessi flumine*): Virgil's Gallus, then, must likewise be leaving elegy for a higher sort of poetry. Leaving aside the question of what Propertius *does* mean, I do not think we are justified in drawing this conclusion, simple and obvious though it may appear. In the first place, in the opening line of the poem Propertius had referred to Helicon, a mountain which can only be Hesiod's: *Sed tempus lustrare aliis Helicona choreis.* Propertius does not say that now is the time to *approach* Helicon (i.e., to write epic at Hesiod's fountains), or to *climb* Helicon, or to be *transported* there, or anything of the sort, but rather simply that it is the time 'to celebrate' (*lustrare*) Helicon (where presumably he has been for some time) with *other* (i.e., epic) choruses: the distinction does not lie in a choice of poetic localities, but rather in the sort of verse to be composed. The simple identification of epic with Hesiod's fountains becomes even more difficult, or impossible, when a few poems later Propertius places his love elegy with no uncertainty in Hesiod's grove:

> hic [Amor] me tam gracilis vetuit contemnere Musas,
> iussit et Ascraeum sic habitare nemus
>
> (2.13.3–4)

a passage to which we will return shortly. If there can be no question of an opposition between the *Ascraeos fontis* (2.10.25) and the *Ascraeum nemus* (2.13.4), and if both clearly refer to Hesiodic verse, then either Propertius is to be found guilty of hopeless inconsistency in saying first that his songs have not yet become acquainted with the Hesiodic fountains, then that Love has ordered him to frequent the Hesiodic grove; or something is wrong with our reading of 2.10.25–6 when we make so clear an opposition between the (elegiac) stream of Permessus and the (epic)

Hesiodic fountains. Perhaps, though, all we can say for the moment is that we should not conclude from Propertius 2.10.25–6 that Virgil's Gallus has been called to abandon elegy.

Furthermore, the Permessus is in origin neither an elegiac stream nor distinct geographically or poetically from Helicon. Hesiod begins the *Theogony* with the Heliconian Muses (by whom he will be initiated as a poet); then,

καί τε λοεσσάμεναι τέρενα χρόα Περμησσοῖο
ἤ ᾿Ίππου κρήνης ἤ ᾿Ολμειοῦ ζαθέοιο
ἀκροτάτῳ ῾Ελικῶνι χοροὺς ἐνεποιήσαντο.

(5–7)[1]

There is no distinction here between the Permessus and Helicon itself, and Virgil, for whom this scene of Hesiod's initiation was of such importance, could hardly have attempted to draw one in the face of Hesiod's text. The identity of the Permessus and Helicon can be followed still further: we know from Servius Auctus (on *Ecl.* 10.12, *Aonie Aganippe*) and the scholiast on Juvenal (7.6) that Callimachus had mentioned Aganippe as the '*fons Permessi fluminis*', and we now know for certain where this mention occurred: as had been suspected, it is to be placed in the introduction to the *Aetia*, in the context of Callimachus' own dream, in which he was transported to Helicon.[2] Finally and significantly, in the only other occurrence of the Permessus in Greek poetry, Nicander too connects it with ᾿Ασκραῖος ῾Ησίοδος (*Ther.* 11–12).

From a review of these contexts it seems impossible that Virgil (or perhaps Gallus previously) could have meant the Permessus to represent 'subjective love elegy' opposed to Helicon and Hesiodic-Callimachean aetiological poetry. Such an interpretation cannot stand: the Permessus and Helicon are topographically and poetically identical wherever they occur together in Greek poetry, and those occurrences are all in poets and scenes intimately connected with Virgil's poetic genealogy and Gallus' initiation. Instead of assuming that Gallus has been called from elegy to a loftier poetic genre, we must infer (a) that the geographical details (both the Permessus and Helicon) are presented by Virgil to refer

---

[1] See M. L. West, *Hesiod Theogony* (Oxford, 1966), 153–4: wherever Hesiod's Permessus actually was, there is no doubt about its being in the immediate vicinity of Helicon.

[2] Pfeiffer (on *Aetia* fr. 696), following a conjecture first made by Hecker, had suggested, 'fort. in Aetiorum "somnio"'; see also his comments on the Schol. Flor. to fr. 2. Confirmation is given by P. Oxy. 2262 fr. 2 (published by Pfeiffer, *Call.* vol. 2, pp. 101–3, with commentary). For Callimachus' dream, see *Anth. Pal.* 7.42. It is important, in this context, to note the association of *Aonie Aganippe* with Gallus again in *Ecl.* 10.12 – a further indication not to oppose, but to unite, the *Permessi flumina* and *Aonas montes* in *Ecl.* 6.

in no uncertain terms to the scene of the initiations of both Hesiod and Callimachus, and therefore (b) that Gallus, wandering by the Permessus, had already written Hesiodic-Callimachean poetry which he is being rewarded and recognized for, not initiated to.

The inference that Gallus had already written Hesiodic-Callimachean poetry (in some form), and that this was recognized by Virgil in the Sixth Eclogue, can be given additional support by a different approach. A question was suggested earlier about Virgil's precedent for the figure of Linus, whose new role was created by Virgil so quietly that modern scholars have understandably overlooked its significance. Yet it seems doubtful that even the complete context (now lost) of Linus' appearance in Callimachus would have made more significant, or explicable, to contemporary Roman readers of the *Eclogues* the importance Linus suddenly assumed, for the Callimachean Linus, though a shepherd, seems only to have been an incidental figure created with literary wit for a single aetiological episode, having nothing of the ritual solemnity he emerges with in the *Eclogues*; likewise the Theocritean Linus, though a precedent of sorts, would hardly have illuminated the Virgilian context. We must assume, I think, that we have lost an important stage in Linus' transformation, that this development occurred elsewhere with fuller detail in a source which Virgil could draw on and suggest.

It seems more than likely that that source was Gallus. Scholars have suggested that some of the details of *Ecl.* 6.64–73 owe something to Gallus, that he himself had perhaps written of his own initiation by the Muses.[1] We may return now to a passage referred to previously, a pronouncement by Propertius on his own poetry:

> hic [Amor] me tam gracilis vetuit contemnere Musas,
> iussit et Ascraeum sic habitare nemus,
> non ut Pieriae quercus mea verba sequantur,
> aut possim Ismaria ducere valle feras,
> sed magis ut nostro stupefiat Cynthia versu:
> tunc ego sim Inachio notior arte Lino.
>
> (2.13.3–8)

The whole poem contains unmistakable Callimachean terms:[2] the *gracilis Musas* represent Callimachus' 'slender Muse' of the *Aetia* pro-

---

[1] R. Reitzenstein, 'Properz Studien', *Hermes* 31 (1896), 194–5; F. Skutsch, *Frühzeit*, 34 ('Nicht eigene Erfindung ist es, was Vergil hier giebt; vielmehr wiederholt er nur, was Gallus selbst in einem eigenen Gedicht von sich erzählt hatte, einem Gedicht, das eben die Schilderung seiner Dichterweihe als Prooemium und danach die Geschichte vom gryneischen Hain enthielt'); W. Wimmel, *Kallimachos in Rom*, 235 ('Vielleicht stammt die Szene in ihrer elegischen Ausformung aus Gallus selbst').

[2] On the following terms and others, see L. P. Wilkinson, 'The Continuity of Propertius

logue (τὴν Μοῦσαν λεπταλέην, fr. 1.24 Pf.); shortly after this passage Propertius mentions a *docta puella*, who will approve his poetry *auribus puris* (11–12) – καθαρός is another key term for Callimachus[1] – and then scorns the *populi confusa fabula* (13–14).[2] At the same time the *personae dramatis* of Propertius' lines all seem to enter directly from Gallus' initiation in the Sixth Eclogue: the Muses, Hesiod (the *Ascraeum nemus*), Orpheus with his power to charm the oaks and wild beasts,[3] and finally Linus, distinguished in his 'art'. It may be asked, though, why Propertius should import his poetic characters wholesale from Virgil and specifically from the *Eclogues*, a tradition in which he has no need to stress his literary individuality (*non ut...sed magis ut nostro stupefiat Cynthia versu: tunc ego sim...notior arte Lino* is after all a challenge to a precedent in his own genre). If Gallus, however, had first brought these poetic exemplars together somewhere in his elegies, there is then every reason for Propertius' doing so here in this context.

That both Propertius and Virgil derive their passages from a common source, and that this source is Gallus, can be demonstrated positively, I believe. It would be gratuitous to point to details which occur in Propertius but not in Virgil (such as the specific epithet *Pieriae* (*quercus*) or the mention of the *ars* specifically of Linus), were it not that one such detail provides an essential clue that amounts almost to proof: *Inachio... Lino*.[4] Virgil, as we have seen, gives no information anywhere about Linus' provenance, and indeed provides so little information of any sort that we might well feel uncertain about the claim made previously that Callimachus' Linus, 'reared amongst lambs', provided the reason for Linus' role as *pastor* in Virgil. But the story related by Callimachus and the mythographer Conon differs in several essential features from other, both earlier and later, accounts of the attributes and activities of Linus, one of which is the setting in *Argos*, where Linus is the son of the *Argive* princess Psamathe. Had Propertius taken Linus (with the others) directly from the cast of participants in Gallus' initiation in the Sixth Eclogue, it would appear extremely unlikely that he would himself have then

---

ii.13', *CR* 16 (1966), 141–4, who argues convincingly for the unity of this poem largely from the Callimachean elements in it.

[1] καθαρή τε καὶ . . . ὀλίγη λιβάς, *Hymn* 2.111–12; cf. above, p. 29 n. 1 for the term in Aratus (with λεπτός), translated as *purus* by Virgil.

[2] σικχαίνω πάντα τὰ δημόσια, Call. *Ep.* 28.4 (Pf.) = e.g. *odi profanum vulgus et arceo*, Hor. *Od.* 3.1.1.

[3] Cf. *feras, quercus,* and *Ismarus* all with Orpheus at *Ecl.* 6.27–30. E. Reitzenstein, though, refers the lines to Hesiod (see above, p. 26 n. 2).

[4] Commentators have missed the point of *Inachio* entirely (just as they have overlooked the general significance of Linus; *Inachio* is interpreted to mean, simply, 'Greek' (e.g. Camps, *ad loc.,* 'i.e. Greek, Inachus being a legendary of Argos').

made a connection, independently, with Callimachus' Argive Linus and come up with the proper epithet *Inachio* – there is no evident reason that would have prompted him to have taken such an uncharacteristic step. If, however, it was Gallus who had introduced the *pastor* Linus to Latin poetry (and it has been argued above that the Virgilian Linus would hardly have been understandable even to a literary contemporary without a previous exemplar), then Gallus' Linus must have been a form of the Callimachean Linus, complete with his Callimachean provenance, and perhaps even with the epithet *Inachius*.

We have seen that Virgil, with his initiation scene, sets Gallus directly in the tradition of Hesiod and Callimachus. We can assume, in all probability, that Gallus had taken over the *pastor* Linus from Callimachus and made him a figure of some importance: when in the Sixth Eclogue Linus acts as the Muses' representative in handing on the pipes to Gallus, he may well be re-enacting a role he had performed earlier in Gallus' own poetry, and when he instructs Gallus to sing of the Grynean Grove, he is in fact relating what had already been performed. Finally, as we can infer from a comparison with Propertius 2.13.3–8, it is more than likely that the entire initiation scene and the actors in it come more or less directly from Gallus.[1]

What we said about a unified poetic tradition inherited by Gallus will now have to be modified in one important respect: it is not Virgil who was responsible for this conception (at least not entirely), but rather Gallus himself. In his poetic genealogy Virgil may have rearranged and organized various pieces, and may have expanded, connected, and suggested other relationships, but I do not think he can be credited with the original conception of a poetic unity. Callimachus, after all, had clearly established a single tradition for what can be termed scientific poetry; it may have been Gallus who saw Orpheus as the archetypal cosmic poet,[2] the founder of the line of Hesiod and Aratus. Linus' function is parallel, the semi-divine exemplar of the pastoral.[3] Whoever devised the position of one of these two legendary singers most likely also established the other in his corresponding role.

Whoever first enunciated what particular detail is of little importance

[1] To speak of an 'initiation' scene in Virgil is now no more than a convenience: Gallus may have related a proper initiation, but, as we have argued, for Virgil the scene is one of recognition and reward, not an initiation to a new poetic course.

[2] This assumption rests on my arguments for the common exemplar (Gallus) for *Ecl.* 6.64–73 and Prop. 2.13.3–8 (proved, I think, at least for the figure of Linus): the chances are, then, that Orpheus played a role of some importance in Gallus.

[3] The pastoral element in Gallus, as has often been suggested, must have been considerable.

(since we can never be certain of all the facts) beside what was actually achieved. The idea that all poetry arises from a single impulse (Apollo, the Muses) and, whatever form it may take, never departs from a single demonstrable tradition, and that the true poet of the present (the received, initiated poet, that is) inherits this unified tradition, was perhaps never before clearly realized and expressed, even by Callimachus. It has become a commonplace to say that what primarily motivated classical (and especially Roman) poetry was the expression of individuality within a confining genre. The discovery of a single unified tradition comprehending a variety of forms and genres means that genre need no longer count for much. As long as the poetic impulse is pure and the tradition undefiled – that is, as long as the poet can claim to have been initiated to the canons of Callimachean art – then, no matter what formal genre a poet assumes, there can be a universality of time and space, of reality and unreality. There is no better demonstration of this new freedom than the *Eclogues* of Virgil, in part pure Theocritean pastoral, in part disturbingly divorced from the pastoral world, set now in a timeless past, now in a present all too real, in a landscape which shifts in a similar fashion. We may assume, though, that Virgil in the *Eclogues* was not the first to have experienced the new freedom with such confidence. Everything suggests that Gallus had seen the real unity behind apparently diverse traditions, and had gone far in formulating it. We can expect his elegies to have reflected this discovery.

'*Carmina quae vultis cognoscite*,' says Silenus to his captors (line 25), and the following songs are indeed a perfect demonstration of the possibilities of the new poetry. We have mentioned precedents and associations, both literary and scientific, for the eclectic cosmogony with which Silenus begins.[1] The themes which follow defy neat classification – purposely. There are indications of epyllia. The brief mention of the Proetides (line 48) within the story of Pasiphae resembles the panel within a panel of, for instance, Catullus' epyllion;[2] the repeated *a, virgo infelix...* (lines 47 and 52) comes from Calvus' epyllion *Io* (*a, virgo infelix, herbis pasceris amaris*, FPL p. 85, Morel); and there is a direct speech by the heroine (55–60). Other notable features of neoteric poetry are not difficult to find. F. Skutsch has called attention to the way certain themes are presented: Silenus tells *at what fountain* Hylas was lost (*quo*

---

[1] The cosmogony should include lines 41–2 (after which – *his adiungit* – a new *carmen* begins: cf. Orpheus' song in Apollonius, which continues in the same way with Cronos and Zeus (*Arg.* 1.503–11)). In support of this (not generally accepted) division, see G. Jachmann, *Hermes* 58 (1923), 288–94.

[2] Noted by F. Skutsch, *Frühzeit*, 42.

fonte relictum, 43), and is concerned with the specific details of Philomela's flight and plumage (*quo cursu…quibus…alis*, 80–1), both of which suggest aetiological poetry.[1] It is often observed that in lines 74–7 Virgil has conflated the two separate stories concerning a Scylla (one the monster daughter of Phorcys, the other the daughter of Nisus who became the *ciris*), but the allusion to a different tradition in the relating of another is a recognized feature of learned poetry, which Virgil makes clear with the Alexandrian *quam fama secuta est*.[2] At the same time, there is no need to point out the pastoral motifs of, for instance, the stories mentioned in lines 45–63,[3] or to do more than mention that a good case can be made for regarding Love as the prime concern of Silenus' songs:[4] the neoteric interest in the darker aspects of erotic experience is certainly evident, and many of the stories concern metamorphoses.

This summary does little justice to the richness of detail in Silenus' song, but the lines have been discussed at length by many scholars in various attempts to find a controlling unity. There seems to be a purposeful variety in the poetic forms and poetic stories Virgil suggests, so that no category, no matter how broad, can include them all comfortably.[5] Yet obviously Virgil must have had some purpose in putting them all into Silenus' song, and enough similarities and points of contact obviously exist between the separate songs to convey the impression of a whole. Gallus' initiation, I have argued, provides the clue, and Gallus' poetry supplied what is now missing to us, the discovery that behind poetic diversity, behind the variety of purpose, form, theme, or genre, lies a unity of poetic tradition, a direct line of descent from divinity to contemporary poet, represented by the pipes of the poet, '*hos tibi dant calamos, en accipe, Musae…*' Whatever is played on these pipes will necessarily be real poetry, for style and expression are determined by the instrument. The Sixth Eclogue is itself the demonstration of the unity of poetry, and the Eclogue Book is the example of what can be achieved by the discovery that real poetry is circumscribed and defined not by genre or form, but only according to a poetic genealogy.

---

[1] *Frühzeit*, 32–3.

[2] See E. Norden, *Aen. VI*, 123–4 (on line 14, *ut fama est*).

[3] Cf. again Elder's comments on the pastoral elements throughout the poem, *HSCP* 65 (1961), 116–20, though many of the motifs he lists I cannot accept as 'pastoral'.

[4] F. Klingner, *Virgil*, 109–10.

[5] To find the unity of Silenus' songs in the force and development of Love, for instance, or in metamorphoses, is to have distorted, or to leave unexplained, the opening cosmogony and Gallus' initiation.

3

Gallus the elegist

Of the entire poetic production of Gaius Cornelius Gallus only one pentameter line survives: *uno tellures dividit amne duas*.[1] The loss of Gallus' poems, so important for our understanding of the development of Augustan poetry, and so highly valued by Virgil (among others), may perhaps be due in some way to the *damnatio memoriae* he suffered after his disgrace and suicide in 27 or 26 B.C. But Gallus has had his revenge: modern scholarship has produced such a mass of speculation and discussion that, from a glance at a bibliography, it would appear to an outsider that his poetry is better known today than at any other time since his death.

This impression, though, would be dispelled at a second look. All that has been written about Gallus' poetry is based on only two sources: Virgil's Sixth and Tenth Eclogues, and the meager 'testimonia' of later grammarians and scholars, together with the scattered mentions of Gallus by other Augustan poets. The two Eclogues were mined at the turn of the century by F. Skutsch,[2] who read them as catalogues of passages from Gallus – the Tenth from his four books of elegies, the Sixth of themes from his other works – and was therefore able to attribute to Gallus a hoard of epyllia (many of which, he notes, might well have been shorter than Catullus 64), a poem *de rerum natura*, and the *Ciris* of the Virgilian Appendix. There is still considerable sympathy for the suggestion that the Tenth Eclogue contains genuine pieces of Gallus,[3] but few scholars are now willing to see poems of Gallus imbedded in the mosaic of themes in the Sixth.

Skutsch's real contribution can be said to be the realization that Gallus'

---

[1] The line is cited by the geographer Vibius Sequester (see *FPL*, p. 99, Morel). The subject of the line is the Scythian river Hypanis, dividing Asia from Europe; the reference is both learned and exotic (cf. the Hypanis in the catalogue of rivers, *Geo.* 4.370, and Prop. 1.12.4; and Norden's comment, *Ennius und Vergilius* (Leipzig/Berlin, 1915), 23 n. 4).

[2] *Aus Vergils Frühzeit* (Leipzig, 1901) and *Gallus und Vergil* (Leipzig, 1906). The first and most effective of the many attacks on Skutsch's hypotheses was by F. Leo ('Vergil und die Ciris', *Hermes* 37 (1902), 14–55). In the mass of modern discussions of Gallus' poetry, however, Skutsch's two *libelli* remain the most stimulating.

[3] Servius' comment on *Ecl.* 10.46 cannot, after all, be ignored: '*hi autem omnes versus Galli sunt, de ipsius translati carminibus.*'

poetry and poetic interests are an integral part of the weave of the two Eclogues, that more can be learned about Gallus from the poetry of these Eclogues, and from what must have produced it, than from any other statements we may have about Gallus and what he wrote. Subsequent scholarship, however, undoubtedly as a reaction to Skutsch's conclusions, has tended to rely heavily on the 'testimonia' – dry, contradictory, and debatable though they are – and has used the Eclogues in much the same way, only as further testimonia *about* Gallus' poetry. We have already discussed the Sixth Eclogue as a statement and demonstration of a new poetic *credo*, in devising which Gallus can be seen to have had no small part. We must now look briefly at the testimonia, to see what may, and what may not, be safely deduced from them before we can turn to Propertius' *Monobiblos* and the Tenth Eclogue.[1]

> ibo et Chalcidico quae sunt mihi condita versu
> carmina pastoris Siculi modulabor avena.
>
> (*Ecl.* 10.50–1)

These two lines are crucial for our understanding of Gallus' speech in the Tenth Eclogue, but while they give the appearance of simplicity itself, a number of questions, all but unanswerable, cluster around them. By position they stand at the beginning of the second half of Gallus' speech (but do they mark the beginning of a new movement? or should we say rather that they are simply central?), and they seem to sum up Gallus' preoccupation with elegy and pastoral. Skutsch thought them originally part of a programmatic passage by Gallus (with the following three lines, from a poem like Propertius 1.18).[2] But does *Chalcidico versu* mean

---

[1] The following survey of the testimonia (though all are mentioned) is incomplete in that certain aspects of Gallus' poetry which they suggest are not mentioned: my discussion is selective in order to emphasize lines of interpretation developed above and below; and, because so much has been written so inconclusively on Gallus' poetry that little can be added on many (sometimes important) points, I have tried to avoid the repetitive monotony that any thorough review involves. I have found two studies which, to my delight, generally support many of my own conclusions: L. Alfonsi, 'L'elegia di Gallo', *Riv. di Fil.* 71 n.s.21 (1943), 46–56; and J.-P. Boucher, *Caius Cornélius Gallus*, Bibliothèque de la Faculté des Lettres de Lyon XI (Paris, 1966), esp. pp. 69–101. In addition to discussions of Gallus in the standard literary histories and the article in *RE* 4.1, 1342–50 (by Stein on his life and F. Skutsch on his poetry), the following recent studies are relevant and contain further bibliography: E. Bréguet, 'Les *Élégies* de Gallus', *REL* 26 (1948), 204–14; H. Bardon, 'Les Élégies de Cornélius Gallus', *Latomus* 8 (1949), 217–28 (and in *La littérature latine inconnue*, vol. 2 (Paris, 1956), 34–44); A. Barigazzi, 'Euforione e Cornelio Gallo', *Maia* 3 (1950), 16–25; R. Coleman, 'Gallus, the Bucolics, and the ending of the Fourth Georgic', *AJP* 83 (1962), 55–71; L. Alfonsi, 'Euforione e l'elegia', *Miscellanea di Studi Alessandrini* (Turin, 1963), 455–68, with a full bibliography; 'Euforione e i poeti latini' (discussions by Della Corte, Treves, Barigazzi, Bartoletti, Alfonsi), *Maia* 17 (1965), 158–76. In what follows I have not indicated the positions taken by these and other scholars on all the various points considered.

[2] *Frühzeit*, 17–20.

'elegiac couplets'? did Euphorion then write elegies? if not, who is the poet from Chalcis?[1] Is Gallus proposing to abandon elegy for Theocritean pastoral? had he already done so, or is Virgil urging him to do so? Or does *Chalcidico versu* mean hexameter verse in the manner of Euphorion (that is, epyllia)? Should the mention of pastoral be read only in the context of the Tenth Eclogue itself (that is, that only in the dramatic situation of the Eclogue – not in his own poetry – does Gallus become concerned with pastoral)? As such questions multiply, certain solution becomes more and more difficult; but since so many of the answers that have been proposed are based on the testimonia, we may hope at least to limit the number of valid questions by sorting out the worthy testimonia from the unreliable.

Servius' comment (on *Ecl.* 10.50) identifies (a) the island of Euboea and (b) its city Chalcis, (c) names Euphorion as the poet of the *Chalcidico versu*, (d) whom Gallus 'translated' – that is, 'made use of'[2] – and offers a paraphrase of the sense of the lines (in which Theocritus is identified as the *Siculus pastor*):

(a) Euboea insula est, (b) in qua est Chalcis civitas, (c) de qua fuit Euphorion, (d) quem transtulit Gallus. et hoc dicit: ibo et Theocritio stilo canam carmina Euphorionis.

Servius had anticipated these remarks in his comment on *Ecl.* 6.72:

...hoc autem Euphorionis continent carmina, (d) quae Gallus transtulit in sermonem latinum: unde est illud in fine, ubi Gallus loquitur [10.50] *ibo et Chalcidico quae sunt mihi condita versu carmina*; nam (b) Chalcis civitas est (a) Euboeae, (c) de qua fuerat Euphorion.

We may observe (1) that Servius appears to be drawing on the same source for both comments, (2) that there is no question in his source or in his own mind that Euphorion might not be the poet referred to in *Chalcidico versu*,[3] and (3) that there is no indication whatsoever that Servius knew Euphorion as an *elegiarum scriptor*.

[1] O. Crusius, seconded by B. Snell, nominated Theocles of Chalcis, and J. Perret admitted, 'Nous ne savons à quel élégiaque originaire de Chalcis Virgile a fait ici allusion': see Boucher, *Caius Cornélius Gallus*, 78 nn. 33–5. These are the proposals of scholars who do not allow that Euphorion composed elegiacs.

[2] There is no need to repeat the observations so often made that *transtulit* need not mean 'translated' (cf. Servius on *Ecl.* 10.46, '*hi autem omnes versus Galli sunt, de ipsius translati carminibus*'): for one example, Servius in his introductory remarks to *Aen.* IV says that the whole of that book is 'translated' ('*inde totus hic liber translatus est*') from Apollonius, *Argon.* III (for details, see Boucher, *Caius Cornélius Gallus*, 80 n. 43).

[3] Though Servius Auctus does report at *Ecl.* 10.50 the speculations of others ('*alii dicunt... alii volunt...*') that '*per Chalcidem Theocritum significari*', for several, all equally absurd, reasons. The recognized importance of Euphorion for Gallus makes it entirely unnecessary, and even perverse, to hunt for another poet of Chalcis, or to claim ignorance (see above, n. 1): on this identification we may have complete confidence in Servius' source and judgement.

The most common assumption made about these lines, however, is that *Chalcidico versu* means 'elegiac couplets, that is, the meter of Euphorion's verse'. Here, in an ideal world, some decision would be made, for it is of basic importance at this stage of our investigation to know whether or not Euphorion did write elegy (or at least extended poems of some sort in elegiac couplets): because if Euphorion did *not* write elegiacs, then Gallus *either* wrote elegies influenced by Euphorion in some way other than in meter, *or* wrote hexameter poems influenced by Euphorion and, in addition, the four books of elegies not necessarily influenced by Euphorion. But in a world short of ideal, our decision on this crucial question can only be one with a strong likelihood of being correct.

What is the evidence for or against Euphorion's having written elegies? Against: among the 500 verses we now have of Euphorion, not a single one is a pentameter or part of a pentameter.[1] (The law of probability is playing strange tricks indeed, if in this number of surviving lines no pentameter, by chance, has been left to us, while the single preserved line of Gallus happens, again by chance, to be a pentameter.) For: two later comments on *Ecl.* 10.50, one by the pseudo-Probus ('*Euphorion elegiarum scriptor Chalcidensis fuit...*'), the other by Filagrius (or Philargyrius), repeated from one scholarly discussion to another, with no indication of context or of any textual uncertainty, in the form '*Euphorion distichico versu usus est*'). Before we can let ourselves be persuaded by these two statements, we must be assured that they have a good chance of having preserved genuine and valid information.

The commentary of 'Filagrius' is preserved in two parallel versions. I give here the complete text of each version of the comment on *Ecl.* 10.50, adapted from Hagen's text and apparatus:[2]

I	II
CHALCIDICO idest (b) Chalcis civitas (a) in Euboea, (c) in qua fuit Euphorion, qui Euphorion [-ius *LNP*] distichico versu [sidus illi a conversu (conversi *N*) *LN*, sidiis iliaco ūsu *P*] usus est.	*CHALCIDICO* idest civitas enim (a) in Euboea (b) Chalcis dicitur, (c) in qua fuit Euphorion, (d) quem transtulit Gallus.

It is clear, first, that Filagrius' comments go back to Servius or his source, and therefore any item of information not also found in Servius

[1] So Barigazzi, *Maia* 17 (1965), 169, who fifteen years earlier had counted 300 verses (*Maia* 3 (1950), 17).

[2] *Servii Grammatici...Commentarii*, ed. G. Thilo and H. Hagen, vol. 3.2 *Appendix Serviana* ed. H. Hagen (Leipzig, 1902), pp. 184–5. The three MSS (*LNP*) are of the ninth and tenth centuries.

is to be regarded in this particular case as highly suspicious. All four items offered by Servius are found in Fil. II, but (d) is missing in Fil. I, where in its place is found the relative clause repeated in isolation with such confidence by modern scholars, '*qui Euphorion distichico versu usus est*', a piece of information having no parallel in any other scholion. The clause is further marked as an intruder by the nominative (*Euphor*)-*ius* given by all three MSS, though elsewhere in both versions the nominative is (*Euphor*)-*ion*. But the origin of the clause naming Euphorion as a writer of elegiac distichs is for our purposes irrelevant, for the crucial words, *distichico versu*, turn out to be an attempt (Hagen's?) to make sense of the nonsense syllables of the MSS – none too successful, when one realizes that the *Thesaurus* has no entry for *distichicus*: there is, indeed, a better case for emending to *Chalcidico versu* than there is for retaining the unsatisfactory conjecture *distichico*.

The statement by pseudo-Probus[1] ('*Euphorion elegiarum scriptor Chalcidensis fuit, cuius in scribendo secutus colorem videtur Cornelius Gallus*') cannot be dismissed as easily or with such finality, but its lonely position is open to attack. F. Jacoby long ago pointed to the likely explanation: 'Wenn Euphorion nun bei Probus... als Elegiker erscheint... so erregt schon der Wortlauf den dringenden Verdacht, dass es sich hier um einen Rückschluss handelt: Euphorion wird Elegiker, weil er von Gallus benutzt ist.'[2] One might feel more confidence too if the appositive *elegiarum scriptor* were anchored more firmly in its context as an essential part: as it is, the purpose of the comment is not to assert that Euphorion was a writer of elegies, but that Gallus *seems* (*videtur*, indicating second-hand information) to have followed the *color* ('flavor') of Euphorion – nothing, it should be noted, about meter. The weight that the pseudo-Probus is asked to carry (and now alone, without what little help Filagrius once lent) is too great: the assumption that Euphorion did not, after all, write elegies is entirely reasonable.

Once we have decided that this is a reasonable enough assumption on which to proceed, the next questions to be considered are clearly: did Gallus write *only* elegies (in which case *Chalcidico versu* carries no reference to meter, but to something like the pseudo-Probus' *color*), or did he write *both* elegies (with little or no regard for Euphorion) *and* hexameter verse in the manner of Euphorion? It will be important, once again, to arrive at as reasonable an answer as possible, for what is in

---

[1] *Appendix Serviana*, ed. H. Hagen, vol. 3.2, p. 348.
[2] 'Zur Entstehung der Römischen Elegie', *RhM* 60 (1905), 70. Cf. F. Skutsch, *RE* 6.1, 1177, who accepts Jacoby's explanation.

question, after all, is the nature of the first Latin elegy. A reasonable answer is once again all we can expect: we can hardly hope for any reliable statement from antiquity such as 'Gallus wrote only elegies.'

Yet something close to such a statement can be had from several of the testimonia. The grammarian Diomedes, in writing of Latin elegy, names only three poets:[1]

...quod genus carminis praecipue scripserunt apud Romanos Propertius et Tibullus et Gallus, imitati Graecos Callimachum et Euphoriona.

Though Diomedes is undoubtedly repeating and simplifying at second-hand an earlier tradition or scholar,[2] two observations can be made with confidence. First, that Gallus is said to have 'imitated' Euphorion *in elegy*, just as Propertius 'imitated' Callimachus *in elegy* (we know, of course, that Propertius wrote no hexameter verse).[3] Secondly, that the only apparent reason for these three elegists to have been singled out ('...*praecipue scripserunt apud Romanos*...') is that they alone composed elegy and nothing else: this we know to be true for Propertius and Tibullus, and we know that Catullus and Ovid (not to mention others such as Calvus and Varro of Atax) wrote other forms of verse as well; it is reasonable, then, to assume that Gallus' total poetic production consisted of elegy – at least until we find some good contradictory evidence.

Diomedes' canon of the three elegists may go back ultimately to several passages in Ovid. At *Ars Amatoria* 3.333–4, as elsewhere,[4] Gallus, Propertius, and Tibullus are all included together as elegists in one couplet of a passage cataloguing other poets as well. Quintilian's famous pronouncement on the elegists – as overworked in the examination room as in the literary histories – must form part of this same tradition,[5] and includes Ovid because Ovid himself had drawn up the canon of three in

---

[1] *Grammatici Latini*, ed. H. Keil (Leipzig, 1857), vol. 1, p. 484.

[2] Cf. Alfonsi, *Riv. di Fil.* 21 (1943), 46: 'da Svetonio o da testi già antecedentemente nel I secolo d. Cristo fissati.'

[3] One can assume that Gallus and Euphorion are meant to be linked in Diomedes' statement, as are Propertius (the *Romanus Callimachus*) and Callimachus. Bardon's quibble with Alfonsi (*Latomus* 8 (1949), 220 n. 3) – 'que fait-il de Tibulle?' – need hardly be considered seriously, though on the other hand there is no need to refuse (as does Alfonsi) to grant Gallus an interest in Callimachus. Cf. Jacoby's sensible remarks, *RhM* 60 (1905), 59 n. 2.

[4] Identical are *RA* 763–6, *Tr.* 4.10.51–4 (in a passage of poets Ovid had known) and 5.1.17–18, in all of which Gallus, Propertius, and Tibullus – and only they – appear together as elegists.

[5] Quint. *Inst. Or.* 10.1.93: '*Elegia quoque Graecos provocamus, cuius mihi tersus atque elegans maxime videtur auctor Tibullus. Sunt qui Propertium malint. Ovidius utroque lascivior, sicut durior Gallus.*'

reference to his own elegy. These passages offer some confirmation of the supposition that Gallus wrote only elegies, though absolute certainty cannot go beyond the statement that he was *primarily* an elegist.

Other passages in Propertius, Ovid, and Martial, while including Gallus in lists of various poets (elegiac, amatory, or otherwise), refer specifically to his Lycoris and therefore to his four books of elegies.[1] It is striking that all these passages from the poets mentioning Gallus (we have catalogued ten) specifically refer to his elegies, and that there is no indication of any other sort of verse (though many of them include references to the work of different poets from Ennius on – Virgil, for instance, is credited with pastoral, georgic, and epic poetry in Propertius 2.34.63–80 and Ovid *Am.* 1.15.25–6). Had Gallus written verse other than what was included in the four books of elegies, we might reasonably expect to hear of it; and, what is more, had the famous *aetion* on the Grynean Grove occurred in an independent poem (such as an epyllion), we could certainly expect to have some reference to that poem. We still have found nothing to contradict our supposition that Gallus wrote only elegies, and much to support it.

We have left for last two testimonia which have most often been called upon to credit Gallus with poems other than elegies. First, Servius on *Ecl.* 10.1:

Gallus...fuit poeta eximius; nam *et* Euphorionem, ut supra diximus [6.72], transtulit in latinum sermonem et amorum suorum de Cytheride scripsit libros quattuor.[2]

Does this statement imply two sorts of poetry, epyllia in the manner of (*transtulit*) Euphorion *and* the four books of elegies (the *Amores*)? Not necessarily. To begin with, Servius is explaining here *why* Gallus was a *poeta eximius* (*nam* clearly indicates the explanatory purpose of what follows), a fact often overlooked: Servius is not saying 'these are the two (*et...et...*) kinds of poetry Gallus wrote', but rather 'this is what made Gallus unique in his day, that he had an interest in Euphorion and wrote four books of elegies.' What I have explained here is actually the text of Servius Auctus; Servius omits the first *et*, which makes the whole question much simpler. Furthermore, as has frequently been pointed out, Servius is actually only adding (*et...*) one new point (that Gallus wrote *Amores*) to his previous statement (*ut supra diximus*) about Gallus'

---

[1] Prop. 2.34.91–2; Ovid, *Am.* 1.15.29–30, *AA* 3.537, *Tr.* 2.445–6; Mart. 8.73.5–10; finally, Ovid, *Am.* 3.9.61–4 (the elegy on the death of Tibullus), though not referring to Lycoris, does present Gallus (along with Catullus and Calvus) as an elegist (cf. line 3, *flebilis indignos, Elegia, solve capillos*).

[2] Cf. the almost identical notice in the *vita* of Donatus Auctus (*Die Vitae Vergilianae*, ed. E. Diehl (Bonn, 1911), 31) – not in Donatus.

use of Euphorion: two separate kinds of poetry are not implied.

Finally, we must mention Parthenius' Preface, in the form of an introductory epistle addressed to Gallus, to the Ἐρωτικὰ Παθήματα, a collection of stories from the more obscure Hellenistic poets suitable for Gallus' use, as Parthenius says, 'in epic and elegy': αὐτῷ τέ σοι παρέσται εἰς ἔπη καὶ ἐλεγείας ἀνάγειν τὰ μάλιστα ἐξ αὐτῶν ἁρμόδια.[1] The question, of course, is whether εἰς ἔπη καὶ ἐλεγείας is descriptive or prescriptive, whether Gallus had actually composed 'epics' (that is, epyllia) or whether Parthenius is merely inviting him to do so. Obviously this notice can no more be used, by itself, to furnish evidence for epyllia by Gallus (though it is strange how often it has been made to do so) than it can prove that he wrote only elegies.

It seems, then, that there can only be one reasonable conclusion to be drawn from the testimonia: that Gallus wrote four books of elegies, and nothing more. No other sort of poetry by him was known (or at least thought of any importance) either to Propertius, Ovid, or Martial, or to the later scholarly tradition. If Gallus did dabble in other forms and genres of verse, the results could hardly have been widely published or held to be of any importance, any more than any of the poems of the *Catalepton*, if by Virgil, influenced in the slightest his subsequent reputation or influence. But the important conclusion to be drawn concerns the sort of poetry his four books of elegies must have contained. The teaching of Parthenius, the influence of Euphorion, the poetic interests he shared with Virgil, all this must now be seen to have been contained and expressed in his elegies.

Before we turn to Propertius' *Monobiblos*, we may speculate further on Gallus' elegies from the viewpoint afforded by Catullus. Most of what has been written about Gallan elegy has been the result, quite naturally, of working back from extant Latin elegy, of assuming that the most obvious characteristics found in Propertius, Tibullus, and Ovid necessarily were already present in Gallus' *Amores*. Such assumptions, however, have not always led to a better understanding of the origins of Latin elegy, for they leave the obvious questions, though transposed one step back, precisely as they were before: how, if there was no such thing as subjective love elegy in Alexandrian poetry, did it develop at Rome, and how are we to see Catullus' position in this development? Since in

---

[1] See the convenient edition and translation by S. Gaselee in the Loeb Library volume of Longus, *Daphnis and Chloe* (ed. J. M. Edmonds); or in *Mythographi Graeci*, vol. 2.1 suppl., ed. E. Martini (Leipzig, 1902).

this chapter we have been discussing likely possibilities rather than probable observations, a few more such generalities may be in order, with the warning that they are offered with hindsight and will, I hope, in the light of what follows become more than possibilities.

The underlying question to be considered in the next chapter is how Propertius came to assume the role of the poet-lover, writing subjectively about what appear to be his own experiences in elegies in which myth and mythological *exempla* reveal as well the learning and tastes of Alexandria; and subsequent chapters will deal with Propertius' inability to remain in the role of the poet-lover and with the quite different sort of poetry that elegy became. What precedent did Gallus offer elegy that will explain its diversity, and what precedent did Catullus offer him? Is it likely that Gallus began by writing elegy about personal experiences with his Lycoris in the same manner as Propertius wrote of his Cynthia? To suggest a likely framework into which the arguments and conclusions presented later may fit, we should consider the void between Catullus and Propertius and how Gallus may reasonably be supposed to have filled it.

At the end of chapter 1 we outlined the poetic character of each of the three groups of poems written by Catullus and what each group offered subsequent poets. Catullus wrote directly of his Lesbia in his epigrams and polymetrics, though we should remember that there is far more in most of these poems than the revelation of personal amatory experience. His epigrams, though set exclusively in pentameter couplets, provided little or no precedent for the Augustan elegists in manner: their poetic diction and the use they make of the meter derive from a far different tradition, nor can any similarities be seen in general tone or even in content, when one considers the significant absence in the epigrams of mythological suggestions, characteristic display of learning, and the like. The polymetric poems, on the other hand, do reveal such traits later to appear consistently, though often altered, in the elegists, and what is particularly obvious is that again Lesbia is either the addressee or the subject of polymetric poems; but why then did the next two generations of poets make no further use of this form, why did Horace, who alone of the major poets wrote short poems in meters other than the pentameter couplet, claim an entirely different background and precedent for his *Odes*, and why did Catullus' polymetrics lead only to occasional diversions, such as can be found in the collection of *Priapea*?

The answer lies in the importance for subsequent poetry of Catullus' longer poems: here was the language and tone of the polymetrics turned to serious purposes without solemnity, here was a way in which previous Latin poetry could fuse with Greek to produce a new and flexible mode of expression, refined and allusive while it retained the directness and vigor of the Roman character. Above all, Catullus' longer poems showed how the artificiality of literary conventions could be made to serve, rather than suppress, individual expression: in particular, the dignity inherent in the impersonality of the higher genres had been won, but with no loss of personal identity.

What remains before us, however, is still a void to be filled, for there is a tremendous distance between Catullus' marriage poems, or the *Attis*, or his translation of Callimachus, or, especially, his epyllion, and the subjectivity of the *Monobiblos* of Propertius. In these longer poems the poet is only to be seen behind the abstractions set before us, though what is remarkable is that he is to be seen at all: in the *Monobiblos* the poet occupies stage center and delivers all the speeches himself, while other characters, even his Cynthia, are hardly more than props; and the abstractions – the mythological *exempla* – are presented only as *tableaux* illustrating the condition or situation of the poet. In manner of expression likewise Catullus' longer poems consist of a basic formality of elevated poetic diction, relieved occasionally – and often observably to bring out the personal or affective behind the formal façade – by the new infusion of contemporary idiom found in the polymetrics; whereas in Propertius what has been seen quite rightly as informality of diction devised by the elegiac poet for his new *genus tenue* is occasionally elevated by the introduction of a cluster of epic or archaic elements, often observably associated with his mythological *exempla*. We may now try to fit Gallus logically into this void, referring to what we have thus far deduced about his poetry and anticipating what is suggested later.

We have seen in the preceding chapter that in lines 64–73 of the Sixth Eclogue Virgil could not have meant that Gallus had been called from elegy to write another, higher order of verse, and we have argued here that if there is any reasonable conclusion to be drawn from the testimonia, it is that Gallus wrote only elegy. Furthermore, as we can gather from both the Sixth Eclogue and the testimonia, Gallan elegy was rich in myth, capable of such highly sophisticated aetiology as that on the Grynean Grove, could become on occasion pastoral, and defined self-consciously a new role for the poet as the representative of a long tradition of inspired singers. All of this follows quite easily as a logical consequence of Catullus' longer poems, and in fact takes us half-way towards the *Monobiblos*. What Gallan elegy shares with Propertius' first book but not with Catullus' longer poems (or at least not all of them) is the elegiac form itself, the exclusive use of the pentameter couplet in a book of separate, rather short, independent poems. In common with Catullus' longer poems, and opposed to the *Monobiblos*, is the position of the poet, who, it would seem, has not yet become a lover entirely preoccupied with his own experience and emotions, not yet in this role occupying stage center.

But to state the position of Gallan elegy in these terms is far too black and white. If we wonder why Gallus decided on a book of elegies as the most suitable form, many possible reasons come to mind. Philitas and Callimachus (especially his *Aetia*) were important precedents undoubtedly for the adaptability of the meter to the sort of content we can imagine was primary in Gallus' first elegies; and the figure of Parthenius could be invoked here too. The poetry book itself had suddenly become an object of importance; Virgil's *Eclogues* is the first such book we have from Rome, but Gallus may have had some part in shaping the idea, perhaps even providing a demonstration: in any case, the concept of a book composed of separate elegies would obviously have recommended itself. Showing the way were the four poems in the elegiac meter by Catullus, 65–68, so different from his epigrams, and so different from each other. What might have been the most important consideration of all was the fact that the form had not previously been so used at Rome and might thus yield itself easily to content that was not only new, but which also intentionally unified much that previously had been restricted to separate genres.

If it was for such reasons that the first book of elegies was conceived and composed at Rome, we are still a long way from the Propertian poet-lover. I think it unlikely, for reasons to be presented later, that Gallus appeared in any such role, at least in his first book of elegies. If Lycoris appeared in this book, her role must have been minimal. Catullus' precedent here was too important. Lesbia is not named in any of Catullus' longer poems and appears only in poem 68, in which personal experience is reflected rather than directly presented: myth in this poem has a function quite unlike its function in the polymetrics – the *exempla* provide the central focus around which personal experience clusters. In addition, Alexandrian poetry offered no precedent for subjective elegy (if we no longer accept the version manufactured *ex nihilo* by scholars who saw no other alternative), and it is difficult to believe that Gallus, as conscious as we know him to have been of the art of the Alexandrians and Euphorion, could have invented subjective elegy immediately and completely, rather than, as we will argue below, coming upon it slowly and by degrees. From what we have observed thus far, we can hypothesize that myth and Alexandrian learning must have been the outstanding characteristics of his first book of elegy, with Lycoris, if she was present at all, serving only as a point of departure for the development of a few elegies.

These black and white contrasts may be made even less distinct, however. That we see Propertius' position in his *Monobiblos* as poet-lover as a reality may be due to our own particular focus, a fault in our perception. I have referred to Propertius as the principal actor on a stage and to his position as a role he plays; if such he is, then there is considerably less of a difference between him and Gallus as elegists, and the course and development of elegy are easier to understand. The poetry of the *Monobiblos* is indeed subjective, but in a way that has not been clearly understood, and unless we can see precisely what this subjectivity really is, we will not understand the poems themselves properly, nor how they came to be written following the example set by Gallus' *Amores*.

4

Propertius' *Monobiblos*

The historian of classical literature must learn to live with two sources of difficulty and frustration, neither of which can he ever have much hope of avoiding or overcoming. First, his own literary *milieu* is so vastly different in so many ways from that of any of the ancient poets that, even if it were possible to catalogue and describe the traditions, backgrounds, literary values and impulses behind the work of any ancient poet (which of course it is not), there would still remain the almost impossible task of turning this set of facts into appreciative understanding. Even a modern temperament that might be expected to react sympathetically to any particular ancient poet cannot be counted on to do so: in many ways, for instance, T. S. Eliot seems to be a modern Alexandrian; yet Ezra Pound, who thoroughly understood and actually shaped *The Waste Land*, could find nothing to respond to in Virgil. Generally, as it has become a commonplace to point out, our literary reactions are still colored by Romanticism more than we care to admit. Secondly, what we have left to us of the literature of antiquity is so little, a bare outline of what existed and was important; but an outline can easily assume a misleading importance of its own and convey the mistaken impression of a detailed whole. It is easy to forget, when reading an author whose work we have in its entirety, that we have little of (and often know next to nothing about) the work of many others which was of real importance for him.

So it is that we regard Propertius primarily as a love poet writing poems in which passion predominates, heart over head. In this century two questions about Latin elegy can perhaps be singled out as having chiefly exercised scholarly ingenuity and represented critical attitudes. The first, which has just about (but not quite) been laid to rest as a futile preoccupation with an improper question, concerned the origins of Latin 'subjective' love elegy. Much was learned from the discussion, though little was settled, but perhaps the most remarkable aspect apparent to one following it now is that the validity of the term 'subjective' was never questioned.[1]

---

[1] For a review of this discussion with refs., see A. A. Day, *The Origins of Latin Love-Elegy* (Oxford, 1938), 1 nn. 4–7; cf. Butler and Barber, *The Elegies of Propertius* (Oxford, 1933), xxxv–lxvi (esp. xlviii–l).

Yet, if one were to meet Propertius, Tibullus, or Ovid, and to ask what it was that made their poetry original or different, I suspect that the answer 'Its subjectivity' would be dragged forth only after considerable Socratic questioning, and perhaps to their surprise. *We* know that love poetry must be subjective, and we don't like to be told that Cynthia, Delia, and Corinna may never have existed apart from the world of the poems. More recently, much has been written to quiet an uneasiness over the elegists' 'sincerity': love poetry, we feel, must be a genuine reflection of the poet's passion, but there is no escape from the feeling that so often in Latin elegy the passion appears thin or conventional, indeed of secondary importance in the poem. But the question of sincerity, like that of subjectivity, is of such importance only to a mind conditioned by romanticism.[1]

The apparent development of Propertius from his first published book to his last has encouraged the view that he began, at least, as a proper love poet. Subjective love poetry of direct emotion and Alexandrian artificiality of learned refinement represent for us two opposite poles, as any review of Catullan scholarship will show only too clearly. Propertius' *Monobiblos*, we are most often led to believe, has not yet become contaminated by Alexandrian conceits and mannerisms: 'Book I might be expected to show the germ of the developed style... But traces of it... are difficult to see...' 'It is my suggestion that the Roman and Propertian equivalent of this Callimachean style becomes more and more noticeable and controlled between the *Monobiblos*, where its presence at all is very debatable, and Book IV.'[2] The argument can continue by pointing out that if the poet meant the *Monobiblos* to be read as an Alexandrian or Callimachean production, he certainly does not tell us so, nor do any of the *topoi* we associate with Callimachean poetry at Rome appear: Callimachus and Philitas are not mentioned, there is no *recusatio*, no elaborate initiation ritual for the poet, who is not yet termed a *vates*. It is easy to assume, then, that Propertius indeed began

---

[1] See A. W. Allen, '"Sincerity" and the Roman Elegists', *CP* 45 (1950), 145–60, reworked as 'Sunt qui Propertium Malint' in *Critical Essays on Roman Literature: Elegy and Lyric*, ed. J. P. Sullivan (London, 1962), 107–48: Allen argues well against biographical criticism, defines 'sincerity' as the *fides* of Roman rhetoric, and then looks for 'the kind of sincerity which lies in a consistency between the style of their poetry and the emotional condition their elegy depicts' (*Crit. Essays*, 121).

[2] J. P. Sullivan, 'Propertius: A Preliminary Essay', *Arion* 5 (1966), 8–10. Sullivan cites Prop. 1.3 as the only example of 'the developed style', 'But other than this, marks of the later style are difficult to discern.' On p. 21 he speaks of 'the "serious" tone of the *Monobiblos*' in contrast to 'the λεπτότης that Propertius gradually developed.' Cf. the summary statement of Butler and Barber (*The Elegies of Propertius*, lxvi), 'He has advanced [from Book I to IV] from the subjective style of a Catullus to the more objective art of Callimachus...'

as a subjective poet of love, and that only after his first book was completed and published did he discover, and begin to be influenced by, Alexandrian principles (as in 2.1), only later still that he felt the need to proclaim his new role publicly and loudly (as in 3.1 and 3.3), until finally, as he becomes the *Romanus Callimachus* (4.1.64), Cynthia is abandoned and Roman themes and aetiology become his sole concern.

Not only may our conditioned inclinations persuade us to accept this picture of Propertius' development from a poet of love to a poet of learning, but the fact that we have the complete elegiac corpus of Propertius, Tibullus, and Ovid is in itself seductive: the natural temptation is to forget that the work of the recognized head of the tradition, Gallus, is lost almost completely. Propertius comes to be viewed in effect as the first Roman elegist, and in much modern criticism the *Monobiblos* is made to spring fully armed from the head, or rather the heart, of the poet. But Propertius did not found elegy at Rome, and two generations of poets had fundamentally changed the course and altered the nature of poetry, a ferment which was just reaching its peak when Propertius began to write.

We may now assume that Gallus had a share in creating the complexity of Virgil's poetic genealogy, and also that there is no compelling external evidence that need force us to divide Gallus' work in two distinct halves, one of learned, Alexandrian epyllia, the other of subjective elegy. Furthermore, if we take into account that Catullus and the neoterics, prompted by Parthenius, discovered that Alexandrian poetry and Callimachean principles meant primarily a means of expressing a variety of personal emotion, that Latin poetry became, suddenly, both sophisticated and sensitive, then we will not be far from seeing that Gallus must have been of real interest and importance for Propertius at the very beginning of his career as an elegist: Gallus, the student of Parthenius and friend of Virgil, had found in elegy, we may be sure, a means of continuing and developing neoteric principles while integrating that quality of personal emotion we associate primarily with the shorter poems of Catullus.

If we can accept for the moment the not unreasonable assumption that Propertius *must* have begun where Gallus' four books of elegies left off, we may look with some confidence for certain indications that he wrote from the beginning as a conscious neoteric poet. If the *Monobiblos* can be seen as the work of a *doctus poeta* fully aware of and involved in the sudden maturity of Latin poetry, then certain further questions about the development of Propertian elegy will demand consideration.

We may begin with a look at 1.3, followed by some scattered observations, then proceed to a more detailed look at three complete poems. Style and presentation may be more revealing initially than what is being said. After all, the amatory content of the poems is not in question, and it is all too clear that Propertius says surprisingly little – almost nothing in fact – about poetry in this first book, in contrast to what he will write later. But a Latin poet has other means of establishing his place and purpose.

The third poem of the *Monobiblos* has recently been the object of acute analysis, and deservedly, for it is a masterpiece.[1] Interest has naturally focused on the three mythological *exempla* with which the poem opens, and on the interpretative question of their relationship to Cynthia and Propertius in the 'real' world of the poem. Observations have been made on certain clear Catullan elements in the poem (and on some far less clear),[2] but as yet there has been no satisfactory discussion of how the poem relates to previous Latin poetry,[3] Catullan or otherwise, and thus a danger of misconstruing the purpose of the opening *exempla* remains.

Let us first look at lines 19–26, to ask the question, 'By what sort of a poet, under what influence, were they composed?' Propertius has just set the scene of his return, urged on by Bacchus and Amor, and has expressed, from previous experience of her ferocity, his fear of waking Cynthia:

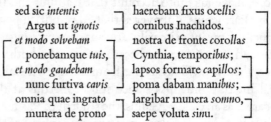

The elaborate sound patterns (as I have indicated them) are brought to the ear's attention by the anaphora *et modo...et modo...*, and by the three successive (quasi-)diminutives at the end of the hexameters. Where had Propertius learned this technique? Catullus 64 opens with an even more complex sound pattern:

[1] A. W. Allen, *Crit. Essays*, 130–4; L. C. Curran, 'Vision and Reality in Propertius 1.3', *YCS* 19 (1966), 189–207; R. O. A. M. Lyne, 'Propertius and Cynthia: Elegy 1.3', *PCPhS* 16 (1970), 60–78.

[2] In addition to the scattered parallels given by commentators, see the allusions to Cat. 64 noted by Curran (esp. pp. 196–7, 207), several of which, however, seem to me doubtful.

[3] I feel no need to say anything about *Anth. Pal.* 5.275 (Paulus Silentiarius), supposed by most to derive from a common Hellenistic source: Paulus' sketch can only serve to illustrate how little Prop. 1.3 has to do with such pieces.

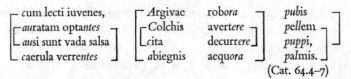

(Cat. 64.4–7)

Undoubtedly a few of the nine years Cinna devoted to his *Zmyrna* were spent evolving such lines. There are further suggestions of Catullus: the *furtiva... poma*, followed by *munera de prono saepe voluta sinu*, calls to mind Catullus 65.19–20, *ut missum sponsi furtivo munere malum* | *procurrit casto virginis e gremio*, just as *omnia quae ingrato...* is a reflection of Catullus 76.9, *omnia quae ingratae perierunt credita menti.*[1] The form *largibar* is paralleled in Propertius only by *operibat* (3.13.35; *lenibunt*, 3.21.32); in Catullus occur *custodibant* (64.319), *scibant* (68.85), *audibant* (84.8).[2] Similarly unusual are the two syncopated perfects, *duxti* (27) and *consumpsti* (37), found in this poem and not elsewhere in Propertius (except for the participle *imposta*, 4.2.29); in Catullus, however, occur *misti* (14.14), *luxti* (66.21), *subrepsti* (77.3), *duxti* (91.9), *promisti* (110.3).[3] Further Catullan flavor is given this second half of the poem by the frequent molossus occurring after the caesura in the hexameters.[4] Perhaps, too, behind the epanalepses *munera somno* | *munera...* (25–6) and *luna fenestras* | *luna* (31–2), occurring so close together, may be heard echoes of the similar use of this Alexandrian device in Catullus 64.[5]

None of these suggestions of Catullus, however, seems intended to recall any specific context; indeed, it might be argued that Propertius hardly expected, or even wanted, a reader to linger over the thoughts of Catullus that inevitably must come to his mind. There is a great difference between these echoes, fleeting and elusive, and those of a purposeful, conscious sort such as, for example, Virgil's reworking (*Aen.* 6.179–82, *itur in antiquam silvam...*) of an Ennian passage (*Ann.* 187–91, *incedunt arbusta per alta...*) or re-application of an Ennian simile (*Aen.* 4.402–7).[6] Here the only reasonable explanation of the suggestions of Catullus

---

[1] *omnia quae* is the emendation of Dousa pater (*omniaque* codd.), to be preferred for sense alone: in Cat. 76.9 the *Veronensis* too read *omniaque*; but cf. *omniaque ingrato* correctly at Prop. 1.17.4.

[2] See Tränkle, *Die Sprachkunst des Properz*, Hermes Einzelschriften 15 (1960), 33–4: though such forms survived colloquially, their occurrence in Prop. must be considered archaic; they do not occur in Hor., in Virg. only in the *Aen.*

[3] See Tränkle, *Die Sprachkunst*, 32–3, for a thorough discussion; again, Virgil's employment of such forms in the *Aen.* suggests that in Prop. too they must be considered literary archaisms.

[4] In lines 5, 19, 25, 29, 31, 37, 39, 41; cf. the opening lines of Cat. 64.

[5] Cf. *prospicit, eheu,* | *prospicit...* (61–2); *perfide ab aris,* | *perfide...* (132–3); *orgia cistis,* | *orgia...* (259–60).

[6] In which *Aen.* 4.404 *it nigrum campis agmen* = Enn. *Ann.* 474: see Serv. *ad loc.*

would seem to be the assumption that Propertius had recently read him completely and carefully, with particular attention perhaps to the epyllion, but with an ear receptive to elements of phrase, language, or style occurring in the other poems. This explanation may suggest, too, that the point of other apparent references to Catullus in the poem should not be pressed too far:[1] the opening *exempla* are consciously mannered and neoteric in style and presentation, and Catullus 64 is certainly brought to mind by the first couplet; but that Propertius wants Ariadne's situation in Catullus' epyllion to be remembered by the reader, or that the other two heroines had similar poetic precedents, seem to me false critical assumptions.

If, then, in a poem with so many clear suggestions of the matter and manner of Catullus, and which indeed opens with what would have been recognized immediately as Catullus' Ariadne, it was not Propertius' purpose to evoke responses to specific Catullan passages, what can we conclude? First, I think, that Propertius produced an entirely original poem, in no way derivative, absorbed though he obviously was at the time in the poetry of Catullus. Secondly, that he had completely assimilated and accepted as a whole what strikes modern scholars and critics as a poetic diversity – the Alexandrian, neoteric Catullus opposed to the poet of personal, subjective love. Not only do elements of language and style from both the 'learned' and the 'personal' poems appear thoroughly mixed in this elegy, but also there is clearly no separating the world of poetic myth from the reality of the personal experience (a 'reality' which, after all, may well have been created by the poet for the poem). Finally, that the creation of such a poem as this means that we can properly speak of Propertius as a neoteric poet, not because of devices or mannerisms employed, but because it represents the work of one who has thoroughly absorbed, and can re-use in an original and personal manner, the essential nature of neoteric verse. Propertius, then, has no need to point to or proclaim his indebtedness to Catullus: the poem itself obviously would have been impossible without his precedent.

If we read the poem again as the work of such a poet, we can see clearly what has been achieved. The event, or dramatic situation, is in itself all too likely to lead to the cold statement of Paulus Silentiarius' treatment (*Anth. Pal.* 5.275), or perhaps to comedy (the modern cartoon type in which the drunken husband returns late to the irate wife, is not far removed): poet returns drunk and late, finds girl sleeping, is moved to rape (but, here, decides against it), girl wakes and expresses anger and

[1] See above, p. 54 n. 2 for parallels Curran finds meaningful.

indignation. The transformation of this unpromising material is performed almost magically, but our eye at times can be faster than the
magician's hand. Neoteric techniques (here absorbed by the poet largely
from Catullus) transform what appears to be a real event into an artificial
literary setting – we are made to feel, half consciously and half without
realizing it, that we have observed the scene and heard the overture
before. Already, then, simply through the poet's use of language and
techniques (which we sometimes regard simply as affected mannerisms
and pointless stylistic tricks), we are at one remove from any actual situation: we experience, with a rather vague uncertainty, a flash of Catullus'
affair, and at the same moment more precise suggestions of the abstract
distillation of his personal experience, his Ariadne. The language and
style of the epyllion are paralleled at another level by poetic myth itself:
the poet, as he stares at Cynthia asleep, becomes Argus watching Io,[1] a
momentary suggestion of a scene from a different world, almost an
inebriate's fancy. The poem opens suddenly with the three *exempla*
('there is deliberate postponement of the object of the comparison and
whether this be a person, situation, or occasion'),[2] the poet's purpose
being to suggest immediately by beautifully stylized and rapidly shifting
mythological images a world of poetic universality.[3] The neoteric
discovery was, in fact, the means of giving personal experience just this
expressive dimension.

We may now consider briefly what Propertius does say about his poetry
in the *Monobiblos*, and how he says it. The seventh poem is addressed to
Ponticus, an epic poet at work on a *Thebaid*, who is warned not to
depreciate Propertius' amatory verse and is told what would be his lot
should he himself fall in love (which, in the parallel ninth poem, indeed
happens). But clearly the point of the poem is the contrast between epic
and elegy: it is in fact a *recusatio*, a refusal to write epic, but one so under-
stated as to be hardly noticeable without a bald statement of content, such
as this. Relevant and familiar terms are to be noted in both the seventh and
ninth poems: epic is *tristis* (*arma...tristia*, 7.2; *tristis istos...libellos*, 9.13)
and *gravis* (*grave...carmen*, 9.9), while elegy is *mollis* (*mollem versum*,
7.19); the poet can depend on the conventional propriety of the terms for

---

[1] Lines 19–20: it would be unreasonable not to allow Calvus' *Io* to be seen behind this
simile, but here again, it seems to me, there could have been no *specific* suggestion or
allusion intended.

[2] So Curran, *YCS* 19 (1966), 190.

[3] I should add again that I do not consider these *exempla* to be related further to the dramatic
situation as it develops: they (and the one in lines 19–20) neither parallel nor interpret
the specific situation of the poem.

each genre when at the beginning of the seventh poem he playfully reverses their application, calling for *mollia fata* for Ponticus' epic verse (line 4) and referring to his own *duram dominam* (6) and *aetatis tempora dura* (8). Seldom, however, in either poem does Propertius openly and directly confront epic with elegy:[1] the point is made almost entirely within the dramatic situation of each elegy – that is, (in the seventh) the warning to Ponticus, who *happens* (we might put it) to be an epic poet, and in the ninth the warning fulfilled, Ponticus in love – and thus the purpose of the poems as *recusationes* is neatly disguised.

Here, then, are two points about the *Monobiblos* it may be helpful to keep in mind (both of which were implied throughout our discussion of 1.3). First, it is clear that the poet can assume that his reader is aware of the poetics of the day; suggestion by a key word or concept, therefore, rather than open discussion and pronouncement, can convey the point to be made when poetry is the real subject of a poem. Secondly, we may gather from the seventh and ninth poems (and confirm by a quick reading of the others) that the method of presentation in the *Monobiblos* is the dramatic situation, a point which is perhaps not as obvious as it might appear. Just as 1.7 and 1.9 might seem at a quick reading to be about what might happen were Ponticus to fall in love and what then does happen, so is it possible for a modern reader, who can never be completely confident about his receptivity to nuance of tone or play of ideas in ancient poetry, to miss the essential purpose of other poems through his inability to penetrate behind the dramatic situation. What we read, then, as spontaneous subjective love poetry of personal experience may only be such in so far as Propertius has chosen so to set the stage: the poems themselves may in fact be far less spontaneous and far more objective, conscious creations.

I should make clear that I do not intend to reveal the poems of the *Monobiblos* as masks of allegory, nor to examine in detail every poem. Caution at this point is as much a necessity as a virtue. For instance, it seems to me possible to make a case for reading 1.2 as another poem about poetry, with 'Cynthia' (who is not in fact mentioned by name, but addressed only as '*vita*' in the first line) standing for his elegy. In the center of the poem occur two different sets of exempla, natural (9–14) and

---

[1] *Plus in amore valet Mimnermi versus Homero* (1.9.11) is such a statement, that is, one that can be read independent of the dramatic situation. Similarly, Propertius' statement in the seventh about his own elegy is an open contrast between the genres, and one, furthermore, that depends on the accepted contrast between the *ingenium* of the epic poet and the *ars* of the Callimachean poet: *nec tantum ingenio quantum servire dolori | cogor* (1.7.7–8) – cf. *tum me non humilem mirabere saepe poetam, | tunc ego Romanis praeferar ingeniis* (1.7.21–2).

mythological (15–22), which obviously must then represent, in both style and content, proper poetry, and which in fact are superbly neoteric.[1] *Vulgo* (line 23) may well refer to the idea of the *profanum vulgus* shunned by the Callimachean poet, and a few lines later (27–8) Apollo and Calliope present 'Cynthia' (*tibi*) with their poetry (*sua carmina*) and the Aonian lyre (*Aoniam...lyram*). Yet even if such a reading of the poem were entirely consistent (which it is not),[2] and even if it could be justified by appeal to the two points raised in the preceding paragraph, there remain other poems in which Cynthia might seductively call for the same sort of interpretation, but which would inspire even less confidence. We must remember, however, that the name 'Cynthia' was chosen by Propertius for its association with the supreme deity of Augustan poetry, Apollo.

A few poems, however, allow us to make some valid observations and inferences, I think, about the nature of the poetry of the *Monobiblos* as Propertius wrote it, and about his place and part in the poetic development of the time as he saw it, particularly with reference to Gallus. In looking closely at these few poems we will have opportunity to add some remarks on other poems and passages, thus perhaps conveying some idea of the book as a whole.

The first elegy of the *Monobiblos*, set beside the opening elegies of the other three books, appears at first to be a very different sort of poem. *Cynthia prima suis miserum me cepit ocellis*: here there is no Apollo or Calliope, no inspirational drink from the proper poetic fountain, no rites of initiation, no allusion to Callimachus or poetic doctrine; but it would be wrong to draw the conclusion that Propertius is ignorant of, or has no interest in, the poetic ideas which will play so important a part in the obviously programmatic poems of each of his later books of elegies. Take, for instance, Apollo and Calliope. The rejection of both at the opening of Book II (*non haec Calliope, non haec mihi cantat Apollo:* | *ingenium nobis ipsa puella facit*, 2.1.3–4) implies, of course, the expected assumption that they would be responsible for such poetry as Propertius is writing; and in Book III both deities go through elaborate motions to

---

[1] For an exemplary discussion of 1.2.9–14 as neoteric, see Tränkle, *Die Sprachkunst*, 25–6, the details of which I need not repeat; the nature of the mythological *exempla* of lines 15–22 should likewise be clear (on *Eueni patriis filia litoribus*, see below, p. 77 n. 2).

[2] In line 2, is the *Coa...veste* then a reference to Philitas (cf. *Coe poeta*, 3.9.44)? or is *tenuis* (*sinus*) to be taken as the key term for neoteric poetry? If so, I cannot make consistent sense of the whole. Points of this reading of 1.2 may in fact be quite correct, but, if so, what may have been clear when Propertius wrote the poem is no longer so, and we should try at this stage not to confuse what little we can call fact with a great deal of plausible fiction.

initiate and advise the poet. Cynthia alone, with no nonsense, is the inspiration of Book 1; but if there seems to be a progression from book to book, a turning away from Cynthia and an acceptance of Apollo and Calliope, it is certainly not because Propertius was unaware in his first efforts that a real poet should look to Apollo and the Muses for his inspiration. Both Apollo and Calliope inspire Cynthia herself in the second poem of the *Monobiblos* (*cum tibi praesertim Phoebus sua carmina donet | Aoniamque libens Calliopea lyram,* 1.2.27–8); both deities first appear together in the Fourth Eclogue, as we have seen (*Orphei Calliopea, Lino formosus Apollo,* 4.57), in a context of primary importance for Virgil's poetic genealogy, and both may therefore have appeared together in Gallus: it is impossible to imagine, then, that Propertius was unaware of the most important contemporary statements about poetry.[1]

The first poem of Book 1 would appear at first to be concerned with love rather than with poetry, and as such might just as well have been the fifth of the Book, or the tenth, or the fifteenth,[2] but I believe that, in a way characteristic of the whole Book, more of the contemporary literary background than can be readily apparent to us is understood and suggested by Propertius and would have been clear to readers of the time, and that when we too can put certain details in their proper literary context, the poem is just as programmatic as any of those to his subsequent Books. The difference, though, lies in the fact that the poetic principles set out for the whole book are here assumed rather than stated, and the poem itself is a representation, rather than an exposition, of why the poet is writing, what his models are, what sort of poetry is to follow and how it is to be read.

The structure of the poem seems purposely clear and simple. There are two halves of twenty lines each.[3] The first half consists, equally neatly, of five couplets introducing Cynthia, Propertius, and his *furor* (1–8, 17–18), into which five couplets (originally) are set containing the mytho-

[1] I will argue below that it is wrong, too, to understand from this progression (with other details as well) that Propertius begins in Book II, and especially in Book III, to write a new and different sort of poetry.

[2] B. Otis ('Propertius' Single Book', *HSCP* 70 (1965), 12) does call the poem programmatic, but only as regards theme: 'Furthermore, it is clearly a programmatic piece: this is the theme of a whole *book* of poems, the proem to a literary work that sets the key for the whole.'

[3] Housman's lacuna (a pentameter and hexameter) after line 11 is certainly right (it can be supported by grammatical usage, by sense, by the parallel context in Ovid, *AA* 2.185–96, and by structure): see Housman, *JP* 16 (1888), 19–22 and on Man. 1.898, and also Shackleton Bailey, *Propertiana* (Cambridge, 1956), 2–3 – though he 'perhaps' prefers *saepe* for *ille* in line 12 as a solution to the grammatical difficulty. On the structure, cf. P. J. Enk, *Mnem.* 3 (1936), 149–52, who uses a structural argument (somewhat different from mine) to support Housman's lacuna; and B. Otis, *HSCP* 70 (1965), 39 n. 12.

logical exemplum of Milanion and Atalanta (9–16). The second half begins with two groups of three couplets each (*at vos*. . . 19–24, *et vos*. . . 25–30), followed by two couplets of summary and contrast (*vos*. . . 31–2, *in me*. . . 33–4), and finally two couplets in conclusion (35–8). The transitions between these sections are smooth and natural, and the precise divisions suggested here should not be insisted upon beyond their usefulness in indicating the development of the programmatic content of the poem.

The two sections of the first half present a striking stylistic contrast. The lines introducing Cynthia's first devastating effect on the poet (1–8) are written in a language which can only be described as simple, pure elegiac, totally different from the oddly archaic and highly poetic tone of the *exemplum*:[1]

> Milanion nullos fugiendo, Tulle, labores
>   saevitiam durae contudit Iasidos.
> nam modo Partheniis amens errabat in antris,
>   ibat et hirsutas ille videre feras;
> ille etiam Hylaei percussus vulnere rami
>   saucius Arcadiis rupibus ingemuit.
> ergo velocem potuit domuisse puellam:
>   tantum in amore preces et bene facta valent.
>
>   (1.1.9–16)

Various archaisms and poeticisms of vocabulary in these lines have been admirably collected and discussed by Tränkle, among them *saevitiam contudit* (10), *antris* and *amens errabat* (11), *hirsutus* (12), *Hylaei* as an adjective (13), *domuisse* (15); and of grammar, such as the ablative *fugiendo* with an object (9), *ibat* with an infinitive of purpose *videre* (12),[2] *potuit* with the perfect infinitive *domuisse* (15). Few passages of equal length in Propertius contain so many peculiarities of style, but Tränkle is certainly right in clearing Propertius of the charge of vulgarisms: all these features clearly represent an attempt to reproduce an artificial poetic language, stylized and somewhat archaic. It remains, though, to ask why Propertius has done so, and what his model might have been.[3]

Some further observations on the language and presentation of the

---

[1] See P. Fedeli, 'Osservazioni sullo stile di Properzio', *SIFC* 41 (1969), 81–94, who discusses the stylistic difference between lines 1–8 and 9–16 (pp. 83–6), comparing the opening section to Meleager, *Anth. Pal.* 12.101 ('Nei vv. 1–8 la lingua è quella tipica della poesia amorosa', p. 83); his comments on lines 9–16 are mostly repeated from Tränkle, *Die Sprachkunst*, 12–17.

[2] *Videre* is probably right – see Shackleton Bailey *ad loc.*

[3] A. La Penna, *Properzio* (Florence, 1951), 178–9, sees the Milanion *exemplum* derived from Hellenistic models, but few have bothered to inquire further.

exemplum may be made. One striking neoteric feature occurs in line 15. Propertius has been relating a variant of the Milanion–Atalanta story which we hear of elsewhere only infrequently, that Atalanta was finally won through Milanion's perseverance and faithful service.[1] The usual form of the story has it that a suitor's success will depend on his beating Atalanta in a foot race, a victory Hippomenes is able to win by the stratagem of throwing the golden apple in front of the girl, which she of course stops to pick up. This version has nothing to do with the one Propertius relates (and in fact some ancient mythographers are careful to explain that there were two Atalantas), but he does allude to it in line 15 by the epithet *velocem... puellam*; it is a feature of Alexandrian learned poetry to point, in some such way, to versions of a myth other than the one being told: we have mentioned above an example of this, Virgil's treatment of Scylla in *Ecl.* 6.74–7, where he relates in outline the story of the monster daughter of Phorcys, but by calling her *Scyllam Nisi* points to the other, who became the *ciris*.

Another neoteric detail has not, as far as I am aware, been noticed. The avoidance of a common proper name is, of course, a 'learned' mannerism in neoteric poetry: to use a patronymic or a geographical designation is far more elegant. So in these lines Atalanta is never allowed the simplicity of her own name, but in line 10 appears with her patronymic and epithet, *durae Iasidos*. We have seen that there is a reason for the other epithet she receives in these lines, *velocem*: is there any reason for this one? At *Aen.* 4.247 Virgil gives the same epithet to Mt Atlas (*Atlantis duri...* | *Atlantis* – the repetition of the name seems pointed), where it is recognized as an etymological gloss explaining the Greek name (ἀ - τλα-), 'unyielding'. Propertius had previously used the same gloss, with the same significance, though with the further refinement that the proper name Atalanta is to be supplied by the reader aware of such things.[2]

The details of another line demand particular attention: *nam modo Partheniis amens errabat in antris*. First, Tränkle notes that *errans... amens* occurred previously in Cicero (*Arat.* 420–1, *ut quondam Orion manibus violasse Dianam* | *dicitur excelsis errans in collibus amens*) and suggests (though without apparent reason) that it may go back to Ennius; he

---

[1] Cf. esp. Ovid, *AA* 2.185–92, obviously using the same source (and *Am.* 3.2.29 = *AA* 3.775); see *ThLL* s.v. *Atalanta* for other references.

[2] The identical function and purpose (*durus* = ἀ - τλα-) in Propertius and Virgil, and Propertius' priority, seem to suggest a common 'source'. If the Milanion *exemplum*, as is argued here, comes directly from Gallus, then I would postulate that *dura Atalanta* occurred in Gallus, then *dura* but without the key proper name in Propertius, then *durus* but applied to Atlas in Virgil: a fine example, if so it happened, of originality within a specific detail. (See my note in *Mnem.* 26 (1973), 60–2.)

also, however, cites Ovid, *Ars Amatoria* 1.527, *Cnosis in ignotis amens errabat harenis*, where the words occur in exactly the same position as they do in Propertius, but this need not indicate that Ovid remembers the line directly from Propertius – the context is not so simple. *Antrum*, as Tränkle also notes, is a poetic word (as the *Thesaurus* says, 'vox a poetis novellis ex Graeco tracta'), but there is more to it than that.[1] It first appears in Virgil's *Eclogues*, more often than not with the special meaning 'glen' (rather than 'cave'), or, as the *Oxford Latin Dictionary* now nicely defines it, 'a hollow place with overarching foliage'.[2] One further observation can give support to Norden's suggestion that *antrum* did not begin its poetic career in Virgil: here again the epithet, *Partheniis in antris*, seems far from otiose. Mt Parthenius (in Arcadia) occurs for the first time, and for the only other time in Augustan poetry, in the *Eclogues*, specifically at that point in the Tenth Eclogue where Gallus himself speaks of hunting (*non me ulla vetabunt | frigora Parthenios canibus circumdare saltus*, 10.56–7),[3] and the similarity of the two contexts as well suggests that they are not independent (Gallus, in Arcadia, sick with love, proposing to hunt; Milanion, in Arcadia, *amens errabat*, actually hunting). Now, since there is little reason for Propertius to be referring to the Tenth Eclogue here (or to any of the others, for that matter, where the special sense of *antrum* occurs), it is reasonable, if not inescapable, that he and Virgil both refer to a poem or passage by Gallus himself. This hypothesis can be given further support. It was on Mt Parthenius that Atalanta was exposed as a child, and in fact its name was commonly derived from this event.[4] Gallus, writing of Milanion and Atalanta would then certainly have had cause to set the scene on Parthenius, just as does Propertius; but there can be only one reason or explanation for Virgil's setting Gallus on Parthenius – that Gallus had used the Atalanta–Milanion *exemplum* in an important passage about his own amatory situation, and only by such an assumption can the similarity of the contexts in Virgil and Propertius be understood.[5]

---

[1] Norden is, as always, instructive (on *Aen.* 6.10): 'Uns begegnet *antrum* zuerst in V.s buc. I, 75; da es aber für Vergil und die anderen Augusteer schon ganz geläufig ist, wird es von den Neoterikern aus der zierlichen hellenistischen Poesie, in der die ἄντρα ja eine grosse Rolle spielten, übernommen worden sein...' I would suggest Gallus again (the word does not appear in Catullus), whom Norden goes on to suggest as the source for Virgil's *spelaeum* in *Ecl.* 10. 52: cf. the discussion immediately following.

[2] *Ecl.* 1.75, 5.6, 19, 9.41 must have this meaning (rather than 'cave'), and it is more fitting at 6.13 as well; neither the *ThLL* nor Lewis and Short recognize this meaning clearly.

[3] See D. C. Swanson, *The Names in Roman Verse* (Madison, 1967), 245. Propertius, it should be noted, substitutes the Virgilian (Gallan?) word *antris* with its special sense for Virgil's *saltus*.

[4] See *ThLL* vol. 2, 1012.55–9 (s.v. *Atalanta*) for refs.

[5] Why the Arcadian Mt Parthenius, then, in Propertius, Virgil, and presumably Gallus,

The entire *exemplum*, then, may come directly from an important programmatic passage by Gallus. This would explain the highly stylized, archaic-poetic tone of the lines, and why this particular variant of the story was chosen for a position of prominence in Propertius' first poem (the variant alone would immediately direct an Augustan reader to Gallus); this also explains the neoteric features of expression and presentation we have observed – why, for instance, Propertius calls the daughter of Iasos '*dura*', why *amens errabat* should have stuck in Ovid's mind, why Propertius should have used *antrum*, and particularly why these glens should have been 'Parthenian'. What is the function and purpose of this extended and elaborate *exemplum*, taken from Gallus, in Propertius' first poem?

We have suggested that the five couplets of the Milanion *exemplum* should be regarded structurally as an inset in the frame of 1–8 and 17–18 – the last couplet of this first half of the poem returns to the poet's own situation and serves also to establish the point of the *exemplum*, almost as if it were a simile. Here, somewhat unexpectedly, the comparison of Milanion's case to Propertius' situation is a negative one – things are *not* going as they once did:

> in me tardus Amor non nullas cogitat artis,
> nec meminit notas, ut prius, ire vias.
> (1.1.17–18)[1]

ut prius, as Rothstein noted, refers to the time of the *exemplum*, and the *notae viae* are the ways along which the world has always moved and should still be moving; but *tardus Amor* with his 'tricks' complicates the

---

but nowhere else? I would with some confidence support the suggestion that originally Gallus hit upon it as a compliment to his mentor Parthenius (see J. Hubaux, *Les Thèmes Bucoliques dans la Poésie Latine* (Brussels, 1930), 96 n. 1, for this suggestion): it then comes easily enough into its two other contexts, but would be inappropriate otherwise for the Augustan poets. This would suggest, too, that Gallus used the *exemplum* in a programmatic context, and thus would explain why it was so obviously important for Virgil and Propertius – the context of the *exemplum* in Gallus must have been something more than casual.

[1] *non ullas* (codd. dett.) is read by modern editors against the *non nullas* of the older MSS, and must mean, as Enk paraphrases (*ad loc.*), 'nihil comminiscitur quo Cynthiam mihi conciliare possim,' but there are certain objections to this. Milanion won Atalanta not by *artes* (μηχαναί, 'tricks'), but by *preces* (read *fides*? – Fonteine's conjecture approved by Housman) and *benefacta, nullos fugiendo labores*, and thus it would be strangely forgetful of Propertius to have emphasized the diligent and faithful service of Milanion only to complain immediately afterwards, 'But in my case Love doesn't supply me with any tricks'; furthermore, the meaning Enk wants (and presumably other commentators, who are silent on these lines) would demand a dative 'for me', such as *sed mihi tardus Amor non ullas cogitat artis*. *Non nullas*, on the other hand, gives perfect sense: 'Milanion's hard work and perseverance were fine *then* (*prius*), but *in my case* (in spite of my diligence) Love plots tricks *against me*, and doesn't go the way he always used to' (*in me* can be taken with both ablative and accusative force simultaneously).

ancient scheme of things, and no longer can service as faithful as Milanion's produce results. The first half of the poem, then, is a neatly contained unit: the *exemplum*, which presents the ancient and natural order of the lover's world, when frustration could be overcome by devotion, is framed by the poet's own situation, a time of unhappy complications. Moreover, we can begin to see now just how the poem is programmatic: not only is the originality of Propertius' amatory experience established (as we have just described), but by taking the *exemplum* directly from Gallus, literary debt and descent are acknowledged, and originality within the tradition is proclaimed. The marked stylistic contrast between the two sections of this first half intentionally reflects this same programmatic purpose.

One would expect the second half of the poem (lines 19–38, which would be 21–40 of the original) to be programmatic in much the same way, and I believe it is. On the level of content, the structure and progression are relatively simple. First, three couplets addressed to what appear to be magicians ('I will believe in your powers if you can make Cynthia respond to me'), balanced by three couplets addressed to his friends ('Go look for a cure – for all the good it will do – but take me far away'). Then, by a smooth transition, Propertius addresses those (*vos*) to whom the god nods easily (31–2); in his own case (33–4) both Venus and Amor are harsh. Finally, there are two concluding couplets as a general admonition.

Why, though, does Propertius spend so much time addressing magicians in the first section of this second half?

> at vos, deductae quibus est fallacia lunae
>   et labor in magicis sacra piare focis,
> en agedum dominae mentem convertite nostrae,
>   et facite illa meo palleat ore magis!
> tunc ego crediderim vobis et sidera et amnis
>   posse Cytaeines ducere carminibus.
>
> (1.1.19–24)

Presumably we must suppose that Propertius wanted desperately to be converted to a belief in magic, or that among his close friends he had a number of magicians: they are given a place of prominence in the poem (these six lines are not a casual reference), and the obvious structural correspondence with the following three couplets demands an explanation. One hint from the poet is enough. *Ducere* (line 24) has caused commentators some trouble,[1] but the slight oddity of the word in its context

---

[1] Beginning with Housman (*JP* 16 (1888), 27–30), who wrote *tunc ego crediderim et manes et*

was intentional: here, just after the half-way point in the last line of the passage, it is meant to recall *deductae* of the first line (19) just before the caesura, and, what is more, is to be understood as *deducere* by a common linguistic feature native to Latin and exploited by the Latin poets, whereby a prefix is to be understood when the simple verb is repeated (or even with a different verb of similar meaning).[1] This is a poet's way of underlining his intention: the poetic device of the repetition of the simple verb, to be taken as the compound, and the placement of the two forms to frame the passage, are characteristic neoteric details.

Nothing was easier than for a poet to use a form of *deducere* after Virgil's Sixth Eclogue to suggest in a fitting context the special poetic significance given the verb there (lines 3–5, as we have discussed above), and that the verb is played upon and repeated by Propertius here is an invitation to remember Virgil and the Callimachean *recusatio*.[2] Moreover, it is no chance recall when (as we have seen) *deducere* occurs later in the Sixth Eclogue, applied to the magic power of Orpheus' song over nature ([*hos calamos*] *quibus ille solebat | cantando rigidas deducere montibus ornos*, 70–1, where the verb is also emphasized by position). In these three couplets Propertius is obviously doing more than expressing interest in the magician's craft (and we should note that, in fact, no magicians are referred to – there is no restricting word such as *magi*, the only vocative is a general *vos*): those who have power over moon, stars, and streams by their songs are poets, and the repeated *deducere* makes this clear. Propertius is referring to one important complex of Virgilian poetics, in forming which Gallus must have played an important part, that of the magical power of neoteric song, of 'scientific poetry'. If such poetry could charm Cynthia, then Propertius would welcome it.

The next three couplets are a corresponding structural unit:

> et vos, qui sero lapsum revocatis, amici,
>   quaerite non sani pectoris auxilia.
> fortiter et ferrum saevos patiemur et ignis,

sidera vobis | posse Cytinaeis ducere carminibus on the grounds that *amnes ducere* is 'one of the commonest operations of Italian agriculture', entirely out of place in a context of magical incantation: I agree, but suggest that Propertius did not in fact imply the agricultural operation when he wrote *amnes ducere*. Butler and Barber feel some difficulty they find hard to express, and Enk glosses *ducere* with ἐφέλκεσθαι (note the prefix).

[1] See W. V. Clausen in *AJP* 76 (1955), 49–51, and 86 (1965), 97–8: this feature occurs in the Twelve Tables and in Roman comedy, and has been noted in Greek poetry. That it may have been a common Indo-European construction is argued by C. Watkins, 'An Indo-European Construction in Greek and Latin', *HSCP* 71 (1967), 115–19.

[2] In Propertius *deducere* occurs only once after Book II (1.1.19, 6.15, 16.41; 2.20.21, 25.9, 33.38; 4.3.13). One should note 1.16.41, *at tibi saepe novo deduxi carmina versu*, and 2.33.38, *et mea deducta carmina voce legis*. In the other occurrences, the context does not allow the poetic meaning to intrude – intentionally, it would seem.

> sit modo libertas, quae velit ira, loqui.
> ferte per extremas gentis et ferte per undas,
> qua non ulla meum femina norit iter.
>
> (1.1.25–30)

Two 'themes' are involved (a medical cure for the lover, *non sani pectoris auxilia*; and the removal of the lover to the ends of the earth), but the relationship of one to the other is none too clear, and the lines are more difficult than the general silence of commentators would suggest. If Propertius, in the first two couplets, says, 'Look for medical aid, I can stand any surgery,' then why does he say in the third, 'Take me far away,' as if medical attention has been futile? What he *should* be saying, instead of 'Look for a cure' (*quaerite. . . auxilia*), is 'Don't waste your time looking for a cure – there's no cure for love – and since this is so (in elegy), then take me far away.'[1] Before we can resolve these difficulties, we must again try to place these themes in their proper poetic contexts.

We can be sure of the first theme; it is suggested again in the next poem,

> crede mihi, non ulla tuae est medicina figurae:
> nudus Amor formae non amat artificem
>
> (1.2.7–8)

though in a very different context. Later, however, a similar pentameter occurs in a context identical to that of 1.1:

> omnis humanos sanat medicina dolores,
> solus amor morbi non amat artificem.
>
> (2.1.57–8)

And to these we may add (Propertius speaking to 'Gallus'):

> non ego tum potero solacia ferre roganti,
> cum mihi nulla mei sit medicina mali.
>
> (1.5.27–8)

From these parallels we may be quite sure that Propertius intends 1.1.25–8 to be understood as, 'There is no medical cure for love.' In a programmatic poem a simple, abbreviated statement of a theme antici- pates its later, more extensive development; we are justified in attempting to understand the theme here from these subsequent contexts.[2]

Shackleton Bailey objects to the text of 2.1.58 (*solus amor morbi non*

---

[1] Perhaps the *auxilia* called for by the poet is (metaphorically) a passage booked for the ends of the earth: but why then the specifically medical operation of the middle couplet? Enk, who does seem bothered by the lines, stretches *quaerite* to get an acceptable meaning, 'verbum significat poetam non credere talia remedia inventum iri.'

[2] That Propertius seems to say the opposite in 1.10.17–18 (*et possum alterius curas sanare recentis,* | *nec levis in verbis est medicina meis*) should not mislead: this is a reversal of the normal elegiac expectation, the sort of reversal used so frequently and effectively by Ovid.

amat artificem) on the grounds that 'Nowhere else does Propertius so echo himself as the Vulgate here echoes 1.2.8 *nudus Amor formae non amat artificem...*'[1] But the unusual echo may be a sign that the poet, in fact, is not repeating *himself*. Tränkle points to the rarity of the word *medicina* in poetry, and goes on to suggest a source for the lines which we may regard as certain.[2] Gallus in the Tenth Eclogue speaks of *nostri medicina furoris* (line 60, cf. Prop. 1.1.7, *furor hic*). Adding this hint to the unusual repetition of 1.2.8 and 2.1.58 (both with *medicina* in the preceding hexameters), and considering other suggestions of the poet Gallus in 1.5 (where, at line 28, we have *medicina mali* – cf. 1.1.35, *hoc malum*),[3] we may be quite sure that an elegy or elegies of Gallus are referred to in 1.1.25–8, though unfortunately, without the original passages, complete understanding is impossible.

The third couplet of this section again is a bare statement of a theme more fully developed later, as, for instance, in 1.18 (discussed in more detail below) or in 1.20.13–14: natural solitude reflects in its desolation the situation of the unhappy lover. The juxtaposition of this theme to that of the *medicina furoris* of the preceding two couplets can only be understood from the Tenth Eclogue. Briefly, Gallus there is dying of love (*amore peribat*, 10.10), and when attempts by Apollo, Silvanus, and Pan to offer words of comfort fail (cf. *et vos, qui sero lapsum revocatis, amici,* Prop. 1.1.25), as they are bound to, Gallus finds himself thinking of natural solitude (*iam mihi per rupes videor lucosque sonantis | ire...*, 10.58–9) and the ends of the earth (lines 65–8, *Hebrum, Sithonias nives*, the *Aethiopes* – cf. *ferte per extremas gentis et ferte per undas*, Prop. 1.1.29). These three couplets, then, seem to be a statement of two elegiac alternatives open for the unhappy lover, both of them understandable as such only when seen as prominent themes in Gallus' elegies, and to be developed later by Propertius himself. The stark juxtaposition ('Look for medical help: take me far away') is perfectly acceptable in a programmatic poem.

Finally, before considering the programmatic purpose of the poem as a whole, there is one further indication afforded by the Tenth Eclogue of Propertius' concern with Gallus. *Cura* (*sua quemque moretur | cura,* 35–6) with the meaning *'amica'* first occurs in *Ecl.* 10.22:

---

[1] *Propertiana*, 63. He goes on to argue that *'dolor non amat medicum* is near to nonsense,' and emends *artificem* to *auxilium* ('only love rejects all remedy for its disease'), though he does not cite 1.1.26, *non sani pectoris auxilia*.

[2] Tränkle, *Die Sprachkunst*, 22–3.

[3] Propertius similarly echoes himself in 1.5.24, *nescit Amor priscis cedere imaginibus* = 1.14.8, *nescit Amor magnis cedere divitiis*; if we suspect again that Propertius is not echoing himself, Tränkle confirms the suspicion (p. 23) and attributes the lines to Gallus.

omnes 'unde amor iste' rogant 'tibi?' venit Apollo
'Galle, quid insanis?' inquit 'tua cura Lycoris
perque nives alium perque horrida castra secuta est.'

It may well be that Gallus himself had first used the word with this meaning, as it is specifically connected with him here; yet Virgil has his own purpose. These three lines (21–3) are an exact translation of Theocritus (1.81–3); when Virgil translates so precisely, there is usually a reason. An observable part of Virgil's reason here is an elaborate etymological play on *tua cura Lycoris* and the Greek of Theocritus at the end of the same line:

πάντες ἀνηρώτευν τί πάθοι κακόν. ἦνθ' ὁ Πρίηπος
κἦφα 'Δάφνι τάλαν, τί τὺ τάκεαι; ἁ δέ τυ κώρα
πάσας ἀνὰ κράνας, πάντ' ἄλσεα ποσσὶ φορεῖται.'

Virgil has put *Lycoris* in the same position in his line as Theocritus' κώρα, and glossed it with *tua cura* (κούρη, Ionic and always in Homer = κώρα).[1] If this play on *cura* = κούρη / κώρα = *Lycoris* originated with Gallus (as we might suspect),[2] Virgil, by introducing it in his translation of Theocritus, has at least given it remarkable prominence, and makes certain that any poet using *cura* in the new sense of *amica* must be doing so with this passage in mind. Propertius, once again in his first poem, can be seen looking to the Tenth Eclogue, or to the poet Gallus behind it.

Gallus, then, can be seen clearly behind each section of Propertius' first elegy. The elaborate *exemplum* of the first half must reproduce not only the style of Gallus, but must be derived from a similar Milanion *exemplum* which will have occurred in a programmatic context in Gallus' elegies. In Propertius the *exemplum* serves two general purposes: through it he establishes originality of approach to amatory verse – past experience as presented in the *exemplum* being contrasted with his own situation; and by pointing to Gallus as his precedent, he defines his own place in the elegiac tradition. If the first half, then, is primarily concerned with the situation and experience of the elegist, the second half looks to poetry.

---

[1] Virgil's fascination with the word *cura* can be seen also at the beginning of *Aen.* 4: *At regina gravi iamdudum saucia cura | vulnus alit venis et caeco carpitur igni* (1–2), lines which introduce the controlling imagery of the book, the fire and the wound. Servius, in a comment ignored by most moderns, notes, '*cura...quod cor urat*': that this is no fanciful etymologizing, but one which would have been known to Virgil and therefore calculated as part of the imagery here, is clear from Varro's identical etymology (*LL* 6.46).

[2] Gallus may be seen behind the *tua cura* of *Ecl.* 1.57 (*raucae, tua cura, palumbes*; cf. Prop. 3.3.31, *et Veneris dominae volucres, mea turba, columbae*): on this neoteric appositional construction, see Norden on *Aen.* 6.7 (p. 117); and on Gallus here, O. Skutsch, *RhM* 99 (1956), 198–9.

The poetry of magic or science (whatever name we may choose for it will be inadequate) is dismissed – though not denied – as ineffective for his elegy: Gallus had been initiated to the mysteries of Orphic magic and Hesiodic science, to poetry as the power over nature and the understanding of it, a unifying conception of the poet's control over physical reality and pure mythology – 'ἴδμεν ψεύδεα πολλὰ λέγειν ἐτύμοισιν ὁμοῖα | ἴδμεν δ' εὖτ' ἐθέλωμεν ἀληθέα γηρύσασθαι', as the Muses said to Hesiod the shepherd (*Theog.* 27–8). Propertius' position is, for the moment, more humble, his claim less exalted. His elegy (*Cynthia prima...*) demands of him total submission, for which there is no medical cure, which can find its poetic image only in the desolate solitude of nature: this is the aspect of Gallan elegy which Propertius will follow and develop. The Gallus of the Tenth Eclogue had finally submitted: *omnia vincit Amor: et nos cedamus Amori* (10.69, his last words): from this point Propertius begins his elegies (*Cynthia... me cepit*).

It is remarkable to what extent the themes suggested by Propertius dominate the movement of the Tenth Eclogue, and how specific stylistic features point so consistently to Gallus. We began this discussion with the claim that the poem is as programmatic (that is, as much concerned with poetry and how it is to be written) as any of the later, obviously programmatic poems (2.1, 3.1 and 3.3, 4.1), but that it is so in a very different way, a way we noted above as characteristic of the *Monobiblos*, in which content or meaning is presented solely by the dramatic situation of a poem, though indications of a poem's ultimate purpose are afforded to the initiated through key words or ideas. In his later statements about poetry Propertius seems so much more self-conscious, so much more intent on emphasizing and defining his role: here at the beginning of his first book he appears to take for granted what poetry had come to be, and hence feels no necessity to parade the symbols and tokens of the poet's calling. He neither denies nor proclaims the neotericism of Gallus and Virgil: he is part of it, thoroughly and naturally, and writes as one within an accepted tradition, the only tradition conceivable; he sets limits for himself within established territory, but does not deny, or even question, the validity of what he excludes. His first poem assumes an awareness of the important poetic ideas and movements of the time, that there is but one way poetry can be written: there is no need for the poet to preach, for there is no possibility of his poetry being misconceived.

We may now look at some examples of how the acceptance of the new poetry works in his first book, and, where possible, at Gallus as a precedent.

> ferte per extremas gentis et ferte per undas,
> qua non ulla meum femina norit iter.
>
> (1.1.29–30)

What Propertius proposed in the first poem of Book 1 becomes a reality in 1.18: the setting of the poem (lines 1–4) is an empty grove (*vacuum nemus*), deserted and silent (*Haec certe deserta loca et taciturna querenti*), where the desolation corresponds to the lover's abandoned solitude (*hic licet occultos proferre impune dolores, | si modo sola queant saxa tenere fidem*). Propertius, in this entirely unreal landscape, then asks three questions about the cause of Cynthia's sudden anger: does she think she has been replaced by someone else (9–16)? does he himself seem less responsive to her (17–22)? has some injury done by her to him caused her anger in bad conscience (23–6)? After these almost mundane probings into what has no more dignity, humor, or interest than a housewife's bad temper, the poem closes with a return to the operatic stage scenery of natural desolation (27–32), Propertius alone, lamenting to the birds, the woods echoing 'Cynthia'. What explains this curious mixture of stylized fantasy with the all too real?

Propertius' solitude, however, is not as desolate as this first impression has it. Lines 5–6, which introduce his questions, have a close enough parallel in Theocritus to make the suggestion of pastoral seem intentional:

> unde tuos primum repetam, mea Cynthia, fastus?
> quod mihi das flendi, Cynthia, principium?
> νῦν δὴ μώνα ἐοῖσα πόθεν τὸν ἔρωτα δακρύσω;
> ἐκ τίνος ἄρξωμαι; τίς μοι κακὸν ἄγαγε τοῦτο;
>
> (Theocr. 2.64–5)

Corydon, the crossed *pastor* of the Second Eclogue, likewise repeatedly seeks wild solitude for voicing his distress:

> tantum inter densas, umbrosa cacumina, fagos
> adsidue veniebat. ibi haec incondita solus
> montibus et silvis studio iactabat inani.
>
> (*Ecl.* 2.3–5)

Propertius' barren rocks do in fact yield to a more sylvan scene in lines 19–22:

> vos eritis testes, si quos habet arbor amores,
> fagus et Arcadio pinus amica deo.
> a quotiens teneras resonant mea verba sub umbras,
> scribitur et vestris Cynthia corticibus,

lines which allow us to see further into Propertius' purpose. First, the *Arcadius deus* is clearly the pastoral Pan of the *Eclogues* (as in *Ecl.* 10.26,

Pan deus Arcadiae, who comes to console Gallus). The *fagus*, though, has caused commentators some difficulty, as there is no love story associated with it as there is for Pan and the pine. We have recently been shown, however, that Propertius' *fagus* comes from Callimachus' treatment of Acontius and Cydippe.[1] Moreover, the *fagus* is, beyond all others perhaps, the tree of the Eclogues: Tityrus begins in its shade (*Tityre, tu patulae recubans sub tegmine fagi*, 1.1); Corydon sings his lament among the beeches (*inter densas, umbrosa cacumina, fagos*, 2.3), which later seem to represent the shattered illusion of the pastoral world (*et veteres, iam fracta cacumina, fagos*, 9.9), both of which lines prominently display the neoteric appositional construction;[2] one may wonder why Menalcas 'shattered' the bow and pipes of Daphnis 'at the old beech grove' (*aut hic ad veteres fagos cum Daphnidis arcum | fregisti et calamos*, 3.12–13); and in *Ecl.* 5 the bark of the beech is carved with pastoral poems (*. . . in viridi nuper quae cortice fagi | carmina descripsi. . .*, 5.13–14). One final suggestion of pastoral poetry may be noted: line 31 (*sed qualiscumque es resonent mihi 'Cynthia' silvae*) looks back to line 21 (where *resonant* stands in a corresponding position), and also to *Ecl.* 1.4–5 (*tu, Tityre, lentus in umbra | formosam resonare doces Amaryllida silvas*). It is clear that Propertius was very much concerned with pastoral, and specifically with the *Eclogues*, when he set his poem in the wilderness, to the extent that the wilderness, almost in spite of itself, becomes far less wild.

But how are we to understand this intrusion of the pastoral, and can we see further into the literary background of the poem? Ample demonstration has lately been provided that Callimachus' story of Acontius and Cydippe furnished Propertius the material for much of the elegy:[3] we have Callimachus' own lines from the *Aetia* about Acontius' wanderings in the wilds[4] and his carving of Cydippe's name on the bark of trees,[5] and further points of correspondence are provided by Aristaenetus' paraphrase of Callimachus.[6] Such observations are particularly valuable

---

[1] See F. Cairns, 'Propertius i.18 and Callimachus, *Acontius and Cydippe*', *CR* 19 (1969), 133.

[2] See above, p. 69 n. 2, and H. Pillinger, *HSCP* 73 (1969), 184.

[3] The details owed to Callimachus have been neatly observed by Cairns, *CR* 19 (1969). See also A. La Penna, *Properzio*, 167–72, for good observations on the pastoral elements in this elegy; and F. Solmsen, 'Three Elegies of Propertius' First Book', *CP* 57 (1962), 73–88. But none of these studies even mentions Gallus as a possible precedent.

[4] ἄγραδε τῷ πάσῃσιν ἐπὶ προχάνῃσιν ἐφοίτα (fr. 72 Pf.).

[5] ἀλλ' ἐνὶ δὴ φλοιοῖσι κεκομμένα τόσσα φέροιτε | γράμματα, Κυδίππην ὅσσ' ἐρέουσι καλήν (fr. 73 Pf.): this motif, of course, occurs in Greek comedy, epigram, and bucolic frequently (see, e.g., Enk on Prop. 1.18).

[6] Among other details, Cairns shows that the setting of Propertius' elegy (lines 1–6) must come from Callimachus, as must the lines (21 and 31) where the trees echo (*resonare*) Cynthia's name, and lines 19–20 (mentioned above).

as a reminder that, from the very beginning, 'This is the work of the Callimachus Romanus,' as Cairns puts it. But here again we are able to see clearly enough that Propertius wrote the elegy not simply as an exercise in translating Callimachus' objective treatment into a subjective elegiac form, but because a nearer, Roman precedent called for his attention. Tränkle has suggested (it can be no more than a suggestion) that line 8 (*nunc in amore tuo cogor habere notam*) is derived from Gallus.[1] We can feel more confidence, I think, in attributing lines 21–2 to Gallus. In the Tenth Eclogue Virgil's Gallus decides to live in the woods among the dens of wild beasts and to carve his *amores* on the trees:

> certum est in silvis inter spelaea ferarum
> malle pati tenerisque meos incidere amores
> arboribus: crescent illae, crescetis, amores.
>
> (*Ecl.* 10.52–4)

Spelaea, a hapax legomenon, may go back to Gallus, as Norden suggested;[2] and *meos amores* (especially prominent by its repetition at the end of successive lines) may well refer to the title of Gallus' four books of elegies, as F. Skutsch thought.[3] In any case, it is highly probable that Virgil is repeating the sense of these lines, at least, from Gallus, in which case Propertius is looking as much to Gallus' lines, when he refers to inscribing 'Cynthia' on the bark of trees, as to Callimachus. *a quotiens teneras resonant mea verba sub umbras*: the neoteric exclamation *a* provides a further hint; there is no doubt that it was a prominent feature in Gallus' poetry (or at least was a notable feature of a prominent passage), for in *Ecl.* 10.46–9 (the lines which Servius notes are 'translated from Gallus') *a* occurs three times, twice in conjunction with postponed *ne* (cf. *et* postponed in Propertius' next line, *scribitur et vestris Cynthia corticibus*).[4]

We may now draw some conclusions about the background of the poem and about Propertius' purpose. It is evident that the setting and many of the details come from Callimachus, but it is also reasonably clear that Gallus is acknowledged as well; in fact, lines 19–22 for which Callimachean influence has been clearly demonstrated, reveal just as clearly the touch of Gallus, and the general situation of Gallus in *Ecl.* 10.52–4, as noted by F. Skutsch,[5] certainly corresponds to that of

---

[1] P.24: Tränkle notes the similarity in content in Ovid *Am.* 1.7.42, 3.14.34 (*dentis habere notam*) and Tib. 1.8.38 (*figere dente notas*), and the formal agreement of Propertius and Ovid, and argues for 'ein älteres Vorbild', Gallus.

[2] *Aeneis VI*, 119.

[3] *Frühzeit*, 21–2; cf. *Ecl.* 10.34, *vestra meos olim si fistula dicat amores.*

[4] The exclamation *a* occurs 9 times in Prop. I, 10 in II, 5 in III, and never in IV: many of the instances in I may well suggest Gallus.

[5] *Frühzeit*, 13.

Propertius here. It is impossible to say, of course, how Gallus used Callimachus' Acontius and Cydippe episode, or to say with absolute certainty
that he did at all (though the intimate interrelationship of Gallan and
Callimachean elements in Propertius 1.18 make it seem very likely).
It seems certain, though, that the barren and rugged solitude with which
1.18 begins is a setting derived primarily from Gallus, and that the
pastoral landscape suggested later comes through Gallus as well, and
ultimately from Callimachus.

The strange juxtaposition of fantasy and reality in the elegy now can
be seen for what it is: Propertius' own contribution. Propertius' immediate precedent, Gallus, supplied the poetic background, stylized and literary, within which Propertius presents his own troubles with Cynthia:[1]
here is the same contrast of literary precedent and Propertius' own amatory situation that we have observed in the first poem of the book. The
elegist appears in a pastoral setting against a traditional background, but
his own experience is all the more vivid as a result.

The acceptance of Gallan elegy led to a very different sort of poetry
in 1.20.

O. Skutsch discovered the remarkable structure of Propertius' *Monobiblos*:[2] two sets of five poems (A^1 = 1–5, 89 distichs; A^2 = 15–19, 88
distichs) frame two other sets of five poems each (B^1 = 6–9, 71 distichs;
B^2 = 10–14, 70 distichs); these central two groups (B) show a carefully
contrived internal arrangement as well. The Book is concluded with a
group of three miscellaneous poems (C = 20–2, 36 distichs), a fairly long
and elaborate piece on Hylas and two short epigrams. All this is observation and description, pure and simple, and as such cannot be denied;
the arrangement of the poems in the central section (B^1 and B^2) indicates
that Propertius intentionally worked for this structure, and in fact
Skutsch finds evidence of earlier and later poems of corresponding pairs.
Skutsch then points out that A = B+C. How this equation was achieved
(even whether the observable fact was Propertius' design) may still be
wondered: there must necessarily have been a certain amount of re-
writing and editing of, and excision and addition of lines to, individual
poems to achieve such a remarkable formula. But it was certainly Propertius' intention, as Skutsch remarks, to set the last three poems apart

[1] I do not mean to suggest that there is necessarily anything 'real' about Cynthia.
[2] 'The Structure of the Propertian *Monobiblos*', *CP* 58 (1963), 238–9. Skutsch's calculations
involve acceptance of Housman's lacuna of two lines after 1.1.11, and regard 8A and 8B
as separate poems. This elaborate arrangement is in itself sufficient indication of the sort
of poet Propertius was from the very beginning.

from the rest of the collection as a coda. The last two poems have always been regarded as unique, but 1.20 is in some ways certainly the oddest piece in all Augustan elegy, a cadenza before the final chords. What is it, and why did Propertius place it outside the collection?

The elegy appears straight forward and simple. Gallus is addressed by name in the opening line, and *monemus* indicates at once that Propertius has for him some words of advice, that the poem is to be a παραίνεσις. Lines 1–16 tell Gallus why he needs this advice, lines 17–50 (the story of Hylas) provide the *exemplum*, and a final couplet again addresses Gallus by name, *his...monitus*. The *exemplum* itself is equally simple: Hylas goes to seek water (17–24), is attacked by Zetes and Calais (25–32), falls into the nymphs' fountain and is lost (33–50). The elegy says, simply, 'Watch out, Gallus, lest your boy be seduced by girls: this happened to Hercules.' Simplicity, though, ends with the design and the message.

The elaborate language of the poem is often noted,[1] but the standard commentaries give no thorough exposition of the details of diction in this *tour de force*, nor do they begin to indicate therefrom its purpose and place. From the very beginning the poem is magnificently elegant and mannered:[2] why, and whether the poem is simply the work of Propertius *ludibundus*, are questions to be considered after a look at some details of language.

The first six lines contain all that is necessary to make clear the external *raison d'être* of the poem, that it is to contain advice to Gallus on a particular situation. Then come five couplets saying, 'Wherever you go, watch out your Hylas isn't stolen from you, as happened to Hercules':

> huic tu, sive leges umbrosae flumina silvae,
>   sive Aniena tuos tinxerit unda pedes,
> sive Gigantea spatiabere litoris ora,
>   sive ubicumque vago fluminis hospitio,
> Nympharum semper cupidas defende rapinas
>   (non minor Ausoniis est amor Adryasin);
> ne tibi sit duros montes et frigida saxa,
>   Galle, neque expertos semper adire lacus:
> quae miser ignotis error perpessus in oris
>   Herculis indomito fleverat Ascanio.   (1.20.7–16)

---

[1] E.g. Enk, who remarks (in his commentary, p. 176), 'Poetae consilio lusus suos dissimulandi explicatur sermo grandiloquus. Iam Ribbeckius (Geschichte der Römischen Dichtung II, 1900, p. 205) iudicabat Propertium hac elegia Gallum suaviter ludibrio habere ("in anmutig neckischem Tone")', and little more. The best understanding of Prop. 1.20 is that of A. La Penna, *Properzio*, 131–44, who also has systematic, though brief, observations on the style of the poem.

[2] Notable features of the first six lines are the neoteric placement of attribute and substantive in the first three lines, and the similar placement of the two proper names in the

The first four of these lines presumably mention Italian resort scenes, which Gallus may be supposed to have frequented – hardly a likely subject for anyone but a satirist. How does a neoteric poet handle St Tropez or Atlantic City? Cynthia's rowing and swimming at Baiae were the subject of a similar exercise (an exercise, of course, calculated to produce something more than a smile):[1]

> atque utinam mage te remis confisa minutis
> parvula Lucrina cumba moretur aqua,
> aut teneat clausam tenui Teuthrantis in unda
> alternae facilis cedere lympha manu.

> (1.11.9–12)

Obvious, of course, is the length to which Propertius has gone to avoid saying, in so many words, what Cynthia actually was doing, but the language goes still further. The periphrasis *Lucrina. . . aqua* has the proper adjective before the half-way point and the noun at the end; similarly, the *Teuthrantis unda* is proudly 'learned'. The last of these four lines is 'Golden', a fitting climax. Two archaisms are paraded out, *mage* and the dative *manu*,[2] similar to the archaic features discussed above in the Milanion *exemplum* of 1.1. The neoteric diminutive *parvula* is notable, as is the adjective – a striking sign post – *tenui*. This is the work of a neoteric poet (much like the delighted experimentation of Catullus in his polymetrics), four lines of excessive stylization devoted lovingly and almost gleefully to Cynthia's paddling. The geographical periphrases in 1.20.7–10 are splendidly delicate in a similar way and, what is more, take the form related poetically to the geographical element in the hymn or prayer form, as the anaphora *sive. . . sive. . . sive. . . sive. . .* clearly shows.[3] Then comes the point of the warning itself, the first instance of Propertius' outlandish nymphology in this poem – the Italian Adryads

---

fourth; the two-and-a-half foot *Theiodamanteo* in line 6 (elsewhere in Propertius only 3.14.14, 4.9.1); and the elaborate periphrasis of lines 5–6. Such features indicate clearly what is to come.

[1] The first four lines of Prop. 1.11 should be noted as well:

> Ecquid te mediis cessantem, Cynthia, Bais,
> qua iacet Herculeis semita litoribus,
> et modo Thesproti mirantem subdita regno
> et modo Misenis aequora nobilibus. . .

Here again the neoteric features are obvious: proper names before the caesura in 2–4; the poetic. . .*Herculeis*. . .*litoribus*; the elaborate and 'learned' periphrasis of 3–4.

[2] On *mage* (also 3.14.2, 4.8.16) see Tränkle, *Die Sprachkunst*, 35; the dative *manu* also occurs in 2.1.66.

[3] Cf. Prop. 1.6.31–4:

> at tu seu mollis qua tendit Ionia, seu qua
> Lydia Pactoli tingit arata liquor;

are just as dangerous. Should Gallus not heed the warning, he will find himself searching for Hylas just as did Hercules: but the scene of his unhappiness is precisely designated a wilderness area, *duros montes, frigida saxa, expertos lacus*, exactly corresponding to Propertius' (originally Gallus') desolate solitude in 1.18 (especially in lines 27–8, *pro quo divini fontes et frigida rupes | et datur inculto tramite dura quies*).[1]

The *exemplum* itself begins at line 17:

> namque ferunt olim Pagasae navalibus Argon
> egressam longe Phasidos isse viam,
> et iam praeteritis labentem Athamantidos undis
> Mysorum scopulis applicuisse ratem.
>
> (1.20.17–20)

Here again there is no mistaking the tone and expression of the lines: the Hellespont is referred to not only obliquely (*Athamantidos undis* – cf. 1.11.11, *Teuthrantis in unda*, mentioned above), but also by allowing Helle only her patronymic.[2] The language is grand to the point of awkwardness: 'the Argo was said...to have applied the bark to the crags of the Mysians' – that is, 'they landed in Mysia' – has caused some concern;[3] the archaic use of the genitive in *Phasidos isse viam* appears again in an epic passage at 2.1.20, *caeli Pelion... iter*. But most telling are the words which introduce the *exemplum*, *namque ferunt olim*. E. Fraenkel has noted the function of *namque* to introduce a παράδειγμα, equivalent to the

> seu pedibus terras seu pontum carpere remis
> ibis, et accepti pars eris imperii.

These lines, it seems to me, are all but untranslatable: *et* (34) must be a proper connective, and *ibis...eris* are unavoidably parallel; but this would leave the lines without a main verb in the apodosis. I would posit a lacuna of a pentameter and a hexameter after line 33, which would have contained a verb to govern *carpere* and perhaps another *seu* (*sive*) clause; the final line then concludes, 'You will go and be part of...' (or with Housman's conjecture *acceptis par?*). The 'geographical excursus' then totals six lines, exactly as the parallel in 1.20.7–12. My only hesitation, however, is the havoc wrought by this lacuna to Skutsch's neat formula (above, p. 74 n. 2).

1 An almost universal desperation over *divini fontes* has led to numerous emendations, none of which satisfy. But even if *divini* has little or no specific point in the context, it would hardly be merely 'ornamental' (see L. A. Holland, *Janus and the Bridge* (Rome, 1961), for an evocative appreciation of the divinity of water); and if, as I argue, the poet Gallus is Propertius' 'source' for both these descriptions (1.18.27–8 and 1.20.13–14), *divini* (with its reference to the nymphs of 1.20) may well be right. The connection between 1.18.1–6 and 1.20.13–14 is well made by F. Solmsen, *CP* 57 (1962), 74.

2 Cf. 1.1.10, *durae Iasidos* = Atalanta. An even more elaborate variation is found in 1.2.17–18, the second of three couplets of three highly stylized *exempla*: *non, Idae et cupido quondam discordia Phoebo, | Eueni patriis filia litoribus*. Here Marpessa, 'once' (*quondam* = *olim* = ποτέ, see below, p. 78 n. 3) the cause of strife between Apollo and Idas, is not named; furthermore, *Eueni patriis...litoribus* contains a neatly fashioned *aetion* – the stream in which her father drowned took his name.

3 See Shackleton Bailey *ad loc*.

Greek καὶ γάρ;[1] *ferunt* serves as an Alexandrian footnote;[2] and *olim* (or *quondam*) is a common feature of Alexandrian (= ποτέ) and neoteric poetry equivalent to the fairy tale formula 'once upon a time'.[3] All three words, in fact, occur together as here in Catullus 64.212 to introduce the passage on Theseus and his father, and with a variation again at line 76 (*nam perhibent olim...*). It is to the first lines of Catullus' epyllion, however, that these lines look, to what was in many ways the most important description of the sailing of the Argo known to Augustan poets: *Peliaco quondam prognatae vertice pinus | dicuntur...* Propertius' *exemplum* begins with no uncertainty in the manner of a neoteric epyllion.

Hylas' stroll to the nymphs' spring does not proceed without interruption. The attack by Zetes and Calais (strange winged creatures, the offspring of Boreas' rape of Orithyia) in lines 25–32 is a sudden, seemingly pointless intrusion – for the reader as well as for Hylas. It is not anticipated, and Hylas proceeds on his way after line 32 as if nothing had happened; the interlude itself is so compressed, so much a momentary glimpse of stopped action, that it is almost impossible to make sense of it. In only one form of ancient poetry does such a scene have a place: a feature common to most epyllia is a story within a story, or a scene within a scene.

If, then, the language and form of the Hylas *exemplum* suggests an epyllion,[4] we must ask why. Was Propertius himself responsible for this innovation? or was there some precedent in elegy for staging an epyllion in miniature?

Here some further details may help us towards an answer. It would be pointless to list all the examples of neoteric elegance of language: every couplet can illustrate some feature of such poetry. But two features of diction can be related to our previous discussion. In lines 23–4 the infinitive is used with a verb of motion to express purpose (*at comes invicti iuvenis processerat ultra | raram sepositi quaerere fontis aquam*): this is a pure archaism, whose rare appearance in poetry may be due to Greek usage; in Propertius the construction appears only twice elsewhere, in the Milanion *exemplum* at 1.1.12 and in 3.1.3–4.[5] The second feature is the

---

[1] *Horace* (Oxford, 1957), 185–6.

[2] Norden, *Aeneis VI*, 123–4.

[3] See W. Bühler, *Die Europa des Moschos*, Hermes Einzelschriften 13 (1960), 47–8.

[4] This suggestion (see Rothstein *ad loc.*, 'ein Epyllion in alexandrinischer Manier') has had little success. La Penna (*Properzio*, 136–8) considers the question whether 1.20 is an elegy or epyllion useless, and in some ways it is. But it is important to understand the difference between 1.20 and 1.1–19, and if the observable differences lead to what we may call 'an elegiac epyllion' as a precedent for the poem, the question is worth pursuing.

[5] Tränkle, *Die Sprachkunst*, 14–15: 'Es gibt im I. Buch kaum eine Elegie, in der so sehr eine

dative form *nullae* at line 35; such a form occurs elsewhere in Propertius only at 3.11.57 (*toto...orbi*, in an epic context), and must be archaic-poetic.[1] With these two archaisms one should compare certain forms and constructions noted above – *mage* and the dative *manu* in 1.11.9–12 (Cynthia boating and swimming), and the archaic poeticisms in the Milanion *exemplum*. The suspicion is irresistible that such features were prominent in Gallus' verse: one might go further and understand Quintilian's verdict on Gallus (*sicut durior Gallus*, 10.1.93) to refer to such archaic features of diction, and so also understand Parthenius' reference to Gallus' elevated diction (τὸ περιττόν, in the dedicatory letter to Gallus of the Ἐρωτικὰ Παθήματα).[2] If, then, the Hylas *exemplum* depends in some way on Gallus, such features as *processerat quaerere* and *nullae* are not only explicable, but would have been almost a requirement.

The passage describing Pege appears at first to be a conventional treatment of the *locus amoenus*:

> hic erat Arganthi Pege sub vertice montis
> grata domus Nymphis umida Thyniasin,
> quam supra nullae pendebant debita curae
> roscida desertis poma sub arboribus,
> et circum irriguo surgebant lilia prato
> candida purpureis mixta papaveribus.
>
> (1.20.33–8)

There are fruit trees, a watered meadow, splendid flowers, but the length of the description, out of all proportion to its apparent function, cannot simply be explained away by appeal to elegiac ἀσυμμετρία,[3] and raises the question what Propertius' purpose really was. Apollonius and Theocritus (whose description of Pege is but a list of the flowers that grew there) have nothing similar, and it is not from them, at any rate, that this description, especially with its fruit trees, derives. Now there was a poetic grove in which fruit trees played an active part. Servius in his comment on the *Grynei nemoris origo* of Gallus (*Ecl.* 6.72) outlines the story told by Euphorion in the poems 'translated' by Gallus as follows:

in quo [luco] aliquando Calchas et Mopsus dicuntur de peritia divinandi inter se habuisse certamen: et cum de pomorum arboris cuiusdam contenderent numero, stetit gloria Mopso: cuius rei dolore Calchas interiit. hoc autem Euphorionis continent carmina, quae Gallus transtulit in sermonem latinum.

ungewöhnliche Sprachform gesucht ist wie in 1, 20, und 3, 1 ist als Einleitungsgedicht von erhabener Feierlichkeit.'

[1] For details, see Tränkle (pp. 36–7).
[2] So L. Alfonsi, *Riv. di Fil.* 21 (1943), 53 ('una certa epicità di intonazione insita nell' elegia di Gallo'), and J.-P. Boucher, *Gallus*, 71–2.
[3] La Penna, *Properzio*, 136–7.

Moreover, Servius Auctus adds here (undoubtedly at second hand) a brief description (though followed by a different story) which can only be a flat prose summary of a poetic *ekphrasis*:

vel a Grynio, Moesiae civitate, ubi est locus arboribus multis iucundus, gramine floribusque variis omni tempore vestitus, abundans etiam fontibus.

Trees, flowers, springs. There is only one *ekphrasis* that is likely to be the original summarized here, and that is Gallus' own description of the Grynean Grove. If it is not sheer coincidence that Propertius' description of Pege parallels so closely that bald summary given by Servius Auctus, then it must be assumed that Propertius has taken from Gallus not only diction and expression, but an important passage from a very important poem, by reference to which the nature and purpose of his poem would have been made even more clear.

One further possible suggestion of Gallus should be mentioned. The transition from the attack by Zetes and Calais to the *ekphrasis* is neatly made with this couplet (31–2):

> iam Pandioniae cessit genus Orithyiae:
> a dolor! ibat Hylas, ibat Hamadryasin.
> (Hamadryasin *Itali*: hamadrias hinc *vel sim. codd.*, Ephydriasin *Baehrens*)

The elaborate periphrasis *Pandioniae genus Orithyiae* needs no comment: the line itself is spondaic, ending with the Greek proper name,[1] clearly suggesting the style of a neoteric epyllion. *A*, the neoteric exclamation, has been noted above in connection with Gallus.[2] Finally, *ibat Hamadryasin*, a further *recherché* venture by Propertius into nymphology, was emended by Baehrens because of the possible echo of a pentameter of Alexander Aetolus, cited by Parthenius in his collection of erotic stories (*Erot.* 14): αὐτὸς δ' ἐς Νύμφας ᾤχετ' Ἐφυδριάδας.[3] Baehrens' emendation may be correct, but for a line of Gallus rather than here (where there is no need to mistrust the paradosis): if Gallus did use the line suggested to him by his mentor, then Propertius, in referring to it, has perhaps altered the name for his own version. In any case, it would be difficult to find another couplet in Propertius more neoteric than this.

If these suggestions of Gallus are not all illusory, we may form a general answer to the question why Propertius wrote this elegiac epyllion, and what precedent there might have been for it. Hylas, Virgil implies, was a subject for every poet: *cui non dictus Hylas puer?* (*Geo.*

---

[1] See M. Platnauer, *Latin Elegiac Verse* (Cambridge, 1951), 39: elsewhere in Propertius only 1.13.31, 19.13; 2.2.9, 28.49; 3.7.13; 4.4.71.
[2] See above, p. 73 n. 4 and related text.
[3] See Butler and Barber on 1.20.12.

3.6); and the first story related by Silenus after his cosmogony (which should include the accounts of the Saturnian Age, Prometheus, and Pyrrha) is that of Hylas (... *Hylan nautae quo fonte relictum | clamassent, ut litus 'Hyla, Hyla' omne sonaret, Ecl.* 6.43–4) – to be understood, as *quo fonte?* implies, as a neoteric treatment. There is no reason why we should not allow Gallus to have written a version of this popular neoteric subject, though the form it may have taken is a more debatable point. But since Propertius has handled the Hylas story in a book of elegies, in a manner that suggests Gallus both in specifics and in general treatment, it is not unlikely that Gallus had done so as well in his *Amores*.

Is 1.20, then, simply the work of Propertius *ludibundus*, to be read almost as a parody of an elegy of Gallus? Certainly Propertius' handling of the story is not without poetic humor – and a good bit of it at that. But humor cannot be the only reason for the poem's being placed as a cadenza outside the collection of twenty poems. If the poem is early, as most scholars agree,[1] then anything approaching a parody of the master in elegy would be extremely objectionable, as well as unusual. The observable poetic fun seems more the result of carrying one step further every trick and mannerism of one's model in order to make clear just what that model was and just how the derived work differs. It was perhaps as a comparison with what preceded that Propertius placed the poem in such a position, with a purpose ultimately more serious than otherwise. To a reader who has just read through the first twenty poems (particularly to one who is aware of the arrangement of the book), 1.20 seems an entirely different poetic world. Gallan elegy had been assumed in the programmatic first poem (including in the Milanion *exemplum* a good sampling of it) and had received frequent glances throughout the subsequent poems; but here at last is a full-scale Gallan production, a delighted hyperbole in the matter and manner of the master, permitting full realization of just how different, and how personal, Propertius' own book of elegy really is.

We may conveniently summarize here what we have been able to learn or suggest about Gallus' poetry from this investigation of the *Monobiblos*. First, some support has been given the hypothesis that Gallus'

[1] See, for instance, O. Skutsch, *CP* 58 (1963), 239, 'their [1.20–2] metrical technique is old' – in 1.20, 14 of 26 pentameters end with a word longer than an iamb; see also La Penna, who regards the poem as an early production. But the validity of stylistic arguments for an early date is most questionable – as we have argued, the purpose of the poem, an 'elegiac epyllion', demanded a style and tone both archaic (Gallan) and much in the manner of the first generation neoterics.

entire poetic production was his four books of elegies. A precedent for the Milanion–Atalanta *exemplum* in Propertius' first elegy must have occurred in an important, undoubtedly programmatic, context in Gallus: that Propertius uses it for a programmatic purpose in his introduction to a book of elegies must be taken as an indication that in Gallus, too, the setting had been elegiac. Likewise, if Propertius' description of Pege (1.20.33–8) is in fact meant to suggest Gallus' description of the Grynean Grove (as preserved for us in a bald summary statement by Servius Auctus), we may postulate that Gallus' passage occurred as well in a book of elegies, not as a separate aetiological poem (an epyllion or whatever), and the same would most likely be true for whatever treatment Hylas received from Gallus: this can be no more than suggestion, of course, but since Propertius wrote 1.20 so clearly in the manner and style of Gallus and included it as an elegy in a book of elegies (though purposely set off by the arrangement as a contrast with the other poems of the book), it would seem more than reasonable that its model and *raison d'être* had been a similar elegy, perhaps one which first showed how the style and matter of a neoteric epyllion could be distilled further into an elegiac form. Furthermore, we have seen that features of style in Propertius which can be attributed with some confidence to Gallus can be described consistently as archaic poeticisms of the sort expected in serious neoteric poetry, and that lines and passages in such a style occur throughout the *Monobiblos*, suggesting again that it was in such a style that Gallus' elegies had been composed: there is thus no stylistic difficulty in the assumption that subjects or themes sometimes attributed to Gallus' 'epyllia' actually occurred in his elegies. Finally, Propertius 1.18 clearly shows in confirmation of Virgil that in Gallus the pastoral element was important, and was recognized as such: this affords further confirmation that Gallus was to a great extent responsible for, and influential in, the creation of a new concept of poetry, one which would define poetry not according to genre but according to the impulse that produced it; and this is, in fact, the best reason for attributing to Gallus' elegies that diversity of subject and theme which our sources imply.

Propertius, then, while recognizing and referring to this diversity and breadth of Gallus' elegiac precedent, limits his own poetic concern ostensibly to his Cynthia, that is, to the amatory situation. What personal contact there may have been between the two poets remains an open question: there is no clear evidence one way or the other, as there seems to be, for instance, for the strained relationship between Propertius and Horace, or for the affection Horace felt for Tibullus. It is one of the oddities of modern scholarship, however, that the Gallus to whom four poems (5, 10, 13, and 20) of the *Monobiblos* are addressed is seldom allowed even a chance of having been the poet Cornelius.[1] Commentators[2] are satisfied with ruling out the poet on the slight grounds that he was older than Propertius (and so would not have been addressed in such terms of intimacy), and was not of sufficiently distinguished birth to qualify for the *priscae imagines* Propertius grants him in 1.5.24 (a line, with 1.14.8, we have seen good reason for deriving from the poet Gallus himself!). Alfonsi's call for some measure of common sense in this matter seems to have gone unheard:[3] Cornelius Gallus was in Rome in the year 30 B.C.; after the *Monobiblos* this friend of Propertius disappears from the poems (except at 2.34.91–2, where he appears as a figure of literary history), a silence entirely consistent with his subsequent career abroad and suicide in disgrace in 27 or 26 B.C. There is no reason why Cornelius Gallus should not be the addressee of four poems in the *Monobiblos*, and indeed some reason why his case should be heard.

There is at this point little need to argue that the Gallus of 1.20 is the poet: coincidence will hardly allow a poem so obviously in the style of Gallus to be addressed to an unrelated (and unknown) figure of the same name. We have discussed above two lines in 1.5, separated by the space of two couplets, which may well derive from Gallus (line 24, *nescit Amor priscis cedere imaginibus*, and line 28, *cum mihi nulla mei sit medicina mali*), occurring just before the final couplet addressing Gallus for the first time.[4] 1.10 is even more intriguing:[5] can it refer, on one level, to experiments in amatory elegy Gallus may recently have been writing, experiments 'predicted' by Propertius in 1.5? The first ten lines, in fact, are reminiscent of Catullus' evening of poetic experimentation with Calvus recorded in poem 50 (where the language is also erotic), and conclude

---

1 I exclude the Gallus of 1.21.7 from this discussion, for obvious reasons. The poet occurs definitely in the catalogue of 2.34.91–2. The only other Gallus in Propertius is the figure from early Roman history at 4.1.95–6.

2 E.g. Butler and Barber, Enk, Camps.

3 Pp. 54–6: on the important second point, Alfonsi notes, 'la *nobilitas* e le *priscae imagines*, a parte il colorito retorico della frase, possono essere un voluto riferimento al passato dell' attuale posto importante ricoperto da Gallo.' The other point is worth even less consideration: there is no need to demand of Propertius *in his poetry* an embarrassed deference to a senior poet.

4 On line 2 of this poem, see L. A. Moritz, 'Well-matched Lovers (Propertius 1.5)', *CP* 62 (1967), 106–8, who argues convincingly that *pares* does not refer to Propertius and Cynthia, but to Propertius and Gallus (whose identity, however, he leaves unconsidered). The next to last couplet (*sed pariter miseri socio cogemur amore...*) certainly refers to Propertius and Gallus.

5 Note, in passing, lines 17–18, *et possum alterius curas sanare recentis,* | *nec levis in verbis est medicina meis.*

5

Gallus and the Tenth Eclogue

F. Skutsch's conclusions on the Tenth Eclogue have been more generally accepted than any other part of his books,[1] based as they are on sound and valid observations that have become essential to every discussion of Gallus' poetry. Skutsch noted, for instance, certain elegiac themes in Gallus' speech in the Tenth Eclogue. Lines 46–9 (Gallus' words to Lycoris, *. . . a, te ne frigora laedant!* | *a, tibi ne teneras glacies secet aspera plantas!*) are echoed by Propertius 1.8.7–8 (*tu pedibus teneris positas fulcire pruinas,* | *tu potes insolitas, Cynthia, ferre nives?*), as are lines 52–4 by Propertius 1.18, a correspondence we have discussed more fully in the preceding chapter. Lines 42–3 (*hic gelidi fontes, hic mollia prata, Lycori,* | *hic nemus;* *hic ipso tecum consumerer aevo*), Skutsch notes, are similar to many passages in Tibullus 1, and, with the following two lines (*nunc insanus amor duri me Martis in armis* | *tela inter media atque adversos detinet hostis*), present a frequent Tibullan contrast, country peace and love opposed to war. Lines 55–60 are part of a 'Jagdelegie', as in Tibullus 1.4.49–50: we have discussed in detail the connection, noted by Skutsch, between these lines and the Milanion *exemplum* in Propertius 1.1.9–16, as made explicit by the Virgilian *Parthenios saltus* and the Propertian *Partheniis antris*. Skutsch also pointed to certain clear indications of bucolic themes: for instance, in both *Ecl.* 10.65–8 and Theocritus 7.111–14 occur the Hebrus and the Aethiopes; line 42 corresponds to Theocritus 5.33–4 (springs and meadows); lines 38–9 have a parallel in Theocritus 10.26–8 (and Amyntas occurs as well in Theocritus 7.2 and 132). Skutsch is able to conclude, then, 'Vergils zehnte Ekloge hat demnach offenbar den Zweck, einen Überblick über die elegisch-bukolische Poesie seines verehrten Gallus zu geben.'[2]

From his discussions of such parallels, Skutsch suggested that in the four books of Gallus' *Amores* occurred elegies with pastoral content: 'Mit mehr Recht könnte man vielleicht umgekehrt vermuten, dass bisweilen bei Gallus in die elegische Form etwas bukolischer Inhalt gekommen sei. . . Trifft diese Vermutung das richtige, dann hätten wir

1 *Frühzeit*, 2–27; *Gallus und Vergil*, 155–92.
2 *Frühzeit*, 18 (for his preceding observations on elegiac and bucolic themes, see pp. 12–17).

in Gallus nicht bloss einen Vorläufer der Eigentümlichkeiten der Properzischen, sondern inbesondere auch der Tibullischen Elegie zu erkennen, die, wie schon gesagt, mit ihren pastoralen Elementen bisher so gut wie allein stand.'[1] The Tenth Eclogue is thus to be read as a catalogue poem of passages from Gallus' elegies.[2] If this view is basically correct, we may certainly expect to find in the Tenth Eclogue confirmation of what we have thus far been able to infer about Gallus' poetry from Propertius' *Monobiblos*; and if, as we have argued, Gallus wrote no poetry other than the four books of elegies, then what we have suggested about the importance and purpose of his concept of poetry from the Sixth Eclogue (which Skutsch – and others – regarded as concerned with Gallus' non-elegiac poetry) should find a place in the Tenth Eclogue (which, as is generally agreed, is concerned with Gallus as an elegist – though perhaps as an elegist wanting to discover other genres, such as pastoral). What is more, if the suppositions and suggestions we have made thus far are substantially valid, then we should expect to be able to see certain details of the Tenth Eclogue in a new light and perhaps view the whole from a different perspective.

Two assumptions about the Tenth Eclogue should be made clear at the start. Though neither can be proved, it will be impossible to arrive at any valid conclusions without beginning from a reasonable position on each of these two points. First, it will have to be agreed that any poetry by Gallus referred to in the Eclogue had already been written. Whatever interpretation may be offered for Gallus' words in lines 50–1, it must be assumed, I think, that Gallus had actually composed on the reed of the Sicilian shepherd, just as he had already written Chalcidian verse. A similar working assumption was made in our discussion of the Sixth Eclogue – that the subjunctive in *his tibi Grynei nemoris dicatur origo* (line 72) is jussive only in the dramatic context, that in fact Linus must be relating what Gallus had already performed: it would be perverse to maintain that the idea of writing aetiological verse on the Grynean

---

[1] *Frühzeit*, 25. Reconsideration of the questions involved has generally tended to confirm these conclusions; for instance, E. Bréguet, 'Les *Élégies* de Gallus', *REL* 26 (1948), 212: 'je croirais volontiers que, si Virgile mêle à la plainte de Gallus quelques motifs bucoliques, cela n'est pas seulement pour conserver l'harmonie de son poème, mais parce que ce n'est pas en contradiction avec les élégies de Gallus; comme Tibulle qui fut son "successeur", nous dit Ovide, Gallus peut avoir fait place dans ses vers à des motifs de la poésie bucolique. Cela est peut-être confirmé par les vers 69–71 de la *VIᵉ Bucolique*: les flûtes d'Hésiode sont des flûtes de pâtre; c'est en pâtre, en effet, qu'Hésiode se représente au début de sa *Théogonie*, lorsqu'il reçoit des Muses l'invitation à chanter les dieux.'

[2] Servius' comment on *Ecl.* 10.46 ('*hi autem omnes versus Galli sunt, de ipsius translati carminibus*') is correct, says Skutsch, but should be extended to the whole of Gallus' speech.

Grove occurred to Gallus only on reading these lines, and even more perverse to imagine that Virgil, in this important climax to so central a scene, should be referring to poetry which had not yet taken final and significant form. But though this may be obvious enough, it has not been generally agreed that it must be equally perverse not to make the same assumption about poetry by Gallus suggested or referred to in the Tenth Eclogue. Our second working assumption is that the world of the poem is entirely unreal, that the only reality is poetic. No one, I expect, has ever imagined the flesh and blood Gallus actually languishing under some lonely Arcadian crag, surrounded by sheep and shepherds, addressed in words of comfort and advice by Apollo, Silvanus, and Pan;[1] yet at the same time lines 44–5 have been taken more often than not to refer to an actual campaign, or at least to set the real Gallus on a real parade ground, and Lycoris (or Cytheris or Volumnia) has been sent barefoot following actual legions through real Alpine snows. The Gallus of the Tenth Eclogue, we must assume, was not to be met outside the pages of his poetry; he is real only insofar as his poetry was real. It is proper, then, to forget whatever we happen to know about Gallus the soldier or about the actual courtesan Cytheris, and to concentrate only on Gallus the elegist and Lycoris the elegiac mistress, and on what we can make out about the poetic reality of this elegiac world.

We may best begin where the conclusions, both firm and tentative, we have drawn thus far about Gallus' poetry may contribute most toward an understanding of the Tenth Eclogue: if, as most will agree, the Eclogue is somehow concerned with the poet Gallus and would have been understood by those who knew his poetry, then it will be useful to decide immediately what is the *poetic* crisis Gallus finds himself involved in.[2] The second half of Gallus' speech will take us directly to the heart of the matter:[3]

[1] Some scholars have come very close to such a view: see for instance H. J. Rose, *The Eclogues of Vergil* (Berkeley, 1942), 104–16, who finds (following Leo, *Hermes* 37 (1902), 14–22) Gallus in Greece at the time, having 'taken an opportunity for a furlough, which he spends in Arkadia, amid romantic pastoral surroundings, poeticized of course by Vergil' (p. 106). Rose's chapter is a good demonstration of the futility of the factual interpretation of poetic fiction.

[2] I emphasize that it is a poetic crisis for two reasons: first, because poetry does seem to be the real subject of the poem, after all; and secondly because, as we have just assumed, the only reality is poetic – that is, it is not Gallus' *love* that is the poem's subject, but Gallus' *love poetry*, just as in Propertius' *Monobiblos* dramatic situation is often clearly only a formal means of presenting the *real* subject of a poem. Common sense can suggest the best answer to the question, 'Did Gaius Cornelius Gallus *really* go through such agonies of blighted affection that some scholars have imagined is Virgil's subject in the Tenth Eclogue?' G. Williams (*Tradition and Originality* (Oxford, 1968), 233–8) makes the point well.

[3] The punctuation and divisions here are my own, intended to bring out the movement of

ibo et Chalcidico quae sunt mihi condita versu
carmina pastoris Siculi modulabor avena:
certum est in silvis inter spelaea ferarum
malle pati tenerisque meos incidere amores
arboribus – crescent illae, crescetis, amores.

interea mixtis lustrabo Maenala Nymphis,
aut acris venabor apros; non me ulla vetabunt
frigora Parthenios canibus circumdare saltus:
iam mihi per rupes videor lucosque sonantis
ire, libet Partho torquere Cydonia cornu
spicula –

      tamquam haec sit nostri medicina furoris,
aut deus ille malis hominum mitescere discat:
iam neque Hamadryades rursus neque carmina nobis
ipsa placent, ipsae rursus concedite silvae.

                         (*Ecl.* 10.50–63)

In the following discussion of these lines, two main points will be made:
first, that they derive directly from Gallus,[1] then that they refer to three
different sorts of poetry.

Lines 50–4 proceed directly from Gallus' thoughts about Lycoris:
what he has written in the verse of Euphorion, he will now play on the
reed of the Sicilian shepherd. We may quite confidently assume that
Virgil is not far from an actual passage of Gallus here: we have discussed
above the details and implications of a similar passage in Propertius 1.18
clearly derived from Gallus and, through him, from Callimachus[2] –

the lines. I do not mean to imply that I see any structural division in calling this 'the second
half' of the Eclogue: the movement throughout Gallus' speech is one continuity.

[1] This has been suspected by various scholars, who, as Skutsch, have extended Servius'
comment on line 46 to include more than the four lines of related context: e.g. R. Coleman, *AJP* 83 (1962), 62, 'The well-known Servian comment on line 46 *presumably* refers
to more than just the following four lines... In fact it is reasonable to assume that
Servius is relating the whole succession of *topoi* here to various elegies by Gallus, and that
the whole passage serves as a summary of the themes of Gallus' erotic poetry' (italics
mine). I hope that it will be demonstrated positively here that lines 46–69 (at least) are a
close paraphrase of important passages from Gallus. Most of the indications of Gallus
in these lines have already been dealt with above in discussions which should be consulted.

[2] To summarize, Prop. 1.18.19–22 (*vos eritis testes, si quos habet arbor amores,* | *fagus et
Arcadio pinus amica deo.* | *a quotiens teneras resonant mea verba sub umbras,* | *scribitur et vestris
Cynthia corticibus*) shows the following specific correspondences with *Ecl.* 10, esp. lines
50–4: *amores* at line end (twice successively in Virgil) associated with the trees (*arbor
amores* | ∼ *amores* | *arboribus*); the Arcadian 'setting' (real in Virgil, suggested by Prop.
with *Arcadio deo*); the neoteric *a!* with the postponed *et* in Prop. (1.18.21–2), suggesting
almost certainly the Gallan tone as evident from the thrice-repeated *a!* and the postponed
ne (twice) in *Ecl.* 10.47–9; the carving (of *amores* and of *Cynthia*) on the trees; a less specific
(but quite compelling, in the light of the other parallels) correspondence in tone and

nothing short of direct quotation of Gallus would produce as many or as clear parallels and mutual suggestions in these two passages of Virgil and Propertius.[1] We may feel confident, too, that Virgil's Gallus (and hence the poet Gallus) is resolved (*certum est...*) to give his elegies (*meos amores*) a pastoral setting when he refers to carving them on trees:[2] this statement is an elaboration of that directly preceding ('I will go and turn my verse in the manner of Euphorion into pastoral' – the *pastoris Siculi avena* leaves no doubt that pastoral poetry is meant here). Our working assumption that Gallus had actually composed whatever sort of poetry is referred to in the Tenth Eclogue seems substantially secure for the suggestion of pastoral in these lines, since the very means (the terms and the language) of stating Gallus' resolve to write pastoral can be demonstrated to have been taken by Virgil (and Propertius) from an actual passage of Gallus. Finally, we can, I think, be almost certain about this passage of Gallus: somewhere in his elegies he related the Calli-machean story of Acontius and Cydippe (as we can tell from Propertius 1.18), in which Acontius, crossed in love, withdrew to the woods and fields, where he carved his love's name on the bark of trees. Lines 52–4 of the Tenth Eclogue refer to this poem, a sufficiently important poem for Propertius to make use of as well: Gallus for a moment assumes the character and the words of Acontius.

This clear resolve to inhabit in the future a pastoral world[3] is, however, immediately reconsidered.[4] In the dramatic setting the transitional

---

purpose suggested by *teneras...umbras* ~ *teneris...* | *arboribus*, and by *a quotiens...* *resonant mea verba* ~ *respondent omnia silvae* (*Ecl.* 10.8) ~ *...resonent mihi 'Cynthia' silvae* (Prop. 1.18.31).

[1] We may mention again Norden's suspicion (see on *Aen.* 6.10) that *spelaea* (a *hapax*) was first used by Gallus.

[2] F. Skutsch was undoubtedly right in understanding *meos amores* to refer to Gallus' elegies, and in all probability as the title of the collection of four books (*Frühzeit*, 23–4). And that the act of carving poems on trees is itself (for Virgil, at least) pastoral, cf. *Ecl.* 5.13–15 (*Immo haec, in viridi nuper quae cortice fagi* | *carmina descripsi et modulans alterna notavi,* | *experiar: tu deinde iubeto ut certet Amyntas*).

[3] In the dramatic situation of the poem, that is (to make the point once again): Virgil's Gallus in fact is referring to his own elegiac experiments with the pastoral.

[4] The apparent fluctuations of Gallus' resolve have been explained from the dramatic situation: e.g. H. J. Rose, *The Eclogues*, 107, 'the theme after all is, as Virgil himself says, the troubled passion of Gallus, and one does not expect a man in his situation to speak with strict attention to logic and the best arrangement of his thoughts'; or similarly M. Putnam (*Virgil's Pastoral Art* (Princeton, 1970), 377), 'That such fluctuations are the lover's prerogative is one of the lessons of *Eclogue* 2...' But surely the assertions, immediate denials, and vacillations in Gallus' speech are not simply an expression of the state of mind brought on by his *sollicitos amores* (line 6), any more than the apparent lack of unity can be attributed simply (as F. Skutsch) to its being a patch-work of passages from Gallus' elegies. Any interpretation of the poem that fails, not just to explain away, but actually to derive Virgil's fundamental purpose from the shifts in Gallus' thought or the changes of landscape or setting, cannot have much chance of being correct.

adverb *interea* serves to introduce a quite different proposal for the more immediate future: we may understand, therefore, that the following lines present an entirely separate, distinct topic.[1] Virgil's geography here is explicit. *Maenala* immediately indicates Arcadia, but all that this mountain range and Arcadia itself have come to suggest in the *Eclogues* (Pan, pastoral life and song, and the scene of Gallus' languishing in this Eclogue), having been suggested, is immediately given a different, specific focus: the theme of hunting and its setting in the *Parthenios saltus* (a most specific reference) are for us intelligible only from the Milanion–Atalanta *exemplum* of Propertius 1.1. That *exemplum*, set in Arcadia (*Arcadiis rupibus*, line 14) and specifically among the *Partheniis antris* (line 11), contains as we have seen unmistakable signs of Gallus, and had been set prominently by Propertius in his programmatic poem to the *Monobiblos* specifically to suggest Gallan elegy by reference to what can only have been a similarly important programmatic passage in his immediate predecessor. But what amounts to absolute proof that these lines of the Tenth Eclogue and Propertius' *exemplum* not only are intimately related but both derive from the same passage (which can only have been by Gallus) is afforded by Ovid, who uses the same Milanion–Atalanta story as an *exemplum* of *obsequium* (cf. the anaphora of the word in lines 179, 181, 183) precisely as does Propertius:[2]

> quid fuit asperius Nonacrina Atalanta?
>   subcubuit meritis trux tamen illa viri.
> saepe suos casus nec mitia facta puellae
>   flesse sub arboribus Milaniona ferunt;
> saepe tulit iusso fallacia retia collo,
>   saepe fera torvos cuspide fixit apros.
> sensit et Hylaei contentum saucius arcum;
>   sed tamen hoc arcu notior alter erat.
> non te Maenalias armatum scandere silvas
>   nec iubeo collo retia ferre tuo,
> pectora nec missis iubeo praebere sagittis;
>   artis erunt cautae mollia iussa meae.

(*AA* 2.185–96)

---

[1] Critical interpretation of this Eclogue has made almost nothing of this point: lines 55–60 are considered to be as 'pastoral' as those preceding, or as a variation on the pastoral; one exception is Putnam (*Virgil's Pastoral Art*, 374–6), who considers these lines 'an intervening stage between his double life of elegiac poet and soldier and his imagined future existence as pastoral poet and rational lover' (but otherwise I find these pages difficult to follow, and his interpretation of 'hunting' quite mistaken). F. Skutsch's suggestion that the lines were taken from a 'Jagdelegie' by Gallus was however too vague and unspecific to have been of help.

[2] Ovid's *meritis viri* (line 186) ∼ Propertius' *tantum in amore preces et bene facta valent* (line 16); *trux illa* (186) ∼ *saevitiam durae Iasidos* (10); *sensit et Hylaei contentum saucius*

Now there are two details in these lines which do not occur in the Propertian *exemplum* but do appear in the lines from the Tenth Eclogue. Ovid's Milanion hunts fierce boars (*torvos apros*) just as will Virgil's Gallus (*aut acris venabor apros*), and the setting in both Virgil and Ovid is specifically Maenalus (*Ecl.* 10.55, *AA* 2.193). Either these two details have found their way into Ovid's lines completely by chance, or else there is an unmistakable connection between the Virgilian and Ovidian passages; such a connection must mean either that Ovid associated Virgil's lines gratuitously with Milanion's situation, or that the association with Milanion was one that could not be missed, in which case there can be little doubt that Virgil, Propertius, and Ovid all look to an important passage of Gallus.

Certain conclusions are now unavoidable. Gallus had used the Milanion–Atalanta story as an *exemplum* for the power of the *obsequium amoris* (as does Ovid positively and Propertius negatively), undoubtedly applying it to his own amatory situation in a specific elegy. The context in which he did this was in some way distinguished, and almost certainly was in some sense programmatic, since Propertius uses it prominently in his first programmatic poem, and Virgil refers to it not only to indicate a course that his unhappy Gallus may take to overcome the frustrations of his love but (as will be argued) also to suggest a definite form of Gallan poetry. Finally, just as Virgil's Gallus had assumed the character and the words of Acontius in the preceding lines, so there he speaks as Milanion. *iam mihi per rupes videor lucosque sonantis | ire...* : Gallus has slipped into the person of Milanion as if in a dream.

The dream, however, is suddenly shattered, as Gallus realizes that he can find no release by adopting the role of either Acontius or Milanion: *– tamquam haec sit nostri medicina furoris, | aut deus ille malis hominum mitescere discat.* We have previously referred to Tränkle's demonstration that the elegiac *medicina furoris* is traceable to Gallus, and have discussed above Propertius' use of the theme in the first (programmatic) poems of his first two books, and elsewhere. These two lines must originally have been Gallus' own, and this sudden awakening must be a reflection of the course of his own poetry.

In such a context the last eight lines of Gallus' speech must be understood as a summation of the inadequacy of the responses represented by Acontius and Milanion to the domination of Amor:

arcum (191) ~ *ille etiam Hylaei percussus vulnere rami | saucius...* (13–14). One may note also that the two lines Housman offers *exempli gratia* to fill his lacuna after Prop. 1.1.11 (< *multaque desertis fleverat arboribus | et modo submissa casses cervice ferebat* >) are based on Ovid, *AA* 2.187–8.

iam neque Hamadryades rursus neque carmina nobis
ipsa placent, ipsae rursus concedite silvae.
non illum nostri possunt mutare labores,
nec si frigoribus mediis Hebrumque bibamus,
Sithoniasque nives hiemis subeamus aquosae,
nec si, cum moriens alto liber aret in ulmo,
Aethiopum versemus ovis sub sidere Cancri.
omnia vincit Amor: et nos cedamus Amori.

(*Ecl.* 10.62–9)

Gallus concludes by yielding, as does everything, to Love; his *labores* cannot change Love, whether he goes to the frozen north or the torrid south. Skutsch, as we have noted, saw the north–south alternative as another pastoral element in Gallus' speech,[1] but Virgil has extended and transformed the Theocritean suggestion. First, *nostri labores* must mean 'our poetry', as in the first line of the Eclogue, *extremum hunc, Arethusa, mihi concede laborem*. What sorts of poetry are unable to change Love is then suggested by the following geographical opposition of north and south. The heat of the south represents a specifically pastoral world (*versemus ovis*). Sun and warmth are a constant in the pastoral climate – though here, as is to be expected from the context, present in the extreme (*cum moriens alto liber aret in ulmo*). Virgil seems to offer us the pastoral world taken to its logical conclusion, reduced to the impossible (as we will discuss in more detail shortly). The northern cold is similarly emphasized (*frigoribus mediis... Sithoniasque nives hiemis... aquosae*), and seems almost an explanation of a mention of cold (*frigora*) just eight lines earlier: *non me ulla vetabunt* | *frigora Parthenios canibus circumdare saltus*. In neither Propertius nor Ovid does Milanion have to contend with cold: here then is an element of some prominence in Virgil, emphasized further by expression and position. By thus emphasizing the *frigora*, Virgil has underlined the parallelism of these two passages (lines 55–60 and 65–6). Both refer to poetry (we have shown that the Milanion lines are derived from a programmatic passage of Gallus, and that the north–south alternative is an explanation of the *labores*, 'poetry', of line 64, in which the southern heat represents pastoral), and we may now attempt to see what sort of poetry is to be understood by the northern cold.

The suggestion of Parthenius ought to be of some importance.[2] What is to be made of this depends on whatever associations our fragmentary knowledge of Parthenius' work and influence summons up. We may

---

[1] See above, p. 85 n. 2: the *Hebrus* and the *Aethiopes* occur together at Theocr. 7.111–14.
[2] Mt Parthenius occurs only here and in Prop. 1.1.11, and is thus clearly derived from Gallus, where it must have been introduced as a compliment to his friend and poetic mentor Parthenius (see above, p. 63 n. 5).

understand Euphorion and Callimachean poetics, mythological presentation of inner experience, poetry as an art and a *labor* open only to the initiated. But precision, or allegory, was not Virgil's intention in this suggestion.

Somewhat more precise is the mention of the river Hebrus (line 65), where we can see clearly, I believe, Virgil's purpose. The Hebrus is not a common landmark in Latin poetry: it is associated either with Bacchus or with Orpheus, and sometimes seems simply to designate northern cold,[1] but it must be the Orphic associations that Virgil has in mind here. The Hebrus is mentioned nowhere else in the *Eclogues*, and occurs in the *Georgics* only as one of the rivers that mourned Eurydice's death (*Geo.* 4.463) and down which Orpheus' head was carried (*Geo.* 4.524).[2] This possible suggestion of Orpheus is made specific by other associations in the two contexts.

To return to the *frigora* of lines 57 and 65: Gallus, assuming the role of Milanion, says first that no cold will prevent his hunting in the Parthenian glades, but then, when the reality of Love's domination shatters his dream, he admits that not even by drinking the cold (Orphic) waters of the Hebrus can he change Love (nor will pastoral heat be of any help). What Virgil intends here can be understood from the poetic finale to the Second Georgic. Virgil has described 'scientific poetry' (lines 475–82), but suddenly feels that his powers may not extend so far:

> sin has ne possim naturae accedere partis
> *frigidus* obstiterit circum praecordia sanguis,
> rura mihi et rigui placeant in vallibus amnes,
> flumina amem silvasque inglorius.
>
> (*Geo.* 2.483–6)

This appears to be the same poetic chill that Gallus claimed would not prevent his hunting in the Parthenian glades.[3] We have previously discussed the relationship of these lines to Orpheus as he appears at the end

---

[1] Not mentioned, for instance, by Cat., Tib., Prop. (D. C. Swanson, *The Names in Roman Verse* (Madison, 1967), shows that it appears in Latin first here in Virgil). For its associations with Bacchus, see e.g. Hor. *Od.* 3.25.10, Ovid, *Fast.* 3.737; to denote northern cold, e.g. Hor. *Epist.* 1.3.3., 16.13. In general see *RE* 7.2, 2588–9, and Nisbet and Hubbard on Hor. *Od.* 1.25.20, where they argue for *Euro* (Aldine, 1501) for *Hebro* (MSS, Porph.).

[2] So also Ovid, *Met.* 11.50–3. (In the *Aeneid* the Hebrus occurs only at 1.317, associated with Harpalyce, and at 12.331, with Mars.) The poet of the *Culex* played on *Geo.* 4.524 (*Oeagrius Hebrus*) when he wrote *non tantum Oeagrius Hebrum* | *restantem tenuit ripis silvasque canendo...* (*Culex* 117–18: *Oeagrius* Heinsius, *horridus* ΓCL, *horpheus* V): clearly he had in mind Virgil's important association of the river with the mythical singer.

[3] I do not cite *Geo.* 2.483–6 as an explanation of *Ecl.* 10.55–60 simply because of *frigora* | *frigoribus* | *frigidus*: note that the 'pastoral' alternative follows immediately (485–6).

of the Fourth Georgic, but another correspondence is now clear: the world Orpheus inhabits after his loss of Eurydice is desolate, wild, and above all cold:

> solus Hyperboreas glacies Tanaimque nivalem
> arvaque Riphaeis numquam viduata pruinis
> lustrabat...
>
> (*Geo.* 4.517–19)[1]

Orpheus' failure is a human one, his final loss of Eurydice is the direct result of his passion (*'quis tantus furor?'* line 495); after her final disappearance his song still exerts its charm over nature (*mulcentem tigris et agentem carmine quercus*, line 510), but the unending cold of the landscape suggests vividly the impotence of the pure magic of his song when faced with the reality of personal loss.

We are dealing with one of Virgil's most profound and moving ideas, to which no scholarly or critical assessment can do justice, an idea which reappears continually from the *Eclogues* to the last book of the *Aeneid*. Only the one aspect of it which appears in the Tenth Eclogue can concern us here, but to understand this we must refer to the similar terms of the parallel passages at the end of the Second and Fourth Georgics, a later restatement of the themes of the power of poetry and personal loss. We have cited the relevant passages; our summary now can only be descriptive and suggestive.

In his poetic genealogy (as we discussed it in the Sixth Eclogue) Virgil presented an original unity (Apollo and the Muses), an intermediate diversity of scientific poetry (represented by Orpheus) and pastoral (Linus), and a final unifying singer (Gallus). Such a schematization is of course far too precise, but may not misrepresent Virgil's basic intention. Our term 'scientific' poetry is a poor attempt to reproduce what Virgil represented by the figure of Orpheus: first, what we may properly call scientific, the themes sung by Apollonius' Orpheus, or the first ten lines of Silenus' song in the Sixth Eclogue, or what Virgil himself considers the supreme gift of the Muses (*Geo.* 2.475–82); then, 'things like the truth', as the Muses told Hesiod, where myth exerts a power more compelling and truthful than actuality.[2] The magic of Orphic song is the power of

---

[1] Cf. also *Geo.* 4.509, *gelidis...sub astris*. Virgil associates cold with Orpheus once again as the Hebrus bears his head downstream: *...Eurydicen vox ipsa et* frigida lingua | *a miseram Eurydicen! anima fugiente vocabat* (*Geo.* 4.525–6).

[2] See the splendid synthesis by R. Coleman, *AJP* 83 (1962), with the conclusion (p. 58), 'The combination of μίμησις and ποίησις by which the poet embraces "things that are true" and "things that are like the truth" and so reaches out to a universality beyond the limits of rational precision were summed up symbolically in the figure of Orpheus, the archetypal poet who knew the secrets of the universe – cosmogony and science – and was also the father of mythological song.'

understanding – pure intellect, perhaps; and though Orpheus naturally continues to exert this power after the final loss of Eurydice, he is powerless to help himself in his personal loss, a situation movingly symbolized by the frozen landscape in which he sings. Virgil's own description of cosmic understanding, pure and scientific, fails too because of the unhuman cold involved (*sin...frigidus obstiterit circum praecordia sanguis*, *Geo.* 2.483–4): the alternative presented at this point is the pastoral or rural.

The second half of Gallus' speech in the Tenth Eclogue is concerned with these same questions. He first turns to pastoral poetry (lines 50–4), assuming the role of his own Acontius, to suggest the sympathetic response of a warm landscape to his unhappiness. Then (lines 55–60) comes the suggestion of a different sort of poetry, but again drawn from his own work: as Milanion he will withdraw to a wilderness,[1] while *in propria persona* as poet he will write Parthenian, 'scientific' poetry, poetry of mythological truth or abstract universality. Suddenly, however, the reality of personal loss comes home to him again (and again in his own words, *tamquam haec sit nostri medicina furoris...*[2]), with the realization that *Amor* (personal emotion) does not grow any gentler when faced with human suffering.[3] Neither the Hamadryads nor songs have any appeal now; the pastoral landscape itself is abandoned.[4] Finally, the poetic alternatives represented by Acontius and Milanion are clearly

---

[1] *Frigora* is more than enough to convey the idea of an unresponsive wilderness: but it should be clear by now, from our discussions of related passages in Propertius especially (e.g. 1.18 and 1.20), that the original passage(s) by Gallus referred to by Virgil in these lines emphasized this aspect of wild desolation, cold and barren, quite opposed to a 'pastoral' climate in which, for instance, the *teneræ arbores* can receive in sympathy the poet's loves – and grow with them.

[2] Though there is no question of 'recall' or 'echo' involved, it is worth pointing out how Orpheus' personal loss (as mentioned just above) is also termed the result of *furor* by Eurydice (*illa 'quis et me' inquit 'miseram et te perdidit, Orpheu,* | *quis tantus furor'*, Geo. 4.494–5): *furor* in Virgil is often something very close to 'human weakness', 'mortality'.

[3] This line too (*aut deus ille malis hominum mitescere discat*) is Gallus' own (cf. Prop. 1.5.24 and 1.14.8: Tränkle, *Die Sprachkunst*, 23). The generalizing *hominum* is worth noting, and is probably Virgil's, not Gallus'.

[4] These two lines (*iam neque Hamadryades rursus neque carmina nobis* | *ipsa placent, ipsae rursus concedite silvae*) must be understood in the light of what we have developed thus far. The Hamadryads and 'songs' may stand for scientific or abstract mythological poetry. Hamadryads are surprisingly rare in Latin poetry (only here in Virgil); perhaps the *Culex* poet again echoes some passage related to this line of Virgil's when he connects the Hamadryads with the Ascrean Hesiod (*...Hamadryadum, quarum non divite cultu* | *aemulus Ascraeo pastor sibi quisque poetae* | *securam placido traducit pectore vitam*, 95–7). Propertius' nymphology in 1.20, which most likely derives from Gallus, may also provide an indication of the sort of Gallan poetry suggested by the Hamadryads here (cf. esp. Prop. 1.20.32, *a dolor! ibat Hylas, ibat Hamadryasin*, discussed above). *Carmina* is too general a designation to allow the connotation 'scientific-mythological poetry' here, but the emphasis on the word in connection with Silenus' songs in the closely related Sixth Eclogue is striking

seen as impossibilities, the one reduced to a barren frigidity, the other to a desert heat where even the bark of the elm shrivels and dies:[1] the realization of the absolute failure of each poetic alternative is complete in the face of Love's domination. Again we are reminded of Orpheus, destroyed by his own *furor* and equally powerless either to effect a change in his situation or to forget: *omnia vincit Amor: et nos cedamus Amori.*

If Virgil's Gallus has finally been forced to reject the very tradition of poetry he had earlier, in the Sixth Eclogue, been initiated as the representative of, what of the rest of the Tenth Eclogue, and how has Virgil led up to this ultimate denial? Our interpretation of the last half of Gallus' speech demands a consistent explication of the whole.

Virgil's staging of the scene is based on Thyrsis' lament for Daphnis in Theocritus I. When a passage of such length is so thoroughly Theocritean, we would do well to be open to Virgil's originality. For instance, Virgil begins (after the introduction, line 9) with an address to the Nymphs (*puellae Naides*), four lines very similar to Thyrsis' beginning (Theocr. 1.66–9):

> Quae nemora aut qui vos saltus habuere, puellae
> Naides, indigno cum Gallus amore peribat?
> nam neque Parnasi vobis iuga, nam neque Pindi
> ulla moram fecere, neque Aonie Aganippe.

> πᾷ ποκ' ἄρ' ἦσθ', ὅκα Δάφνις ἐτάκετο, πᾷ ποκα, Νύμφαι;
> ἦ κατὰ Πηνειῶ καλὰ τέμπεα, ἢ κατὰ Πίνδω;
> οὐ γὰρ δὴ ποταμοῖο μέγαν ῥόον εἴχετ' Ἀνάπω,
> οὐδ' Αἴτνας σκοπιάν, οὐδ' Ἄκιδος ἱερὸν ὕδωρ.

The point of Virgil's departures can easily be overlooked:[2] Theocritus is concerned with the Nymphs themselves, and with where they might

(*Ecl.* 6.5, 18, 25 twice in bucolic anaphora). *Silvae*, though, in the *Eclogues* clearly stands for the pastoral landscape (e.g. *Ecl.* 4.1–3, 6.1–2), and if our interpretation of Gallus' speech is thus far basically correct, it seems that these two lines must also be read in reference to the two sorts of poetry Gallus has been concerned with.

[1] Does the *moriens liber* here deliberately recall the bark on which Acontius–Gallus' *amores* were to be inscribed at lines 53–4 (cf. again the actual *corticibus* of Prop. 1.18.22, deriving most likely from Gallus)?

[2] A. S. F. Gow, for instance, on Theocr. 1.66 f.: 'The meaning is that the local Nymphs, had they been in their usual haunts, would have intervened to save Daphnis, whom they favoured (141); possibly therefore they were in Thessaly... Virgil's imitation of T. ...either misses T.'s point (for Gallus, at the time of his breach with Lycoris, cannot have been both in Thrace and Boeotia, and seems in fact to have been in Italy), or makes the different one that the Dryads were away from their posts of duty like Homeric gods when they visit the Ethiopians (*Il.* 1.423, *Od.* 1.22), and were therefore out of touch with human affairs.'

have been ('If you weren't in Sicily, then you must have been in Thessaly'), whereas Virgil is concerned not with the Nymphs' haunts (though ...*Pindi*, parallel to Theocritus'...*Πίνδω*, is there to reinforce the allusion to Theocritus), but with poetic mountains and springs. Parnassus needs no comment, nor does the Aonian Aganippe, the Boeotian spring of Permessus discussed above in its connection particularly with Hesiod's initiation on Mt Helicon, with Callimachus, and with Gallus' reception in the Sixth Eclogue. Virgil says, quite simply, 'Neither Parnassus, Pindus, nor Aganippe (Helicon) *delayed you*, Nymphs,' yet the Theocritean parallel has forced commentators to interpret this to mean, 'You were not at any of those locations.'[1] If, though, we pay special attention to Virgil's departures from Theocritus, and if we realize that one of his departures is his concern with poetic places of exceptional importance, then we may take his words to mean what they say, '(You Nymphs were on Parnassus, Pindus, and Helicon, and) they gave you no cause not to go to Gallus': that is, there was no reason why poetic help should not have been forthcoming from those great sources of poetic truth and inspiration.

The next three lines (13–15) do not reproduce anything in the Theocritean model,[2] and are therefore again of particular interest: laurels and tamarisks weep for Gallus as he lies under a desolate crag (*sola sub rupe iacentem*), as does Maenalus and the chill rocks of Lycaeus (*et gelidi fleverunt saxa Lycaei*). The setting is generally assumed to be pastoral (and it is, of course, Arcadian), but this assumption may be questioned.[3] Not only should it be kept in mind that the lines are a remarkable intrusion into a lengthy passage otherwise carefully Theocritean, but there are pointed indications of a poetic world distinct from the pastoral, and one with which we have become familiar: Gallus is alone among the desolate crags of Milanion's Maenalus,[4] by the cold stream of Lycaeus. These

---

[1] E.g. T. E. Page, *ad loc.*: 'they could not have been in any of their wonted haunts, for if so, they must have heard that Gallus was perishing and come to his aid.' Cf. Gow's comment in the preceding note.

[2] Theocritus' Thyrsis passes directly from the address to the Nymphs (66–9) to the wild beasts (jackals, wolves, and lions, 71–2) and cattle (74–5), and then to the gods and herdsmen (76–98) – there is no mention in this sequence of trees weeping, or of the site.

[3] M. Putnam (*Virgil's Pastoral Art*, 351) does question this common assumption: 'Though the *mise en scène* is literally in Arcadia, it can in no sense be considered bucolic. Cold rocks and lonely crags have little to do with the shepherd's inner pleasance'; and in n. 14 (p. 351) he compares this setting to 'Virgil's description of the landscape in which Orpheus wanders after the loss of Eurydice in *Georgic 4*.'

[4] Cf. line 55, and our discussion above (text following p. 90 n. 2) deriving Virgil's and Ovid's (*AA* 2.193) Maenalus from Gallus' Milanion–Atalanta passage. Putnam has seen this connection too (via Propertius), but does not pursue it (p. 353): 'To suggest a definite parallel between Gallus, *sola sub rupe* under the mountains of Arcady, and Milanion,

lines should conclude the paragraph beginning with line 9. The Theocritean coloring serves to bring out the bold outlines of the Virgilian
forms: the scene and all that is associated with Gallus' initiation in the
Sixth Eclogue is evoked by the formally striking... *Aonie Aganippe*, the
Gallan Milanion is suggested (though perhaps only clearly on a second
reading of the Eclogue) and through this figure the poetry of science and
myth (though again these lie dormant until the last half of Gallus'
speech). In summary, Virgil sets the question for Gallus, 'Is your initiation
to poetic truth, your position as the inheritor of Hesiod's Orphic pipes,
to be of no help to you?'

A new paragraph begins with line 16, where again the Theocritean
model is closely followed. Here is the pastoral world, the alternative, by
now expected, to what has just preceded, clearly distinguished by Virgil
as such:

> stant et oves circum (nostri nec paenitet illas,
> nec te paeniteat pecoris, divine poeta;
> et formosus ovis ad flumina pavit Adonis),
> venit et opilio, tardi venere subulci,
> uvidus hiberna venit de glande Menalcas.
>
> (*Ecl.* 10.16–20)[1]

In this setting Gallus' affliction provokes only disbelief and consternation
(*omnes 'unde amor iste' rogant 'tibi?' venit Apollo,* | *'Galle, quid insanis?'*
inquit, 21–2). Silvanus and Pan come with further direct questions that
stress the inordinate excess (*'ecquis erit modus?'*, 28) of Gallus' subjection
to *Amor* – inordinate at least in the emotional scale of their pastoral world;
they can see *Amor* only in terms of their pastoral existence (*'nec lacrimis*
crudelis Amor nec gramina rivis | *nec cytiso saturantur apes nec fronde capellae'*,
29–30). The roles and functions of the figures in this procession, however,
have become effectively blurred. Apollo in the *Eclogues* is, rather surprisingly, never clearly a pastoral deity,[2] but in this setting and company
he does convey a rustic impression. Pan, *deus Arcadiae*, on the other hand,
is made to suggest the prophet-singer Silenus of the Sixth Eclogue,
who repeated Apollo's own songs.[3] Arcadia, the scene of Milanion's

saucius Arcadiis rupibus undergoing the *labores* that finally won him his girl, is to go beyond
what Virgil has already told his reader.' But once the dependence of Propertius' Milanion
on Gallus is demonstrated, this connection (with others) is natural and necessary.

[1] The postponed *et* (*stant et oves circum*) is certainly emphatic, perhaps to mark the important
transition here described – 'here too is the pastoral...'

[2] In the light of this, *Geo.* 3.1–2 (*et te memorande canemus* | *pastor ab Amphryso*) is surprising
and original: 'Ἀπόλλων Νόμιος, who served Admetus, is more often simply a figure of
fun. Cf. Pales and Apollo linked in *Ecl.* 5.35, however, and Theocr. 25.21.

[3] *Pan deus Arcadiae venit, quem vidimus ipsi* | *sanguineis ebuli bacis minioque rubentem* (*Ecl.*
10.26–7) ~ *Aegle...iamque videnti* [Sileno] | *sanguineis frontem moris et tempora pingit*

trial and the home of Pan, similarly has come to include both the scientific-mythological and the pastoral.

Gallus' first words are then addressed to these Arcadians, *'soli cantare periti | Arcades'*. His wish for peace, if only their pipe could play his loves (*'o mihi tum quam molliter ossa quiescant, | vestra meos olim si fistula dicat amores'*, 33–4), is far more than a plea for immortality through the power of their song. As he begins to speak he is as firmly under Love's domination as he is in the end, and he is fully aware of it; his wish, though, is to use the Arcadian pipe to play *his own* loves on (and we may take *meos amores* here as we do in line 53 – as a definite suggestion of his four books of elegies). With this wish he begins to imagine pastoral love, just as later he easily assumes the role of Acontius (and then of Milanion). Finally (lines 42–3) he begins to do just what he had hoped for, that is, to set his Lycoris in the pastoral mode (*hic gelidi fontes, hic mollia prata, Lycori, | hic nemus; hic ipso tecum consumerer aevo*). But the very mention of Lycoris' name reminds him of the dramatic reality, and the pastoral vanishes with his return to his present subjection to *Amor* (*nunc insanus Amor...*, 44).[1] His Lycoris has in fact left him. It is at this point that we began: the progress of the Eclogue thus far anticipates in every detail what is now to follow, but could only be completely understood from an awareness of the poetic crisis which the situation of Gallus represents.

We can now begin to see the reflected outlines of Gallus' poetry from which Virgil began and, far more clearly, the point and purpose of the Tenth Eclogue; we can also see why Virgil chose to begin and end the second half of the Eclogue Book with poetry as his subject and with Gallus in particular as its representative.[2]

(*Ecl.* 6.20–2). Why does Virgil write *quem vidimus ipsi*? Had he seen this Pan in Gallus' poetry perhaps? The association of Silenus and Pan at Apollo's cave in Prop. 3.3 surely is a recall of Virgil (*...et Sileni patris imago | fictilis et calami, Pan Tegeaee, tui*, 29–30).

[1] Lines 44–5 (*nunc insanus Amor duri me Martis in armis | tela inter media atque adversos detinet hostis*) have caused considerable uneasiness, but I find them perfectly natural and intelligible. First, *insanus Amor* should be the proper focus for our attention, as we have been defining and discussing it. Then, if we understand the references to Mars, war, and arms poetically rather than literally (according to the second of the two working assumptions with which we began), and if we grant as well that there is every likelihood that these two lines derive from Gallus' poetry, we may see here a shadow of the Gallan original of the motif of War which so appealed to Tibullus especially (1.3 or 1.10 being the clearest extended examples): War is opposed (in this motif) to (real) rural peace and to (idealized) pastoral existence. Virgil's Gallus, then, ends his pastoral reverie (which, I suspect, also appeared in his own elegies – cf. the Tibullan reverie commonly cited as a parallel, 1.5.19–36) with a motif the poet Gallus had employed, War as the present reality opposed to the illusion of pastoral peace.

[2] What follows here about the development of Gallus' poetry must remain largely speculative, but I believe the positive indications about his poetry discussed thus far make new speculations worthwhile.

In the Tenth Eclogue Gallus finds that the universality of two modes of poetic expression – scientific-mythological and pastoral – can offer no final consolation or solution to the individual experience of personal loss: his Lycoris has left him, and he must finally yield to Amor. To isolate and define different levels of experience behind this simple statement of what the Tenth Eclogue is about is to destroy Virgil's unity, but may help to make clear what he started from and what he achieved. First, what I hope has been proved positively: the dramatic situation – the actors and the staging – is assembled from important scenes and passages in Gallus' own poetry; what Gallus does and says in the Eclogue is to be recognized as no more or less than what he had actually written, though the whole, of course, is Virgil's creation. Gallus becomes his own Acontius and his own Milanion; his own Lycoris leaves him, to which he responds in his own words.[1] At a second level we may see Gallus' published works, the actual four books of his elegies, his total poetic production: does Virgil, in the Sixth and Tenth Eclogues, take for granted his readers' awareness of Gallus' development in elegy from book to book, a progress that for us must necessarily remain hypothetical? Finally, at a third level, we may understand what poetry represents, a way of understanding and expressing human experience: there can be no saying precisely how much of the Eclogue at this level is Virgil's and how much was Gallus', but there is no mistaking Virgil's achievement.

Our second level calls for more attention. If Virgil's Gallus actually wrote (as we have assumed in general and proved in most particulars) the poetry referred to and suggested in the Tenth Eclogue, and if the Eclogue presents him as turning to and then dismissing certain modes of poetic expression, can we then assume that such was in fact the course of his poetic career, or that Virgil at least could have presented his career as such? Was there a clear change and development in the sort of elegies Gallus wrote from his first book to his last, such as is evident in Propertius' career, and does Virgil's Gallus represent this development? All we can do to suggest answers to these questions is to remind ourselves of the character and nature of elegy immediately before and after Gallus, and to see whether the development Virgil seems to be suggesting for Gallus' elegies actually fits into this picture.

Whether elegy existed at all before Gallus was unanswerable to those

---

[1] I neglect entirely what might be said to be a level below this: the real experience, whatever it may have been, of Gallus and Cytheris. For reasons often enough mentioned above, I do not consider that this experience had much relevance or importance for Gallus' own elegies and none whatsoever for the Tenth Eclogue.

who knew best,[1] but the poetic source from which it arose is clearly to be found in the neoteric Catullus.[2] It is not to his epigrams (69–116) that one must look to find this source, but to the polymetrics (1–60) and longer poems (61–68) which represent a new poetic *élan* at Rome, a literary sophistication and expressiveness suddenly made possible by the discovery not simply of Hellenistic poetry, but of Callimachean poetics, introduced (and undoubtedly greatly modified and reformed) by Parthenius himself. There is in Catullus no single poem that can unambiguously be termed an elegy (as could be defined from Augustan elegy), but every important poetic characteristic of later elegy can, I think, be found in some form in his neoteric production. It is generally true that the greater the degree of poetic formality in a poem of Catullus, the greater is its expressiveness, not only in its capacity for abstract and complex meaning, but in depth of emotion as well. Until fairly recently Catullus' epyllion (64) was regarded as a frigid exercise in mannered Alexandrianism, appreciated, if at all, only for its icy elegance and certain, rather quaint, technical innovations; as it is now being read and understood, however, it may be said to have given to Latin poetry the possibility of a vastly extended range of abstract meaning and personal emotion. The formality, both of structure and expression, of poem 68 (at least lines 41–148) is similarly being appreciated in a new way: Catullus' two greatest experiences, his love for Lesbia and his brother's death, are both set together in this poem against the literary abstraction of the Trojan war and the death there of Laodamia's Protesilaus. If Gallus' poetry deserved to be taken as seriously as Virgil so obviously does, then certainly Catullus' achievement in such poems as these must have been a significant precedent for him.

We may remind ourselves too of the tone of Gallan elegy, as far as we have been able to detect it: archaic and artificially poetic, it seems to verify Quintilian's verdict, '*sicut durior Gallus*', and to have been appropriate for a poetic successor to Catullus' more formal and serious poems and to the subjects and themes we know to have been of great importance to him (the Grynean Grove, Acontius and Cydippe, Milanion and Atalanta, a Hylas poem not unlike Propertius 1.20). We should remember, too, Parthenius, not only for the confirmation he gives our impression of

---

[1] Catullus appears as an elegist (or perhaps simply as a love-poet?) in the 'canonical' lists in Prop. 2.34.87, Ovid, *Am.* 3.9.62, *Tr.* 2.427–8; otherwise the list begins with Gallus (Ovid, *Tr.* 4.10.51–4, *AA* 3.333–4, Quint. 10.1.93, Suet.-Diomedes 1.484 Keil).

[2] One can say nothing, of course, about such other neoterics as Calvus or Cinna. I have discussed Catullus as an antecedent of the elegists in *Style and Tradition in Catullus*, esp. pp. 163–9, where discussions of and reasons for the following statements about Catullus may be found.

Gallus' elegiac style (τὸ περιττὸν . . ., ὃ δὴ σὺ μέτερχῃ – we should note again that Gallus was already known for this 'extravagant nicety' of style at the time Parthenius dedicated the collection of erotic stories to him), but for the literary background he inevitably calls to mind – Euphorion, exotic taste and learning, and whatever has passed for so long under the heading of Alexandrian 'objective elegy'. We have, then, a fairly substantial idea of the sort of poetry Gallus must have composed in his first books of elegies.

Propertius' first book, though, is very different, as he himself made clear in its programmatic first poem. Cynthia is his subject and inspiration: his elegies are thus to be personal and immediate. The poet claims to be totally subject to the domination of *Amor* (1.1.3–4).[1] His art is thus unadorned,[2] his language more direct and natural.[3] Propertius' emphasis, then, is on a sort of elegy very unlike the impression of Gallan elegy we have just gained.

How did Latin elegy pass so quickly from something objective, Alexandrian, and neoteric in subject and style to what at least poses as fully subjective and personal, as simple in style as in content? Propertius supplies part of the answer in his *Monobiblos*.

We concluded our discussion of the *Monobiblos* by noting that there is no valid or compelling reason not to assume that the Gallus of poems 5, 10, 13 and 20 is the poet Cornelius, and that in fact there is good reason for this obvious identification. We suggested too that these poems can be read as Propertius' reactions to a change in Gallus' approach to elegy. Poem 5 predicts the *servitium amoris* that is at hand for Gallus (*tum grave servitium nostrae cogere puellae | discere...*, 19–20) and warns him from personal experience (*quare, quid possit mea Cynthia, desine, Galle, | quaerere: non impune illa rogata venit*, 31–2: Cynthia can suggest 'my sort of elegy'). Poem 10, we noted, makes more sense when understood as Propertius' reaction to a first reading of new, properly 'subjective', amatory elegy by Gallus than when the staging is taken literally and Propertius plays the voyeur. Poem 13 is another variation on the theme

---

[1] All this, of course, is poetic fiction. I have belabored the point above that it is wrong to read the *Monobiblos* as the work of a romantic obsessed with his own amatory experience, that it is in fact a work of carefully contrived art owing much to neoteric poetry and Gallan elegy.

[2] Prop. 1.2 can be read as such a comment on his art, as has been suggested above. Note, *inter alia*, the adaptation of Gallus in lines 7–8, the positive *exemplum* from nature (9–14) followed by the negative mythological *exemplum* (15–22), and Apollo and Calliope (27–8).

[3] Again, as discussed previously, not only in 1.1, but throughout the *Monobiblos* there is continual juxtaposition of lines and passages in the neoteric (Gallan) elegiac style and in the more direct and supple language of Propertius' personal elegy.

of Gallus' recent and unexpected subjection to Love, a complete domination surpassing (it should be noted) even mythological passions (21–32).[1] Propertius, in fact, seems to begin where Gallus had left off.[2]

To summarize, there is an intriguing similarity between the *servitium* Propertius first predicts and then observes as Gallus' just deserts and the resignation expressed in Gallus' last words in the Tenth Eclogue ('*omnia vincit Amor: et nos cedamus Amori*'), words themselves which seem to be the beginning for Propertius' first book (e.g. 1.1.3–4). The Tenth Eclogue may thus on one level be a reflection of the course of Gallus' elegiac career. It would in fact be a natural expectation that Gallus should provide the transition from the neoteric beginnings such as we can see in Catullus to the fully-developed 'subjective' elegy of Propertius, whose origins have remained so unclear in spite of so much investigation and discussion. Virgil's Gallus, the divine singer whose initiation we witnessed in the Sixth Eclogue, seems clearly to abandon his poetic inheritance and to accept Love's domination: what we know of Latin elegy before and after Gallus makes it likely that this is an accurate summary of Gallus' development as an elegist.

But the Tenth Eclogue is not simply a new setting for lines or passages from Gallus, or a commentary on his poetic career: it is the culmination of the Eclogue Book, and as such we must expect from it much more. There is certainly some reason, beyond personal friendship or admiration for his poetry, for the prominence Virgil gives to Gallus here and centrally in the Sixth Eclogue: Gallus' poetry has been transformed by Virgil as completely as the man himself.

To say that the Tenth Eclogue is about poetry is to mean something

---

[1] Propertius' delighted surprise, I suspect, is again more fiction than fact: his pose from the beginning has been pride in the novelty and originality of his own *servitium* to Cynthia and Amor; it seems more than likely, however, that Gallus' latest elegies (the ones heralded in these poems) had already and for some time shown him the way.

[2] This outline of the development of Gallus' elegy and its position and significance in the transformation of Latin elegy is perhaps set out here too positively. I do not mean to imply that Lycoris entered Gallus' elegies only in, say, his final book: what seems likely, however, is that her role and significance did change. I cannot assume, with the vast majority, that Catullus' Lesbia is simply an accurate reflection of a real experience and nothing more. Even less can I assume that Lycoris ever had much to do with Cytheris, just as I cannot see in Cynthia (or Delia or Corinna) anything more than an elegiac convention. I imagine that in Gallus' first book of elegies Lycoris served as a convenient point of departure for mythological parallels (compare, for instance, Prop. 1.20), and that in many elegies she would have played no part at all; but I cannot exclude the possibility of some degree of subjective expression even in Gallus' first elegies – he may, of course, have experimented as well with the manner and presentation of Catullus' polymetrics about Lesbia. The above is intended only to emphasize what little can be deduced from what we know: we have no hope of supplying shades and details without Gallus' four books themselves.

far beyond the craft of writing or judgements on what makes verse good or bad. In the ancient world philosophy was the only form of serious writing to rival poetry – and that only since Plato. For Virgil there were no boundaries marking off the limits beyond which the poet should not go; he had not to fear intruding in alien territories. No aspects of human experience could be considered foreign to poetry, and no part of the natural world was unfit for poetic speculation. Through poetry, knowledge and understanding were both completely possible and any aspect of human experience could be expressed.[1]

We have often referred to two modes of poetic expression, the scientific-mythological and the pastoral. Virgil himself defined scientific poetry through his Orpheus: knowledge of nature, expressed in song, is power over nature, or magic.[2] Related to pure magic is mythology, perhaps to be thought of as Hesiod's 'things like the truth', and presented by Virgil through the figure of Hesiod: prehistory, anthropology, psychology. Fortunately Virgil had no need to assemble any such list of modern terms to suggest what mythology embraces: *omnia quae Phoebo quondam meditante beatus | audiit Eurotas*. The scope and purpose of pastoral poetry is of course more difficult to define, and the danger of substituting later terms for Virgil's is very real, but it is easy enough to see what Gallus makes of it in the Tenth Eclogue. Apollo, Silvanus, and Pan ask Gallus, in effect, to cure his insanity by accepting and forgetting Love's domination; the power of the Arcadians' song is such as to make this possible ('*o mihi tum quam molliter ossa quiescant, | vestra meos olim si fistula dicat amores*'), and for a time he does in fact forget, lost in a pastoral dream even with Lycoris herself. Through pastoral what is real can be transformed, pain can cease to matter, and there can be solace for those willing to remain in the shade: Corydon's suffering is, like Gallus', both excessive and a form of insanity,[3] but as a proper inhabitant of the

[1] These remarks must seem resoundingly obvious, but so often the range and capacity of ancient poetry are forgotten. Rome was by nature as unpoetical as it was unphilosophical, and needed a long time to discover and learn to use poetry as a way of thought and expression: Virgil was perhaps the first to realize fully what Greek poetry meant. The development of our own separate subjects for investigation and compartments of knowledge, each with its own mode of expression (scientific, philosophical, historical, political, and so on) has reduced the territory of poetry to one corner of 'literature': we need constantly to remind ourselves, therefore, both what poetry was in the Greek world before Plato, and what the universality of Greek poetry meant for Virgil at Rome.

[2] It is perhaps clearer now why I consider it essential to take *ille* in *Ecl.* 6.70 specifically as Orpheus. All the details mentioned in this summary have of course been discussed at length above.

[3] *me tamen urit amor: quis enim modus adsit amori? | a, Corydon, Corydon, quae te dementia cepit!* (*Ecl.* 2.68–9) – cf. Apollo's words to Gallus, '*Galle, quid insanis?*', and Pan's, '*ecquis erit modus?*'.

pastoral world he easily decides to find another, more responsive Alexis (*invenies alium, si te hic fastidit, Alexim, Ecl.* 2.73). At his initiation in the Sixth Eclogue, then, Gallus inherited a unified poetic tradition which makes possible knowledge and understanding of the real world and also the power to transform the real, if need be, into a painless ideal.

We have seen, however, Virgil's own awareness of the possibilities for failure of both intellect and imagination. Intellectual understanding may be beyond capability, a region where the blood stands frozen.[1] Orpheus himself, faced with a personal loss caused by human weakness, found his powers useless, though undiminished, in a landscape correspondingly cold and frozen (*Geo.* 4.453–527). Intellectual abstractions never led Virgil to forget humanity: however seductive and intriguing are the constructions the mind may build, there is always some human element to render them vain and useless. Gallus, who had inherited Orphic powers, anticipates exactly Orpheus' final powerlessness to respond to human loss.[2] The pastoral imagination, with its ability to transform reality, is a ready alternative to the scientific intellect, a retreat where cool shade is welcome in a warm and responsive landscape.[3] But a pastoral paradise is uninhabitable because of the very reality it attempts to transform:[4] Gallus cannot forget Lycoris, human emotion cannot be ignored, and the pastoral landscape becomes a parched desert.[5] The shade in which Tityrus began his neoteric song is abandoned: *surgamus: solet esse gravis cantantibus umbra* (*Ecl.* 10.75).

The Sixth and Tenth Eclogues are thus concerned with far more than what we mean by 'poetry'. The poet's powers to understand and to give form and meaning to his life are as glorious as their failure is inevitable and tragic: divine song is subject to human weakness, to which all things must yield. The second half of the Eclogue Book begins with the

---

[1] *Geo.* 2.475–84, ending *sin has ne possim naturae accedere partis | frigidus obstiterit circum praecordia sanguis...*

[2] *Ecl.* 10.64–6: *non illum [Amorem] nostri possunt mutare labores | nec si frigoribus mediis Hebrumque bibamus, | Sithoniasque nives hiemis subeamus aquosae...*

[3] *Geo.* 2.485–9, ending *o qui me gelidis convallibus Haemi | sistat, et ingenti ramorum protegat umbra!* That Virgil intends the alternative to scientific poetry here to be understood as the pastoral is made clear by Silvanus and Pan (with the Nymphs) at lines 493–4 (*fortunatus et ille deos qui novit agrestis | Panaque Silvanumque senem Nymphasque sorores*): Pan and Silvanus (with Apollo) come to Gallus in *Ecl.* 10.21–30. Compare, of course, Corydon, whom 'love burns' as he sings alone in the mid-day heat in *Ecl.* 2.

[4] This is implied, of course, in *Geo.* 2.495–540: the golden Saturnian age cannot be reconciled either with the *labor* of Virgil's real country or with the real world, *res Romanae peritauraque regna.*

[5] *Ecl.* 10.67–8, *...nec si, cum moriens alta liber aret in ulmo, | Aethiopum versemus ovis sub sidere Cancri.*

expression of potential power and ends with the realization of failure:[1] there is no theme more Virgilian than this. Gallus' elegies would undoubtedly allow us to attribute to him many more of the details we now assume to be Virgilian, but the controlling concept is one we immediately recognize as Virgil's own, the fabric of both the *Georgics* and the *Aeneid*.

[1] The Sixth Eclogue is primarily concerned with scientific-mythological poetry, though sufficient suggestions of pastoral are included (as we discussed above), just as the Tenth is primarily pastoral in setting; but the emphasis in each case is more a matter of artistic presentation than of actual subject: these two modes of poetry should not always be defined as separately as our argument has perhaps suggested.

6

Propertius:
from *Ardoris Poeta* to *Romanus Callimachus*

The preceding pages were devoted to poetry written before Gallus' suicide and under his direct influence, and had a dual, and often seemingly circular, purpose. Certain deductions about the content of Gallus' poetry, made previously by others, were substantiated and enlarged upon, others were discarded, and some new suggestions were offered. We were then able to discuss Gallus' position and importance in contemporary poetry, and to propose new interpretations of the Sixth and Tenth Eclogues and of the character and purpose of Propertius' *Monobiblos*. To reconstruct the content of a lost poem from an obviously dependent existing poem (a fair enough procedure in itself) and then to use the reconstructed content to interpret the dependent poem is to invite the disbelief of those inclined to scepticism, but at least we have been on fairly firm ground in some respects: neither Gallus' friendship and shared interests with Virgil, nor his importance as a precedent for Propertius' first work, can be denied. After Gallus' death, however, the situation changes. The effect of his disgrace and suicide in 27 or 26 B.C. is impossible to estimate: it is hard to form even a rough idea of the process by which his name was caused to be forgotten, or of the extent to which his poetry was quietly suppressed – if indeed it was.[1] Had Gallus not fallen so heavily, we might perhaps have learned much more from the poets themselves, directly and openly, about his elegy and the precedent it constituted. We can, however, trace the development of Augustan poetry by investigating certain aspects related to questions we have been considering; at the beginning of this survey of Latin poetry after Gallus' death, his precedent will again be of great importance. But the ground

[1] For instance, what truth may lie behind Servius' somewhat conflicting notices (on *Ecl.* 10.1 and *Geo.* 4.1) that Virgil had to remove the *laudes Galli* from *Geo.* 4, '*irato Augusto*', still remains totally unclear: modern opinion tends to see much confusion and little veracity in his remarks (see, e.g., R. Coleman, *AJP* 83 (1962), 55–71, and for a bibliography on the question, his refs. p. 55 n. 1). Again, Gallus disappears from Propertius' poetry after the first book, except for the literary historical mention of him in 2.34.91, and only such mentions occur in Ovid. It seems impossible that we will ever know the process by which neglect of Gallus was officially encouraged and quietly accepted, and whether it is to this neglect that we owe the loss of his poetry.

over which we must proceed is becoming less firm, and the dangers all too obvious, for even if what we have said about Gallan elegy is more or less sound, it must be applied now to poetry which necessarily gives few direct indications of its indebtedness to him.

Gallus' precedent is not merely a matter of scholarly curiosity but is of fundamental importance; we cannot begin to understand Augustan elegy, or even to read it properly, unless we have some idea of the poetry which directly preceded it and from which it developed. The little that we learn from ancient sources might suggest (we have argued the opposite) that Gallus wrote two separate sorts of poems: on the one hand aetiological verse, such as that on the Grynean Grove, most likely in hexameters, some of it perhaps in the form of epyllia, but in any case learned, impersonal, and Alexandrian; on the other, his elegies to Lycoris, stylistically direct and subjective in content, the result of personal experience. If some such dichotomy (which most scholars, though with a number of variations on the theme, have accepted) was in fact the case, then a number of important assumptions are to be made. We would have to set Gallus at the very end of one tradition: no important poet (and I do not call the makers of such poems as the *Culex* or the *Ciris* 'important poets') again composed an epyllion *per se*, so important a form for Catullus and his circle, and we would have to proceed with the expectation that not only the form itself, but other neoteric elements of style and content appeared for the last time in this work of Gallus. Then, we would have to see Latin elegy beginning suddenly, almost *in vacuo*, with a fixed character and purpose, and we would have to attribute its invention to Gallus, along with the supposition (and an important one) that a real experience (his affair with Cytheris) lay immediately behind the invention of the genre. Such assumptions necessarily imply that subsequent poets read Gallus' learned verse with no practical interest, that his elegy alone caught their imaginations as something fresh and productive. We must then see Propertius accepting the genre unchanged from Gallus, but eventually making radical innovations, becoming finally the Roman Callimachus and turning elegy into a vehicle for Roman aetiology – innovations indeed of a large order. These assumptions, and others, are of course all to be found in our literary histories.

We have argued, however, that there is no clear evidence that Gallus wrote two separate sorts of poetry, that there is on the contrary good reason for believing that the four books of elegies were his total production. Quite different assumptions now have to be made, which change entirely the way we approach Augustan elegy. Instead of completing one course begun by Catullus and the neoterics, Gallus, by dealing with such aetiological themes as the Grynean Grove in a collection of elegies and by exploiting the possibilities of mythological narrative in such poems, can be said to have extended the scope of neoteric interests, and in fact to have taken a significant step closer to Callimachus. If we must place all we know of Gallus' poetry in an elegiac context, then Latin elegy begins neither *in vacuo* nor as something predominately subjective or even entirely amatory. And Propertius, in eventually abandoning purely amatory elegy, was not so much innovating as simply reverting to a type of elegy for which there had been a general, and important, precedent.

We have proposed that the very capability of poetry to cut across genre restrictions was the discovery of both Gallus and Virgil, and that, as Virgil's poetic genealogy suggests, the new poetry was intended to unite a diversity of poetic forms and purposes. Elegy began, then, not primarily as an attempt to describe erotic experience, not from any compelling personal concerns of the poet-lover, but rather because, as a new form in Latin poetry, it afforded a means to integrate various poetic traditions and purposes. The song of Silenus, the aboriginal prophet-seer, embraces without distinction universal science, mythology, and pastoral imagination: so, originally at least, did Gallan elegy, and so do the *Eclogues*.

But we have also discussed certain indications that Gallus' elegy changed considerably during the course of the publication of his four books: we have, in fact, interpreted the Tenth Eclogue as Virgil's comment on this change and on all that the change implies – just as the Sixth Eclogue presents the significance of Gallus' poetic reception. Precisely how and why the new character of Gallan elegy evolved we cannot tell,[1] but it seems clear that by the fourth book his poetic mistress Lycoris had assumed a far greater reality and importance than she had previously been granted and that the elegies themselves became more and more concerned with the direct expression of conventional amatory themes and situations – conventional in the sense that so many subsequent elegiac topics find parallels in Hellenistic epigram or Roman comedy. It was this development that turned elegy into what we have been taught to call 'subjective'. We may understand, very generally, that Gallus' first elegies were mythological narratives hung sometimes upon the convenient peg of Lycoris and a personal experience, a procedure obviously

---

[1] In the Tenth Eclogue the more significant and grander aspects of Gallus' final submission to the power of love seem so thoroughly Virgilian that Gallus' own reasons for the change in his poetic attitude cannot be deduced.

allowing great freedom in subject matter, treatment, style and tone; but that in his last elegies Lycoris had become a convention that dominated the poems, with myths serving now only as brief *exempla*: the poet had indeed 'yielded to Love'. Only some such development of Gallan elegy will take us easily and naturally from Catullus 68 to Propertius' *Monobiblos*. To say that Gallus 'invented' Latin love-elegy is somewhat misleading. He did not discover it at once, and may even have been somewhat surprised to find what his poetry had eventually become.

Propertius, as we have seen, began here. The *Monobiblos* is concerned above all else with Cynthia and with Love's domination over the poet; hence it has formed the supreme example of 'subjective love-elegy' for modern scholars, and so persuasively has Propertius handled the conventional amatory topics that most have taken the staging for reality.[1] We can, however, see the reflection of Gallus' older elegy, for Propertius is concerned to emphasize his own originality by referring continually to the Gallan background (and sometimes by recreating it); and we can see as well certain indications of Gallus' newer style. It should be clear now just how and why the *Monobiblos* presents us with the apparent *fait accompli* of 'subjective elegy', which, at the same time that it appears to be personal and erotic, is very much conditioned and postulated by the reformed neotericism of Gallus and Virgil.

Propertius' loud insistence on Cynthia in the *Monobiblos* shows that other directions were not only possible, but even perhaps expected and desirable. The original comprehensiveness of Gallan elegy meant an open invitation for later elegy to explore areas far removed from the amatory. But what must have been particularly trying for the Augustan elegists (including the later Propertius) was the fact that the conventions of personal love-elegy accepted by Propertius were so severely limiting. There are, after all, only a few situations the poet-lover can set himself in, and only a few themes he can deal with: variations on these subjects can quickly become monotonous. More important, though, and what

---

[1] For instance, J. Wight Duff (*A Literary History of Rome*, 3rd ed. (London, 1953), 415): 'Plunged at an inexperienced age into a sea of passion, Propertius was the sport of its currents – dirigible only by the feeling of the moment. Such feeling was of an intensity that wrung expression from him. It fostered the poetic; but it quenched all else. . . . In Propertius one is conscious of that type of unreserved absorption in love and intense sincerity in its expression which has been powerful in Italian literature right down to the novels and poems of D'Annunzio.' Or A. Guillemin ('Properce, de Cynthie aux Poèmes Romains', *REL* 28 (1950), 183), 'Avant tout, la sincérité de Properce, de ses accents tragiques, de ses joies, de ses tristesses est hors de cause. Rien ne fait soupçonner en lui une feinte ou une aventure purement littéraire; il a vraiment joui ardemment et cruellement souffert de l'amour.'

must have been a cause of greater frustration, are the subjects and voices effectively denied the love-elegist. Once the poet has assumed the role of lover, it obviously becomes difficult to speak out of character, and once the dramatic situation of a poem is meant to be accepted as something real, it is hard to soften the sharp edges of this assumed reality. It is one thing for a poet, writing about love, to assume the role of Milanion, as Gallus had done; it is quite another thing for a love poet to agree willingly to relegate Milanion to the occasional *exemplum*.

There is a great difference here between Gallus, writing subjective love-elegy only at the end of his career and as a natural development of his first interests and concerns, and Propertius, beginning emphatically and enthusiastically as a personal love-elegist. Interest in the power of love and in the frustrations of erotic experience was the inheritance of Latin poetry notably from Callimachus, Euphorion, and Parthenius. In Virgil this often morbid Alexandrian fascination with the obscure and perverse becomes something new and powerful: from the *Eclogues* to the *Aeneid* one of his major concerns is the power of an obsession to blind and destroy an individual subjected to it (*furor*). While Virgil was engaged on the *Eclogues*, Gallus too was occupied with similar questions, and in fact thus became for Virgil in the Tenth Eclogue the *exemplum* of an individual destroyed by an obsession. We may, I think, assume that Gallus' change from objective to subjective elegy was partly due to a greater interest in the effects of personal obsession and that he came more and more to express the power of love (the most obvious, convenient, and acceptable manifestation of an obsession) by presenting *himself* in subjection to it – much as Virgil in fact presents him. In the context of Gallus' elegies, then, this subjectivity would have appeared as a natural consequence of the Alexandrian-neoteric interest in the erotic sufferings of the unfortunate mythological lover, *whose characteristically Alexandrian monologue now becomes the very words – the poem itself – of the poet-lover.* But for Propertius, beginning where Gallus had left off, the situation is far different: no further development seems possible; the poet-lover, continuing the pose of expressing personal experience and interested in, and able to present, his own erotic psychology only as far as the demands of reality could permit, is effectively denied myth as a means of enlarging or generalizing this experience. What had been for Gallus a natural and productive development was necessarily, from then on, a literary dead end.

We may see in the work of each of the Augustan elegists various attempts to resolve a tension created by two opposing forces, both set in motion by Gallus. On the one hand the original function of elegy – its creation by Gallus to unify diverse poetic traditions and to express a variety of poetic ideas – meant a compelling precedent for expanding the scope of the genre. One could not expect the Augustan elegists to return to the Alexandrian-neoteric concerns of Gallus and the early Virgil, but one could expect elegy to become an acceptable form in which to deal with the poetic questions of the new era (the years during which the *Georgics* and Horace's first three books of *Odes* were being written). Opposed to this inherited potential capacity of the genre we must see the severe limitations of the new love-elegy, a natural development in Gallus' own case, but which, when accepted as a point of departure by Propertius, was to prove a poetic *cul-de-sac*.

It has become a matter of habit to consider love the proper sphere and concern of Latin elegy, just as its subjectivity has been for so long its most prominent characteristic. Propertius' *Monobiblos* has, of course, been largely responsible for forming this habit, the first familiar landmark from which scholars, looking back, have purified Gallus' elegy of any elements not properly amatory and subjective, and from which, looking forward to later Augustan elegy, anything not conforming to the definition of love-elegy was to be explained away with some embarrassment. Yet it should be obvious enough that love was hardly considered an essential ingredient in Roman elegy. In the last two poems (24 and 25) of Book III Propertius in effect dismisses Cynthia with some contempt, and in Book IV shows just how easy it is to get along without her. Are we to regard Book IV, then, as a daring and remarkable innovation? or as an aberration brought about only by a failure of nerve? or as a perfectly natural example of Latin elegy? A quick reading of Tibullus is enough to make one wonder how it is possible that for so long we have read Latin elegy as love poetry. In his first poem (78 lines) Delia does not appear (nor is love the theme) until line 55, and the reason for her appearance then clearly enough has nothing to do with any intensity of emotion wrung from the poet in love.[1] Comparatively little has been written by scholars or critics about Tibullus, and in much that has been written there is a discernible feeling of embarrassment, an impression that somehow his elegy is not being properly understood. The most obvious reason for this would seem to be that there is in Tibullus so little of what we have

---

[1] The sequence forms an obvious cliché of topics: Wealth (51), War (53), Love (55); just as Love soon evokes the thought of Death (69–70). There is absolutely nothing in Tib. 1.1 that would lead someone otherwise ignorant of Latin elegy to say of it on first reading, 'This is a love poem'; and Tib. 1.1 is, of course, meant to be a programmatic proemium to the whole collection.

been conditioned to expect from a love-elegist. Ovid's contribution was to mock, gently and wittily, the whole convention of the poet-lover: once this was done, he turned to other forms.

The object of the following pages is to discuss some of the consequences, for later Augustan poetry, of the arguments set forth above about Gallus and the beginnings of elegy. We must not lose sight of the Alexandrian-neoteric background and inheritance of the Augustan poets, which pervaded their art not only in stylistic matters but in their total approach to poetry and poetic values. We must recognize that the elegists were continuing a genre which had originally been created for the expression of a comprehensive range of ideas with considerable flexibility of style and manner. The limitations of the conventions observable in the subjective love-elegy of the *Monobiblos* should not be taken as a definition of elegy, demanding blind acceptance and perpetuation: they were the result of a particular and singular development, not the moving cause of the whole genre. We may expect, too, that during the few years when poetry at Rome was speaking for the national character with singular intensity, the elegists would have something to contribute.

> Callimachi Manes et Coi sacra Philitae,
> in vestrum, quaeso, me sinite ire nemus.
> primus ego ingredior puro de fonte sacerdos
> Itala per Graios orgia ferre choros.
> dicite, quo pariter carmen tenuastis in antro?
> quove pede ingressi? quamve bibistis aquam? (Prop. 3.1.1–6)

More discussion has been devoted to these lines than perhaps to any other six lines in Propertius,[1] but the questions they raise are still far from settled. Is Propertius seeking admission to the grove of Callimachus and Philitas to offer worship, or to receive it himself after his death, or to ask for an oracular response to certain questions? What are the *Itala orgia* he carries, and what connection do they have with the *Graios choros*? In what sense is he the *primus sacerdos* – is he saying, 'I am [i.e. have been] the first to...', or 'Now for the first time I...'? Why does he ask information from Callimachus and Philitas about their sources of inspiration – has he not known before this? Above all, is he proclaiming a new beginning for his elegy at this point? or is he merely stating formally,

---

[1] See (among much else) D. R. Shackleton Bailey, *Propertiana*; G. Luck, 'The Cave and the Source', CQ 7 (1957), 175–9; I. M. Lonie, 'Propertius and the Alexandrians', *AUMLA* 11 (1959), 17–34; R. J. Baker, 'Propertius III 1, 1–6 Again. Intimations of Immortality?', *Mnem.* 21 (1968), 35–9.

or calling attention to, a poetic program he has always held?[1] If we are to understand the development of Propertian elegy, we may conveniently take as a focus the questions implicit in these lines: why does Propertius so elaborately call attention to his poetry as he does here in the first and third poems of Book III? and what precisely does constitute the recognizable change in Propertian elegy between Book I and Book IV?[2]

A poet's development over some fifteen years (especially during years so productive of remarkably original poetry as were 30 to 16 B.C. at Rome) may be expected to produce observable changes of various sorts, some of fundamental importance, others secondary or superficial. We would do well to make certain just what sort of changes we are discussing, how basic any one may be, whether it may represent a real change in poetic attitude or may only be the result of other factors; what remains constant (which is just as important) may be equally hard to discern. For instance, Propertius' position as a love poet in Book III involves, as we will see, real contradictions: he still claims the role (or so it is said) as proudly as ever, but, among other things, Cynthia is of far less importance than previously, and he clearly rejects her at the end of the book. The question can only be resolved by considering first what other factors are involved which might make such contradictions not only possible but inevitable. To put it simply, if Propertius from the beginning would have defined his poetry essentially as love poetry, then indeed there is a real and fundamental change in Book III; if, however, he would have singled out other characteristics to define the essential nature of his poetry, and would have added that it was amatory only in outward appearance, then the change in his position as a love poet in Book IV is only of secondary importance, and the observer, overly concerned with this aspect, might miss a more fundamental change or overlook what remained constant. We may best begin by looking at what Propertius says about his own poetic program in Books II and III.

In all his programmatic statements in these two books Propertius is

---

[1] Some of these questions will be answered here only in passing; and a full treatment of the question of the *Itala orgia* and the *Graios choros* is best postponed until we discuss Hor. *Odes* 3.30.13–14.

[2] It is, of course, recognized that Book IV is something different from Book I: but just what is different, and precisely when the change is first to be observed, are questions to which surprisingly little discussion has been devoted; see Lonie's summary of the question, *AUMLA* 11 (1959), 22 and nn. 19–23 (who simply states in conclusion, 'in general I think it is a mistake to regard III 1 and 3 as heralding this new character. The most we can say is that there is a new articulateness about method, and about his place in tradition; but he still sees himself as the poet of love'). We cannot here examine thoroughly all the details of this change, but enough can be said to present a general, and I hope convincing, account within the scope of our main argument.

concerned with two basic assertions. First, he must establish himself as a Callimachean poet: to do this he uses Callimachean language and motifs, both in extended programmatic passages and also often in isolation,[1] and makes full use of what had become the hallmark of Callimachean poetry at Rome, the *recusatio*. Secondly, he had to consider his place within the genre at Rome: his assertions about his relation to Gallan elegy, though they have not received the attention of scholars, are no less important, and no less frequent, than his attention to his Alexandrian masters. In regard to each of these two points he is concerned to stress the amatory nature of his elegy: it is his love poetry that makes him a Callimachean; it is love-elegy that distinguishes his originality within the tradition of Gallan elegy. It was almost inevitable, however, that such simple assertions about place and purpose would lead, over the years, to a tangle of cross purposes.

Book II opens with a far more explicitly programmatic poem than any Propertius had written in the *Monobiblos*,[2] a poem which can properly be termed a *recusatio*. But the Callimachean *recusatio* has obscured one aspect of Propertius' program which is in some ways more important than the stock refusal to write epics on the deeds of kings, past or present. The poem opens with *elegy* (*Quaeritis, unde mihi totiens scribantur amores, | unde meus veniat mollis in ora liber*).[3] The next couplet goes directly to the heart of the matter – to the precedent of Gallus and to Propertius' own distinction:

> non haec Calliope, non haec mihi cantat Apollo,
> ingenium nobis ipsa puella facit.

At *Ecl.* 4.57 Calliope is presented as Orpheus' mother and Apollo as Linus' father, relationships which (as we have argued) are likely to have occurred in a position of prominence in Gallus' poetry, devised perhaps by Gallus and Virgil together for important programmatic reasons; and Propertius had certainly been aware of the significance of Calliope and Apollo in his *Monobiblos* (1.2.27–8). Propertius is doing far more here than simply 'declaring his mistress Cynthia to be an elegant sufficiency

---

[1] For examples of Callimachean terminology in isolation, cf. 2.23.1–2, *cui fugienda fuit indocti semita vulgi, | ipsa petita lacu nunc mihi dulcis aqua est*; 2.33.38, *et mea deducta carmina voce legis*; 3.16.25–30, *di faciant, mea ne terra locet ossa frequenti, | qua facit assiduo tramite vulgus iter! – | …me tegat arborea devia terra coma | …non iuvat in media nomen habere via.*

[2] 1.1, as we have discussed above, is certainly programmatic, but is concerned only with Gallus' precedent, and that only by making use, somewhat indirectly, of Gallan language and topics; Callimachus is ignored, and there is no use of Callimachean terminology.

[3] If, as seems more than likely, Gallus' elegies were titled *Amores*, there is an immediate suggestion of Gallus here in the first line.

for inspiration.'[1] Just as the opening programmatic poem of the *Monobiblos* serves to distinguish his elegy from Gallus', so here as well he contrasts his *puella* with the inspirational divinities of Gallan elegy.[2] The first 16 lines are concerned entirely with elegy: it is the poet's fascination with his mistress that is to distinguish his place within the Roman genre.

At line 17 Propertius first addresses to Maecenas the proper refusal to write on subjects of Greek epic, old or new, or on corresponding Roman themes of ancient or current history. Here begins an entirely new movement within the poem, which ought to be recognized as such. Propertius has left elegy and turns to a more general consideration of Callimachean poetry: hence the formal and elaborate *recusatio*, ending after some 24 lines with the mention and paraphrase of Callimachus.[3] Here again it is his purpose to define his own area of the Callimachean field, which he does, neatly, by the *angusto lecto*, the amatory aspect of his elegy.[4]

The rest of the poem (lines 47–78) is concerned with the overwhelming dominance of his love, and does so in a way familiar to us from the *Monobiblos*: the rapid succession of mythological *exempla* and the formality of the language in which they are presented[5] are reminiscent of the manner and style of Gallan elegy, and in fact a paraphrase of Gallus occurs centrally, one that Propertius had made use of in the first poem of the *Monobiblos* for a similar reason.[6] 2.1, then, is a programmatic poem in which Propertius is concerned primarily to assert the originality of his love-elegy, and in this it is not unlike 1.1. Our familiarity with the Callimachean *recusatio* of lines 17–46 should not be allowed to obscure Propertius' purpose in the surrounding sections, which have Gallan elegy – not Callimachus, not the question of epic versus Callimachean poetry – as their focus:[7] the important programmatic note struck here at

---

[1] S. Commager, *The Odes of Horace* (New Haven, 1962), 5.

[2] Cf., of course, *Cynthia prima...*, 1.1.1.

[3] *sed neque Phlegraeos Iovis Enceladique tumultus | intonet angusto pectore Callimachus* (39–40) = βροντᾶν οὐκ ἐμόν, ἀλλὰ Διός, *Aetia*, fr. 1.20 Pf.

[4] *navita de ventis, de tauris narrat arator, | enumerat miles vulnera, pastor ovis; | nos contra angusto versantes proelia lecto: | qua pote quisque, in ea conterat arte diem* (43–6): *angusto* is, of course, a Callimachean term, repeated prominently from line 40 (*angusto pectore Callimachus*).

[5] Note, for instance, the two polysyllabic pentameter endings (both proper nouns), *Iliada* (50) and *Phillyrides* (60); the two heavy gerunds in successive hexameters, *tangenda* (51) and *pereundum* (53); the anaphora...*pocula Phaedrae, | pocula...* (51–2); the dative form *manu* (66); the 'learned' proper adjectives *Circaeo gramine* (53), *Iolciacis focis* (54), *deus Epidaurius* (61), and others in lines 63, 66, 69.

[6] *omnis humanos sanat medicina dolores: | solus amor morbi non amat artificem* (57–8): cf. 1.1.25–6, with the close parallel in 1.2.7–8.

[7] We may note, in passing, a point essential to our general argument: the very fact that

the beginning of Book II is still that which we were familiar with in the *Monobiblos.*

Despite the neatness and apparent simplicity of Propertius' program, he is beginning to find himself in certain difficulties. Just as he is proud to claim that he is a Callimachean poet, so too he must (and does) emphasize his direct succession to Gallus, his place in the Gallan tradition, and his acceptance of Alexandrian-neoteric poetics. All this would be easy, obvious, and expected, but for one obstacle he was not able to surmount, or to by-pass satisfactorily. To press his claim to originality within the genre – his pose as the subjective love poet – meant that he often had to seem to take issue with Gallus, and even to appear to deny much that was essential to Gallus' neoteric poetics, both in matter and manner. Not only in order to claim a position of prominence, but because there could be no other position for a real poet to take, he had to say, 'I am a true and serious poet, a Callimachean, a poet of learning and substance, and therefore as an elegist I am a faithful adherent of all that Gallus represents,' but at the same time he was forced to assert, 'My elegy is not dictated to me by the lofty divinities of the learned tradition, my subject is neither cosmic nor expressible through the universality of myth – *ingenium nobis ipsa puella facit.*'

Propertius was undoubtedly aware of these apparent contradictions and the possibility of being misunderstood. 2.3 seems to be an attempt to balance any impression of willful independence from Gallus that 2.1 may have conveyed in its assertion of originality against the background of Gallan elegy.[1] Here again it is tempting to understand that in the first half, at least, of the poem Propertius intends the unnamed *puella,* without whom he cannot exist, to be taken loosely as his elegy.[2] She possesses a lyre of remarkable character: *et quantum, Aeolio cum temptat carmina plectro,* | *par Aganippaeae ludere docta lyrae* (2.3.19–20). *Docta* and *ludere* are both unmistakable neoteric terms; and Aganippe, the fountain of Helicon and the source of the Permessus, is a distinguished

---

Propertius lays such stress on the uniqueness of his amatory elegy, which both marks him as a Callimachean poet (though we may well wonder precisely how) and establishes his own territory within the genre of elegy at Rome, shows quite clearly that Gallan poetry could *not* have been 'subjective love elegy'.

[1] Though 2.3 is not explicitly programmatic, it complements 2.1, from which it is separated by one poem – cf. 3.1 and 3.3 (and, to be discussed below, 2.10 and 2.13).

[2] This is a temptation I have been trying to resist, with less and less success, for some time. Here, cf. lines 7–8 [*quaerebam*] *aut ego si possem studiis vigilare severis:* | *differtur, numquam tollitur ullus amor.* There can be no question of anything approaching allegory, but in this poem, as in certain poems in Book I, it seems more than likely that Propertius intended to convey a clear, if momentary, suggestion of 'my poetry' when writing of Cynthia or his *puella.*

feature of Callimachean-neoteric topography, as we have seen.[1] Propertius is here doing no more or less than claiming for his elegy the capacity and character of neoteric Gallan poetry, and the poem ends with a veiled prophecy of wide fame for his own elegy that is set in a Gallan couplet (*sive illam Hesperiis, sive illam ostendet Eois,* | *uret et Eoos, uret et Hesperios,* 2.3.43–4).[2]

Two other programmatic poems in the second book are worth a closer look, 2.10 and 2.13.[3] The relationship between the two poems is one we have just observed between the central part (lines 17–46) and the surrounding sections of 2.1: 2.10 is a proper *recusatio* (that is, the poet refuses on Callimachean grounds to relate epic themes or the deeds of Augustus), while in 2.13 the place of Propertian elegy is defined within the Callimachean tradition and the Gallan precedent. We have already had occasion to discuss 2.13.1–8 and need do no more here than summarize that discussion within our present context.[4] Lines 3–8 present Hesiod, Orpheus, and Linus and depend (indirectly) on *Ecl.* 6.64–73, which in turn can be shown to reproduce a passage of Gallus concerning his own Hesiodic-Callimachean meeting with the Muses; Linus certainly, and Orpheus probably, had played important poetic roles in Gallus. Propertius, then, is unmistakably setting his own elegy in the context of Gallus' elegiac inspiration: he too has been forbidden to refuse the Callimachean Μοῦσαν λεπταλέην (*gracilis Musas*), and he too has been ordered to frequent the Hesiodic grove. If we were to ask at this point

---

[1] See Pfeiffer on Call. fr. 696. Callimachus, we know, named Aganippe as the source of the Permessus: hence Virgil, *Ecl.* 10.12. The proper name occurs only here in Propertius and is a rather bold touch – understandable only from its specific literary connections; when commentators, at a loss for a meaningful translation (how can a fountain have a lyre, after all?), resort to the explanatory paraphrase 'Sc. "of a Muse"' (Butler and Barber; but so also, e.g., Rothstein, Enk, Camps), they miss entirely Propertius' clear suggestion of certain poets, Gallus included.

[2] Cf. Ovid, *Am.* 1.15.29–30, *Gallus et Hesperiis et Gallus notus Eois,* | *et sua cum Gallo nota Lycoris erit* (and *AA* 3.537). I think it likely that Prop. 2.3 ended with this, or perhaps the following, couplet: lines 47–54 have nothing to do with what precedes.

[3] It seems to me probable (in spite of much recent scepticism) that, as Lachmann first suggested, 2.10 had at one time been the opening poem of Propertius' third book. (For those first entering this particular Propertian bog, which cannot be negotiated here, the best guides are Butler and Barber, *The Elegies of Propertius*, xxviii–xxxv, and Enk, pp. 19–29 of his edition of the *Monobiblos*.) I find it hard to explain *tres libelli* (2.13.25) in any other way. The inordinate length of Book II, its obvious lacunae and fragments, and the general state of its text, indicate pretty clearly that something drastic had happened to it at some (perhaps fairly early) stage; and Ovid himself, after all, reduced the original five books of his *Amores* to three. 2.10 certainly reads like a programmatic proemium (in spite of Butler and Barber's reservations), to which 2.13 stands in the same relation as 3.3 to 3.1. The following observations have all the more significance if these two elegies did once stand at the beginning of a book.

[4] On the Callimachean language of this elegy, and on the unity of parts A and B, again see Wilkinson, *CR* 16 (1966), 141–4.

how this position was to be reconciled with 2.1.3–4 (*non haec Calliope, non haec mihi cantat Apollo,* | *ingenium nobis ipsa puella facit*), we would not get an entirely satisfactory answer; but we may be sure, again, that Propertius' primary purpose is to re-assert, in spite of any logical inconsistencies, his position in the Gallan tradition, and the answer he does come up with is poetically, if not logically, acceptable and understandable. It is *Amor* who has issued these commands, and the reason and object is Cynthia (*sed magis ut nostro stupefiat Cynthia versu...*, 7). This is as satisfactory a solution to Propertius' dilemma as could be expected.

Only the final couplet of 2.10 need concern us at this point. The poem is a fairly straight-forward *recusatio*, in which Propertius promises to undertake Augustan epic in his old age.[1] But how are we to understand lines 25–6 (*nondum etiam Ascraeos norunt mea carmina fontis,* | *sed modo Permessi flumine lavit Amor*)? Earlier we discussed what the lines could *not* mean; we are now, I think, in a position to interpret the couplet positively. First, it is clear that Propertius cannot be denying knowledge of the Hesiodic fountains: 2.13.4 (*iussit* [*Amor*] *et Ascraeum sic habitare nemus*) alone makes this perfectly clear. It is equally clear that the Ascrean fountains cannot stand for epic on Roman, Augustan themes: to credit Propertius with such an unparalleled poetic solecism is intolerable, even if common. To claim that the *flumine Permessi* is simply subjective love-elegy is equally misleading: this interpretation, as we have seen, is based on nothing outside this very context, and has been quietly accepted only because it seems to explain *Ecl.* 6.64, a line which can (and must) be interpreted in a very different way; in fact, the Permessus cannot be separated, either topographically or poetically, from the entire context of the setting of the Hesiodic and Callimachean initiations and the landscape of poetic inspiration drawn upon and refashioned by Gallus and Virgil – there can, that is, be no contrast or distinction implied between the Hesiodic fountains and the river Permessus. If, however, the adversative *sed* demands two opposed statements, what *is* the opposition Propertius intends? *Amor*, the last word of both the couplet and the poem, is telling: it is to *Amor* that Propertius has always been subject in his elegiac pose (cf. 1.1.4), and it is *Amor*, as we have just seen, who dictates to the poet the terms and purpose of his own particular form of service to the Callimachean Muses in Hesiod's grove (2.13.1–8). Propertius has been saying, 'I will not now – though I may later – write Roman epic'; he

---

[1] He contrives, however, to make it sound as if he were about to write such poetry at any moment: cf. *nunc...nunc* (with the present tense)...*nunc* (with the future), 9–12; and the definite futures of, e.g., lines 8 and 19–20.

concludes (and this couplet is an explanation of the preceding line, *pauperibus sacris vilia tura damus*), 'I have not even written Gallan elegy, but *Love* (my own subjective, amatory form of elegy) only has bathed in the Permessus.' Propertius never intends to deny his Gallan inheritance, and continually asserts (often straining strict logic to do so) that he is very much a part of the same tradition; he must also, however, define his own special place in that tradition: this we have seen to be his purpose in 2.13. When he says here, in a closely related poem, that his elegies (*mea carmina*) do not yet know the Ascrean fountains, he must mean that he has not attempted the sort of elegy written by Gallus and associated with the ritual initiation of the poet, with Orpheus, Linus, and Hesiod. But he does not deny that tradition: his love elegy has bathed *in the same waters*.[1]

Book III begins with five consecutive poems that are all clearly programmatic. This is in itself worth close attention: why has Propertius felt compelled to devote these first five elegies to setting forth the purpose and place of his poetry, when in his first book he could take for granted that his poetic position was – from the poems themselves – clear and obvious, and had only to stress the amatory nature that was to be the distinguishing characteristic of his verse? An answer should allow us to understand what we are seeking to define – precisely what change occurred between Book I and Book IV.

It is obvious at once that Callimachus is of far greater importance and concern to Propertius than ever before. In the *Monobiblos* Callimachus was never named and the terminology of Callimachean poetics played a surprisingly small part. In Book II Propertius appeals to his Alexandrian master twice by name, and makes limited but appropriate use of a few key Callimachean terms, but the sole function of Callimachus in the book can be said to be restricted to the *recusatio* proper (as in 2.1.17–46) or to the fairly simple statement that Propertius' love-elegy is Callimachean poetry (as in 2.13). From the first line of the third book, however, it is obvious that Callimachus will be a major figure.[2] The first poem is not a proper *recusatio* (though, as in lines 15–16, the rejection of

---

[1] My interpretation of this couplet depends essentially on two points, about which I now feel entirely confident: that Gallan elegy was not primarily subjective love-elegy (this was Propertius' contribution), and that the *Ascraeos fontis* and the *flumine Permessi* are the same waters. Since neither of these points has been argued before in connection with this couplet, this interpretation has never been proposed; but if these two propositions are sound, then the explanation offered here for the couplet is natural, and Propertius can once again be seen to be stating his familiar programmatic position: love-elegy (*Amor*) is his claim to distinction within the Gallan tradition.

[2] I leave Philitas out of account in this discussion (in spite of the fact that he shares the first line of Book III with Callimachus), because it was primarily Callimachus who influenced and formed the concept of poetics at Rome (or at least served as a convenient precedent),

epic themes is suggested in passing), but rather a positive statement of future fame and immortality, to be won by Propertius as a Callimachean;[1] and a far more extensive use is made of Callimachean terminology than in any previous poem. 3.3 is equally loaded with key terms and concepts,[2] but it is a proper *recusatio*, beginning with Callimachus' famous dream. In neither poem, however, is there an observable change in Propertius' attitude towards Callimachus: his insistence on Callimachean poetics in these poems is far more open, but it is only a question of degree – Callimachus had always been the accepted master. What this increased attention, and the explicitness with which it is expressed, may mean, we will consider shortly.

The second basic purpose of Propertius' previous programmatic poems was to make clear his position in regard to Gallan elegy, and this, in fact, had been of greater concern to him than the need to define or emphasize the Callimachean nature of his poetry and had led, as we have seen, to certain major difficulties. 3.3 introduces a rather remarkable *volte face*: Calliope and Apollo, the ultimate sources of Gallus' inspiration rejected previously with a pose of disdain (2.1.3-4), here play important roles as Propertius' poetic instructors. In addition, Apollo points out a cave, in which are hanging symbols of Gallan-Virgilian poetry, prophetic and pastoral: *orgia Musarum et Sileni patris imago | fictilis et calami, Pan Tegeaee, tui* (3.3.29-30).[3] The *recusatio*, which before had occurred primarily as a Callimachean form, now operates through Gallan associations; the rejection of Roman epic now leads to acceptance of the neotericism of Gallus and Virgil. But the significance of this acceptance is likely to be misunderstood once again: we are dealing in fact with another constant. Propertius had always insisted upon his Gallan inheritance, as we have seen, and had only rejected Calliope and Apollo to emphasize his *puella* as the moving force of his *ingenium*.[4] We must not

and because so little is known of Philitas that it is simply impossible to know why Propertius acknowledges him particularly and how his poetry might be reflected by Propertius – if at all.

[1] In so far as Propertius imagines a cult of Callimachus and Philitas in lines 1-2, the subject of the poem (his own fame and immortality) suggests that he will one day receive worship with the two Alexandrians; but the suggestion is vague enough (purposely, I think) to allow the reader, if embarrassed by such presumption, to conceive of Propertius' entering the grove to offer worship or to seek oracular response.

[2] The Callimachean terminology in 3.1 and 3.3 has been so much discussed that no details need be given here. See, e.g., W. Wimmel, *Kallimachos in Rom*, 'Stellenindex' for the two poems.

[3] I have no doubt that these *orgia* explain the *Itala orgia* of 3.1.4, though with further associations from Hor. *Odes* 3.30.13-14.

[4] We should not forget that Propertius had phrased the matter in yet another way in the *Monobiblos*, when Apollo and Calliope gave his *puella* their *carmina* and *lyra* (*cum tibi*

expect rigid consistency, but must try rather to see what Propertius intended at each point. In 3.3 he accepts Gallan poetics fully, but he had never, in any case, rejected this concept of poetry previously: what *has* changed is that there is no longer a place in the program of Book III for Cynthia (or for *Amor*, who had instructed the poet in 2.13.1–8), and there is no longer any insistence on the distinguishing amatory aspect of his elegy.

It comes as a surprise to realize just how small a part love-elegy plays in the first five programmatic poems of Book III. In 3.1 Propertius' poetic triumph is celebrated with the *parvi Amores* riding in his chariot – but these happy creatures have nothing in common with the dominating *Amor* of the previous books: there is otherwise not the slightest indication in this proud claim of immortality that it might come to him as a result of his *love* poetry. The second poem promises a return to his usual concerns (*Carminis interea nostri redeamus in orbem,* | *gaudeat in solito tacta puella sono*, 3.2.1–2),[1] but nothing that follows makes good the promise: Propertius claims only that his verse appeals to the *turba puellarum* (line 10), and that she who is his subject will be happy indeed (*fortunata, meo si qua es celebrata libello!* | *carmina erunt formae tot monumenta tuae*, lines 17–18); again his boast of immortality (even in its Horatian model, *Odes* 3.30.1–5) is in no way based on any achievement in amatory verse (lines 19–26). In 3.3 Apollo mentions that Propertius should write for a girl waiting for her lover (lines 19–20), and Calliope proposes that Propertius become a *praeceptor amoris* (lines 47–50), but this is a far different position, it should be noted, from that of the participating subjective love poet of the first two books. Propertius' usual role is suggested in only one line of 3.4 (15, where he sees himself watching Augustus' triumph *in sinu carae puellae*); and in 3.5, after an opening couplet suggestive of his old style (*Pacis Amor deus est, pacem veneramur amantes:* | *stant mihi cum domina proelia dura mea*), the pose is dropped suddenly and completely.

Here, then, in five consecutive programmatic poems, there is hardly a trace of the one claim that had figured prominently in every previous statement about the place and purpose of his poetry. Yet we suggested earlier (somewhat improperly anticipating our conclusions, to be sure) that the subjective expression of erotic experience was a secondary

---

praesertim Phoebus sua carmina donet | Aoniamque libens Calliopea lyram, 1.2.27–8); that is, he accepts the inspiration *both* of the Gallan divinities *and* of his *puella*.

[1] The *puella* of this couplet should, I think, be translated 'a girl' (that is, 'my gentle reader') rather than 'my mistress'. In these first three poems Propertius is concerned with his audience (cf. 2.2.10, *turba puellarum si mea verba colit*; 2.3.20, *quem legat expectans sola puella virum*), and purposely never refers to his own *puella*.

characteristic, not an absolute essential, of Propertius' concept of his poetry: the two essentials – that it is Callimachean and that it is in the tradition of Gallus' neotericism – remain unchanged in Book III, though receiving different emphases. What did it mean to Propertius to have dropped all claims to subjective elegy? Why, at the same time, do his programmatic poems become so much more formal, elaborate, and explicit, appealing to Callimachus in a way he had not done before and accepting openly Gallus' neoteric poetics?

The usual explanation of the *recusatio* is that official pressure was brought to bear on the poets who enjoyed the patronage of Maecenas to write what is often called, or at least implied to be, propaganda for the new regime. 3.9, for example, certainly seems to make this point:

> Maecenas, eques Etrusco de sanguine regum,
>   intra fortunam qui cupis esse tuam,
> quid me scribendi tam vastum mittis in aequor?
>   non sunt apta meae grandia vela rati.
>
> (3.9.1–4)

Maecenas' insistence is answered in Callimachean terminology: the *vastum aequor* of line 3 is repeated later by the *tumidum mare* and contrasted with Propertius' own *exiguo flumine*;[1] then the *libelli* of Callimachus and Philitas are set forth as *exempla*, immediately followed by mention of Propertius' own elegies, which will make him the object of such worship as he had offered to Callimachus and Philitas in the very first lines of the book.[2] Those who have interpreted poems such as this quite literally have put forward other considerations, too, to make their case that Maecenas enforced his demands for official poetry with a heavy hand: for instance, there is no *recusatio* in the *Monobiblos*, written when Propertius had not yet been invited to join Maecenas' charmed circle; but no sooner is he admitted than 2.1 is wrung from him.[3]

However, it is easy to overemphasize the pressure exerted by Maecenas,

---

[1] *non ego velifera tumidum mare findo carina:* | *tota sub exiguo flumine nostra mora est*, 35–6: the epic formation *velifera* is a nice touch.

[2] *inter Callimachi sat erit placuisse libellos* | *et cecinisse modis, Coe poeta, tuis.* | *haec urant pueros, haec urant scripta puellas,* | *meque deum clament et mihi sacra ferant*, 3.9.43–6. It is notable that in this poem too there is no suggestion of Propertius' old role of subjective love poet: only in line 45 is there a reference to erotic poetry, but even this makes no claim to subjective expression: it is only a matter (again) of the poet's audience (see above, p. 122 n. 1). Propertius is remarkably careful in these poems not to suggest that he cannot undertake epic because he is a *love* poet; he is obviously searching for some other elegiac character.

[3] Likewise, there is no *recusatio* in Tibullus, who was never a member of Maecenas' circle. Butler and Barber give the usual opinion (*The Elegies of Propertius*, lxv–lxvi), 'After Maecenas took him under his patronage, pressure seems to have been put on Propertius to sing the achievements of Augustus and his ministers...His usual excuse (cp. II.i and III.i–iii) is that his Greek models had not ventured on such themes.'

and consequently to misunderstand, or miss entirely, the poetic purpose of the *recusatio*. We know really very little about the actual workings of Maecenas' patronage – what was given and what was expected in return. We cannot say with any certainty what form Maecenas and Augustus could expect, much less demand, the new poetic propaganda to take. The *princeps* and his minister were both, after all, sensitive in literary matters. That they supported Virgil, Horace, and Propertius when they might easily have found a new Archias is a good indication that they were well aware of the quality and ideals of the new poetry: they should not be credited with crass tampering and blatant demands for glorifying epic when they so obviously could appreciate the worth of the best poetry being written. With appreciation of the new poetry must go the realization that it could hardly become a vehicle for modern epic, and that in any case its appeal would not be to the *profanum vulgus*. When Propertius refuses to write an epic on a given historical subject – whether it be Troy, the Alban kings, Hannibal, or Marius – no one imagines that Maecenas suggested such themes to him: it is generally recognized that the rejection of these subjects is simply a matter of poetic convention. Do we have any better reason to believe, though, that Maecenas was urging him to write on the expected defeat of the Parthians, or on Actium, or on the *Romana mei...castra ducis* (2.10.4)? Might not Propertius also have a poetic reason for mentioning modern history? Moreover, Propertius, while a member of Maecenas' circle, can often write lines suggesting apathy or even opposition to matters dear to the heart of the new order. 2.7, greeting with delight the failure and the withdrawal of one of Augustus' marriage laws, sounds at times almost scornful of the *princeps*[1] and of the cherished hope of a Parthian victory.[2] If Maecenas had the power to demand a poem glorifying Actium, surely he would also have been in a position to censor lines which are realistically gloomy about Actium and the course of recent history.[3] It would be foolish to imagine that Augustus and Maecenas had no interest in what their poets were writing about – conversations undoubtedly took place, guided along certain suggestive lines – and we know from Horace how Maecenas

---

[1] *'At magnus Caesar.' sed magnus Caesar in armis:* | *devictae gentes nil in amore valent* (2.7.5–6). Camps' summary of the tone of the poem is good (*Propertius: Elegies Book II*, 97): 'There is a certain extravagance, even shrillness, in the manner in which Propertius here expresses his defiance of ordinary Roman values'; but for 'ordinary Roman values' we could equally well read 'Augustus' own values'.

[2] *unde mihi Parthis natos praebere triumphis?* | *nullus de nostro sanguine miles erit* (2.7.13–14). Cf. his similar, somewhat scornful, attitude to the Parthian business at 2.14.23–4, 3.12.1–4.

[3] Cf. 2.15.41–6 – quite a different impression of what Actium meant than that conveyed by 4.6, though the latter, I hasten to add, is no less 'sincere'.

could make personal demands on time and energy (cf. *Epist.* 1.7). But it would be equally foolish not to enquire further into Propertius' use of the *recusatio*. The reason for the increasingly open and formal character of these programmatic statements must have been a poetic one, not simply, or primarily, a response to official pressure.

We have seen that Propertius no longer makes any claim to be a poet of subjective love-elegy in his program in Book III. This sudden and rather surprising silence is reflected in the changing content of the book, in which the amatory element is not only less, but of a different nature, than in the first two books. Cynthia herself, for instance, plays a far smaller part in Book III than previously.[1] W. A. Camps summarizes the matter well:

This heroine and inspiration of Book I is in the present book [III] named only three times, and then in a context of dismissal (xxiv and xxv) or escape (xxi). Hence it is clear that in this Book the author is no lover in search of a means of expression, but a poet in search of subjects. He seems to feel the need of an identified department of poetry within which to work, and the need of the love-theme to provide the identifying label, and so he persists in presenting himself as a 'love-elegist'. But he proceeds to extend the limits of the department 'love-elegy' in such a way as to make it no longer meaningful.[2]

The fact that Cynthia is actually *named* far less in Book III than previously seems of particular importance when we consider that 'Cynthia' often stood for his 'love-elegy'. We need not comment on any further details of the way love-elegy changes in Book III: the facts, not only of the lessening importance of Cynthia herself but of the more impersonal nature of many of the elegies ostensibly devoted to an amatory theme, are clear. But the significance of the change is directly relevant to our argument and has not received sufficient attention.

Camps' observation that in Book III Propertius 'is no lover in search of a means of expression, but a poet in search of subjects' is an apt and succinct summary of an important crisis in Propertius' elegiac career, but needs, I think, some qualification. He had fixed the character of his elegy so securely in his first book that it became difficult to turn his poetry in any other direction. Gallus had finally arrived at the point of writing subjective love-elegy, but only as the natural development and conclusion of his Alexandrian-neoteric interests and beginnings, and perhaps only

---

[1] The figures are revealing: in Book I Cynthia is named in 13 of 22 poems; in Book II in 12 of (at the very least) 34 poems; but in III in only 3 of 25 poems; and in IV in 2 of 11 poems.

[2] *Propertius: Elegies Book III*, 2. I would only qualify the extent to which Propertius 'persists in presenting himself as a "love-elegist"': our look at the programmatic poems of the book has revealed that he has ceased to think of himself as a love-elegist almost completely.

tentatively. Propertius had accepted completely the role of lover yielding to the domination of *Amor* and concerned only with his Cynthia, but he found that this poetic pose effectively cut him off from the wide range of themes and possibilities of expression inherent in the original purpose of Gallan elegy. By the third book Propertius realized not only that he had pretty well exhausted the possibilities of his own subjective love-elegy, but also that he wanted to treat certain themes and express certain concerns which were totally impossible if he continued to play the elegiac lover. He had perhaps already ended his search for subjects by the time he was writing Book III, but had not yet resolved the difficulties concerning a new means of expression, difficulties which were great.

Even after it was apparent that Propertius had reached a dead-end with subjective love-elegy, he could still write, *haec urant pueros, haec urant scripta puellas* (3.9.45). But does he really mean here that he is writing erotic verse, his former love-elegy? If, as we are suggesting, he was at this time searching for a different means of expressing new concerns, why does he define his audience as *pueri* and *puellae*? The whole context is relevant; after placing his poetry in the tradition of Callimachus and Philitas, he continues immediately with the themes he would sing if he had Maecenas' example to follow:

> inter Callimachi sat erit placuisse libellos
> et cecinisse modis, Coe poeta, tuis.
> haec urant pueros, haec urant scripta puellas,
> meque deum clament et mihi sacra ferant!
> te duce vel Iovis arma canam caeloque minantem
> Coeum et Phlegraeis Oromedonta iugis;
> celsaque Romanis decerpta palatia tauris
> ordiar et caeso moenia firma Remo,
> eductosque pares silvestri ex ubere reges,
> crescet et ingenium sub tua iussa meum;
> prosequar et currus utroque ab litore ovantis,
> Parthorum astutae tela remissa fugae,
> castraque Pelusi Romano subruta ferro,
> Antonique gravis in sua fata manus.
>
> (3.9.43–56)

Jupiter and the Giants, the early history of Rome, Augustus and his victories: the unity and relevance of these themes is clearly something new in Propertian *recusationes*. In Horace's Roman Odes Jupiter, 'splendid in his triumph over the Giants', is the universal counterpart to Augustus, the just wielder of a power used to subdue the forces of unnatural chaos:[1]

[1] Cf. Hor. *Odes* 3.1.5–8; 3.4.37–68; 3.5.1–4.

there can be little doubt that here again in Book III Propertius is respond-
ing to the *Odes*. What is remarkable about these lines is that they are not
simply a list of epic themes, Greek and Roman, from Troy and Thebes
to Hannibal and Marius to the Parthians, which are to be rejected by a
proper poet; they constitute, rather, a clear conception, Horatian in
inspiration, of a philosophy of temporal and universal power.[1] Here in
effect is a palinode to 2.1.39–40, *sed neque Phlegraeos Iovis Enceladique
tumultus | intonet angusto pectore Callimachus*: Propertius' poetry will
remain *inter Callimachi libellos* even though (as he clearly suggests in the
next lines) he accepts the challenge of Augustan themes.[2] If Horace's
Roman Odes supplied Propertius with the poetic conception of Augustan
themes, then we have also found what lies behind Propertius' new definition of his audience:

> Odi profanum vulgus et arceo;
> favete linguis: carmina non prius
> audita Musarum sacerdos
> virginibus puerisque canto.[3]

In 3.9 Propertius makes vividly clear what elegiac role he will accept in
place of the old pose abandoned with eloquent silence in the introductory
poems to the book, and leaves no uncertainty that his new part will be no
less Callimachean.

It is, I hope, not necessary to analyse in detail just what Propertius had
found in his search for subjects. Cynthia's day was over: not only must
Propertius have felt that the thematic possibilities of love-elegy had been
exhausted and that the restrictions imposed by the role of poet-lover were
all too confining, but on the positive side there were questions to be
dealt with and concerns to express which a love-elegist could not
approach. Cynthia had to yield to Rome. It would be interesting to
discuss in detail the third book as a last, and somewhat half-hearted, attempt by Propertius to retain the mask he had so proudly made his own,

---

1 Propertius himself makes a clear distinction in this poem that is worth noting. In lines
35–42 he clearly rejects subjects of Greek epic (*non flebo...nec referam...*); but in 47–56
he actually accepts the Horatian themes (*canam...ordiar...prosequar...*) – the *recusatio*
has been turned into something positive.

2 One couplet is enough to show that Propertius was fully aware of the implications we
have stressed. The programmatic first poem to Book IV repeats from 3.9.49–50 both the
picture of the pastoral Palatine (4.1.1–4) and the unusual expression *ordiar moenia* (4.1.57,
moenia coner disponere): by the time of publication of the third book he had undoubtedly
thought through the new program of the fourth, and we may expect to find some of the
results of this thinking appearing in Book III.

3 Hor. *Odes* 3.1.1–4, the introduction to the Roman Odes, immediately preceding Horace's
most magnificent single stanza, which Propertius took as Horace's *locus classicus* on the
philosophy of political power.

while at the same time he was turning to the new themes he could not, as an Augustan poet, avoid. 3.11 is often cited as a rather curious mixture: it begins as a personal amatory elegy (lines 1–4, *Quid mirare, meam si versat femina vitam...*), proceeds with an appropriate list of Greek heroines, *exempla* of the power of women (9–26), but then (rather unexpectedly – had the poem occurred in an earlier book) presents a vivid picture of Cleopatra and her threat to the noble institutions and victories of Rome's past (31–72). The elegy is a first rehearsal for 4.6, the Actian elegy so often compared with Virgil's description (*Aen.* 8.675–728) and so often regarded simply as a set piece, derivative and made to order: but the introduction, with Propertius in his new role of Callimachean *vates*,[1] makes quite clear that he would have regarded this elegy as a solution to the problem he had considered for so long and a resolution of the difficulties he was attempting to deal with in Book III, in which Cleopatra and Actium still had to be treated by the love-elegist only in an over-weighted, poorly fitting *exemplum* for his own unhappy love-life.

3.13 is a similar attempt to handle Augustan topics in an outwardly proper love-elegy. Again it begins with the rhetorical address to the reader (*Quaeritis, unde avidis nox sit pretiosa puellis...*) concerning a common elegiac subject – we expect, perhaps, a variation on the theme of the poor poet ousted by a wealthy rival. Instead, we meet with an essay on *luxuria*, a large part of which is taken up with a contrast between an idealized bucolic past (*felix agrestum quondam pacata iuventus...*, 25–46) and the venial present (*at nunc...*, 47–58 – with the anaphora *aurum... auro... auro... aurum...*, 48–50). Here, unmistakably, is an Augustan poem, yet Propertius is still wary of assuming the role of the Augustan *vates*: he is still only a rather non-committal *haruspex* (*proloquar: – atque utinam patriae sim verus haruspex! –*, 59). 3.22 is also interesting: Propertius still retains the occasional address to a friend, though the elegy itself may be termed *laudes Italiae*; in the next book such a 'subjective' pose will be dispensed with almost entirely. But Propertius' new concerns are best felt in numerous asides throughout the book:[2] the pose of love-elegist must obviously be abandoned by the poet already well on his way to the Roman and Augustan poems of Book IV.

That Cynthia plays an insignificant part in Book III, that the character

---

[1] *Sacra facit vates: sint ora faventia sacris,* | *et cadat ante meos icta iuvenca focos.* | *serta Philiteis certet Romana corymbis,* | *et Cyrenaeas urna ministret aquas* (4.6.1–4). On 'The *vates*-concept in Propertius', see J. K. Newman, *Augustus and the New Poetry*, Coll. Latomus 88 (1967), 165–78.

[2] 3.4 (*Arma deus Caesar dites meditatur ad Indos*) and 3.5 (*Pacis Amor deus est, pacem veneramur amantes*), which can be called programmatic because of the themes they introduce, are

of the elegies begins to change noticeably, that there is an obvious desire to handle Augustan themes and topics, and that there is a greater formality and explicitness in the programmatic poems, seem to me to be related facts. In the *Monobiblos* Propertius was concerned only to stress the individuality of his own elegy against Gallan elegy: he could take for granted what no one would question, that he was in fact continuing where Gallus had left off, in a tradition in which Callimachus was the recognized master. If Propertius, then, in Book II, and even more in Book III, begins to spell out what had previously needed no explanation or emphasis, surely we must suppose that as the content of his elegy changed (as we have seen, there was no real change in his poetic program), so he felt that there was an increasing chance of his position as a poet being misunderstood. Part of his claim to be considered a Callimachean was based on his subjective love-elegy, and often involved a Callimachean refusal to write epic on subjects past or present; but as he came eventually to abandon love-elegy and to turn to Augustan themes, would it not seem too that he was abandoning, or was at least betraying, Callimachean principles? It is this, then, that explains the elaborate *recusationes* and other programmatic statements in Book III: the *recusatio* had become not a refusal to write on Augustan themes, but the pretext for emphasizing that the same poet, writing essentially the same sort of poetry as before, relying on the same sources of inspiration, will be turning to Roman subjects.

Propertius' fourth book has always seemed something of an oddity. True, what Propertius proposes (*sacra diesque canam et cognomina prisca locorum:* | *has meus ad metas sudet oportet equus,* 4.1.69–70) is certainly more Callimachean in every way than the proper love-elegy of the first two books, but Propertius' fears have been justified – his purpose and his poetry have been misunderstood. There are several obvious reasons why the modern reactions to the fourth book have generally been cool. Much of the book, like the elegy on Actium (4.6), leaves a modern reader with the uncomfortable feeling that Propertius has sold out to the regime. Here again his *recusationes* are largely responsible: 'Thou dost protest too much' is likely to be the response. But whatever praise of the new era may be found in the fourth book (and there is not that much) was a voluntary, not an exacted, contribution, as I hope will be clear when we look at Horace's *Odes*. Then, too, since it has been accepted as a

interesting in this respect. The first words of the first lines are of course meant to contrast, and in the first part of 3.5 these and associated ideas are developed in a very Horatian manner (cf. for instance the ideas associated with Prometheus here and in Hor. *Odes* 1.3).

7

The Roman poetry of Horace and Tibullus

Why did Horace write the collection of *Odes* (I–III) published in 23 B.C.? This question may still legitimately be asked, for the question 'why?' properly involves a variety of considerations: what previous poetry, both ancient and the most recent, was Horace stimulated by, and in what ways? what were the current concerns he felt compelled to deal with in his *Odes*? what did he consider his achievement, his own contribution to contemporary poetry, to be? If we imagine an intelligent student first turning to the *Odes* with such questions in mind, and attempting to find answers with the help of a dozen of the most readily available literary histories and critical studies, we can also imagine the perplexities he would soon find himself surrounded by.

He would be told, for instance, by everyone that Horace had as his primary models in the genre Alcaeus and Sappho; but he would then find a large number of odes with no observable relation to the Aeolic poets, and that in others only a line or two, often at the beginning of an ode, were based on an Aeolic model; he might find L. P. Wilkinson noting that 'it is noteworthy that 140 pages of Pasquali suffice for Aeolic influence and 68 for Roman, while no fewer than 500 are required for Hellenistic;'[1] and a reading of E. Fraenkel's illuminating chapter on the *Epodes* would reinforce his impression of how pervasive Hellenistic influence was even on the poet who claimed Archilochus as his guide and model.[2] If our hypothetical student then set himself to consider Horace's use of or reaction to Hellenistic poetry, and in particular to the poet whom the best Roman poets since Catullus had considered their supreme exemplar, Callimachus, he would find Horace himself making prominent and explicit acknowledgement to Callimachean poetics in his

---

[1] *Horace and His Lyric Poetry* (Cambridge, 1946), 118 n. 2 (referring to the monumental study by G. Pasquali, *Orazio Lirico* (Florence, 1920)).

[2] Fraenkel, *Horace* (Oxford, 1957), 30, writing on *Epode* 10, demonstrates a lesson he returns to time and again throughout his book: 'If he wanted to adopt a theme of Archilochus or of another early iambist, he had no choice but to empty it of its substance of primary life and to turn it into a bare topic of literature;' and (p. 35) 'As if to make up for the resulting loss, he embroidered his own poem with many elaborate devices, most of them derived from Hellenistic poetry.'

Odes,[1] or writing a Callimachean *recusatio* denying his ability to handle epic or Roman themes on the pretext that he is a poet of love.[2] But he might read as well the considered remarks of a scholar who had spent a long life studying Latin poetry, 'the Greek influence which [Horace] attacked was the influence of the late Greek poets of Alexandria, and the familiar traits of that school were learned allusion and the artificial pursuit of love as these appeared in the epyllion and the erotic elegy,'[3] a view he would find often expressed elsewhere. His perplexity would grow if he asked related questions about Horace's relationship with Catullus and neoteric poetry, perhaps intrigued by the dispute referred to in S. Commager's note on *Sat.* 1.10.17–19, 'The often quoted words have been built up into evidence of a deep seated hostility toward Catullus, despite the eloquent protest of E. K. Rand, *HSCP*, 17 (1906), 15 ff.'[4] How would our student, finally, understand Fraenkel's observation, 'At an early stage of his poetic activities Horace, like his admired older friend Virgil, had determined to abandon the pretty trifles which had pleased the preceding generation of poets, and to endeavour instead to produce works of a serious and virile character'?[5] Why then are there so many 'pretty trifles' among the *Odes*? and conversely, how can the political odes, often so powerful and moving, have been written by the same poet who elsewhere refused such themes in favor of the *proelia virginum*?

[1] E.g. in *Odes* 1.1.30–2, *me gelidum nemus...secernunt populo* = 3.1.1. *Odi profanum vulgus et arceo* = 2.16.39–40, *...malignum spernere vulgus* = Call. *Epigrams* 28.4 (Pf.), σικχαίνω πάντα τὰ δημόσια.

[2] Again, e.g., *Odes* 1.6 (esp. the Callimachean protestation in lines 5–9, *nos...neque haec* (i.e. epic themes and the *laudes Caesaris*) *dicere...conamur, tenues grandia*, and the final stanza, *nos convivia, nos proelia virginum...cantamus vacui*), 2.12 (a sort of *recusatio* again involving epic themes and the *proelia Caesaris*, rejected in favor of *lucidum fulgentis oculos et bene mutuis fidum pectus amoribus*, 14–16), or 1.19 (in which the *mater saeva Cupidinum* – a line purposely repeated in the first ode of the fourth book (4.1.5.) where Horace again speaks of his odes as if they were pure love poetry, *Intermissa, Venus, diu | rursus bella moves?* – forbids Horace to speak (again *dicere*) of the Scythians and Parthians). For a perceptive analysis of considerable importance for the *Odes*, see the article by C. P. Jones, '*Tange Chloen semel arrogantem*', *HSCP* 75 (1971), 81–3 (demonstrating how Horace 'extends the notion of erotic poetry to cover all his lyric *oeuvre*, of which love poetry is of course only a part').

[3] C. W. Mendell, *Latin Poetry: The New Poets and the Augustans* (New Haven, 1965), 66 (cf. the similar remarks of a very different sort of critic, K. Quinn, *Latin Explorations* (London, 1963), 154–62, pages headed 'Horace's Assault on Love Elegy'). To be set against the view that Horace 'attacked' Alexandrian poetry, there is now J. K. Newman, *Augustus and the New Poetry*, Coll. Latomus 88 (1967), esp. pp. 303–14, but with many other valuable observations scattered through this large book without an index.

[4] *The Odes of Horace* (New Haven, 1962), 45 n. 94; Rand's article ('Catullus and the Augustans') remains basic.

[5] Fraenkel (*Horace*, 47–8) is referring to *Epode* 16, but his observation would hold good for the *Odes*.

The following pages suggest a solution to such perplexities, following lines developed thus far in our discussion. Only *Odes* I–III are considered, but I believe the poetry he wrote both before and after can be related to the same background; and within Horace's first collection of *Odes*, only a few passages, necessarily, are dealt with, specifically those in which he was obviously intending to speak about the nature of the entire collection, comprehending both those 'pretty trifles' at the one extreme, and at the other, poems of a serious political or universal significance. The following sketch, essentially, tries to comment further on Horace's position as *vates* or *Musarum sacerdos*,[1] a position devised precisely because it could include both the public and private functions of the Augustan poet, and to explain and illustrate a few important aspects of Horace's reaction to the conceptions of the nature of poetry developed by his contemporaries, and of his own contribution to Augustan poetry.

Horace's first collection of *Odes* is concluded with a proud celebration of his achievement (3.30, *Exegi monumentum aere perennius*). His vision of immortality is set in Roman terms still strangely appropriate and moving (*usque ego postera* | *crescam laude recens, dum Capitolium* | *scandet cum tacita virgine pontifex*, 3.30.7–9).[2] Horace's justification for the pride (*superbia*, 14) which he expects the Muse Melpomene to share is suggested in lines 10–14:

> dicar, qua violens obstrepit Aufidus
> et qua pauper aquae Daunus agrestium
> regnavit populorum, ex humili potens
> princeps Aeolium carmen ad Italos
> deduxisse modos.

A suggestion may have been sufficient for Roman readers who were capable of supplying the context and background in which Horace intended his boast to be taken, but modern scholars have generally overlooked the significance of several aspects of this claim to poetic achievement.[3]

Horace is most often understood to be saying, simply, 'I am the first

---

1 See J. K. Newman, *The Concept of Vates in Augustan Poetry*, Coll. Latomus 89 (1967) – basically a repetition of Chap. 4 of his monograph cited above, p. 132 n. 3. I make little reference here to the '*vates-* concept' (the development of which Horace had much to do with – see Newman's table, p. 51 (=p. 136, *Augustus and the New Poetry*)), but Newman's basic argument should be familiar.

2 See Fraenkel, *Horace*, 303–4 ('Horace's boast turns out to be an enormous understatement').

3 Fraenkel's important correction of one misunderstanding will no doubt come to be commonly accepted (so, for instance, by Commager, *The Odes of Horace*, 314 and n. 8): the clauses *qua...et qua...* should be taken with *dicar* (see his discussion, pp. 304–5).

to have used Aeolic meters for Latin verse,'[1] but it would be surprising, in view of what he actually managed to accomplish in the *Odes*, if his claim to immortality went no further than this rather flat commonplace. Horace has phrased his boast to include three specific references to different aspects of his poetic accomplishment: (1) *Aeolium carmen*, (2) *deduxisse*, and (3) *Italos modos*. Each of these three spheres is an important part of this particular ode, illustrating, as is proper in a poem of a programmatic nature, the precise contribution it makes to the poetic whole; in other odes of the collection Horace had made similar claims and had so clearly unified these three spheres that a simple suggestion in the final ode was sufficient for his Augustan contemporaries already well aware of the particular concerns of such poetry.

First, it need not be discussed or argued here that Horace followed Alcaeus and Sappho in much the same manner as he claimed to have followed the Parian iambs of Archilochus in his *Epodes* (*numeros animosque secutus | Archilochi, non res et...verba...*, *Epist.* 1.19.23–5). Aeolic poetry was the general model, the suggestion of a beginning, and other early Greek poets, lyric and choral, were drawn on under the same heading. *Ode* 3.30 begins, as do so many, with reference to Greek precedent, in particular to similar claims for poetic immortality by Pindar and Simonides.[2] The first five lines, a clear statement of the theme of the ode, can be said to be an imitation or adaptation of Horace's ancient Greek inheritance, the *Aeolium carmen* he claims a few lines later to have drawn upon.

Second, the precise poetic connotation of *deduxisse* must be heard. It is no longer possible to misunderstand the metaphor,[3] but the precise relevance of the use of the verb in programmatic contexts has not been squarely faced. I do not think it conceivable that Horace here could not have had in mind Virgil's *deductum carmen* in the Callimachean *recusatio* of *Ecl.* 6.3–5. If subsequent poets (and poetasters) knew precisely what they were doing when they used the word to point to their Calli-

---

[1] *Princeps* need cause no difficulty in view of Catullus' Sapphics (11 and 51). Horace may be claiming excellence, not priority, and in any case his chief concern here is not simply to establish himself as the *inventor* of a genre or form, as he does at *Epist.* 1.19.32–3.

[2] Cf. G. Pasquali, *Orazio Lirico*, 748–50: Pindar, *Pyth.* 6.7.14, ἕτοῖμος ὕμνων θησαυρὸς . . . τὸν οὔτε χειμέριος ὄμβρος . . . οὔτ' ἄνεμος . . . ἄξοισι παμφόρῳ χεράδει τυπτόμενον; Simonides 26.4–5 (531 PMG, Page), ἐντάφιον δὲ τοιοῦτον οὔτ' εὐρὼς οὔθ' ὁ πανδαμάτωρ ἀμαυρώσει χρόνος. Note the obviously intentional formal parallelism in *quod non...non...* and τὸν (τοιοῦτον) οὔτε . . . οὔτε . . . in both models. (See now also V. Pöschl, *Horazische Lyrik* (Heidelberg, 1970), 248–62.)

[3] As, for instance, Wickham (*ad loc.*), 'The use of "deducere" seems akin to that of "deducere coloniam".'

machean pretensions, Horace certainly must have.[1] Horace is claiming a share in the Callimachean-neoteric tradition of Virgil and Gallus and does so in the most precise manner possible: that his intention here has not been clearly recognized is due largely to the long established view that Horace had no time to waste on neoteric nonsense (a view largely derived and supported from a misunderstanding of *Sat.* 1.10.17–19), but also to the artistry with which in the *Odes* he has so completely assimilated for his own purposes neoteric principles and techniques that they are no longer immediately apparent.

Finally, *ad Italos modos* points to Horace's proudest achievement – the composition of Italian poetry. It may well, however, include a more practical reference to Horace's contribution to lyric meter, the innovations he introduced particularly into his Sapphic and Alcaic lines. When Ennius first wrote Latin hexameters, he sought the masculine caesura in the third foot in almost nine of every ten lines, and the percentage of such lines increased thereafter, the feminine third-foot caesura (the most common caesura in Greek hexameters) serving to convey a Greek coloring or other (often emotional) effects. The reason for the growing reliance on the masculine caesura is almost certainly due to the conflict of word accent and verse ictus thus produced in the preceding feet, a tension resolved finally in the last two feet of the line. A similar effect is produced in Sapphic lines by Horace's innovation of fixing the caesura after the fifth syllable: only in Latin does such an innovation have any meaning (Greek had no word accent, or stress). Horace's use of *modos* (freely translatable as 'meter') may thus indicate his 'Latinizing' of Aeolic meters, his discovery of how he could use most effectively the resources of his native language.[2]

But what Horace primarily intended to be understood by the phrase *ad Italos modos* was the process by which he and Virgil had found a way to write about what mattered most, about Italy and the new order (political, religious, and social) being established by Augustus. In 3.30 the Roman world is presented immediately after the Greek precedents of the first five lines: the Capitol, the *pontifex* accompanied by the *tacita*

---

[1] This, however, is the only use of the verb in the *Odes* with this possible significance (the other three draw on different connotations, 1.37.31, 2.7.2, 4.4.19); cf. the complete Callimachean metaphor at *Epist.* 2.1.224–5 (*cum lamentamur non apparere* labores | *nostros et tenui deducta poemata filo*), and also *Sat.* 2.1.4, *AP* 129.

[2] This sketch of Horatian metrical innovations is, of course, too simple, but this is not the place to go further into details useful for the novice or arguments convincing to scholars (especially French) who do not believe in Latin word accent. See E. Zinn, *Der Wortakzent in den lyrischen Versen des Horaz* (Munich, 1940), and the remarks by E. Burck, in Kiessling–Heinze, *Oden und Epoden* (Zürich, 1966), 607 and 627–8.

virgine in solemn procession. Yet it is not just Rome, the center of the new order, that is in Horace's mind: he will be remembered also in the place of his birth, by the river Aufidus in the land of ancient Daunus, sites ennobled by the poetic imagination so as to stand beside the mountains of the Greek Muses or Pindar's Thebes.

We may summarize Horace's statement of achievement by offering a paraphrase of lines 13–14: 'I, principally, claim for my poetry a descent from the ancient Greek lyric and choral poets, especially Sappho and Alcaeus, in spirit and in my verse form; but I write as well in the spirit of Callimachus and his Roman descendants, and in so doing have naturally transformed my original models; further, I write with a special purpose, to make thoroughly Italian, in manner and matter, this double Greek inheritance.' A few years before the *Odes* were published, but after Horace had conceived his role and had written many of these odes, Virgil had made a similar claim at the end of his *laudes Italiae*:

> tibi [Saturnia tellus] res antiquae laudis et artis
> ingredior sanctos ausus recludere fontis,
> Ascraeumque cano Romana per oppida carmen.
> *(Geo. 2.174–6)*

Here the same elements of tradition and purpose are to be seen: the Hesiodic precedent, not simply of subject matter, but in the tradition of the poet's role and descent as it was conceived and reformed by Callimachus and by Gallus and Virgil himself; and (*Romana per oppida*) the purpose, largely new, of making Roman what previously had been still basically foreign and, in a sense, somewhat artificial.

We may, I think, regard Virgil and Horace as collaborators in this new program, just as Virgil and Gallus collaborated previously in shaping and defining the role of the Callimachean poet in Rome. An indication of such a joint effort is afforded us by Propertius, whose third book of elegies bears so many signs of being a response to Horace's *Odes* I–III.[1] At the beginning of his third book (as we have discussed above in greater detail) Propertius, without mentioning love poetry, goes through an elaborate Callimachean song and dance, the second couplet of which, however, offers us a glimpse of what the poet would be undertaking if only he knew how:[2]

---

[1] We should, I think, try to free our minds of the old legend of the 'quarrel' between Propertius and Horace: perhaps they were never close, and perhaps personal relations between them may have been sometimes strained, but we can easily read Horace's few references to Propertius (e.g. *Epist.* 2.2.99–101) as jocular rather than savage; and there is no denying how much Propertius eventually owed to Horace poetically.

[2] As argued above, in Book III Propertius was still unsure how he could gracefully and

> primus ego ingredior puro de fonte sacerdos
> Itala per Graios orgia ferre choros.
>
> (3.1.3–4)

There is no question about Propertius' reference to Virgil here, nor should there be any doubt that he also points to Horace's epilogue,[1] which he paraphrases at length in the following elegy.[2] Propertius' *orgia*, however, as we have seen, are the mystic emblems of the poetry of the *Eclogues*:[3] Propertius is here indicating both the Callimachean tradition of Virgil and Gallus and the new national purpose of Virgil and Horace, and his lines can serve as the first commentary written on Horace's *princeps Aeolium carmen ad Italos deduxisse modos*.[4]

Before we turn to Horace's most complex and purposeful statement of his poetic inheritance (*Odes* 3.4), it will be useful to notice another ode which unites the elements presented in summary form in 3.30 and which is in itself largely programmatic.

> Quem virum aut heroa lyra vel acri
> tibia sumis celebrare, Clio?
> quem deum? cuius recinet iocosa
>   nomen imago
>
> aut in umbrosis Heliconis oris
> aut super Pindo gelidove in Haemo,
> unde vocalem temere insecutae
>   Orphea silvae
>
> arte materna rapidos morantem
> fluminum lapsus celerisque ventos,
> blandum et auritas fidibus canoris
>   ducere quercus?
>
> quid prius dicam solitis parentis
> laudibus...?
>
> (*Odes* 1.12.1–14)

The ode begins, of course, with a clear reference to Pindar's Second

---

convincingly put aside his role of poet-lover in order to write with the national purpose of Virgil's *Georgics* and Horace's *Odes* I–III.

[1] *Sacerdos*, the national poet-priest, undoubtedly looks to Horace's role as *Musarum sacerdos* in the first stanza of the Roman Odes (3.1.3).

[2] 3.2.17–26: here again there is absolutely no need to read into the lines a spirit of animosity.

[3] Prop. 3.3.29–30 (*orgia Musarum et Sileni patris imago | fictilis et calami, Pan Tegeaee, tui*) clearly is a reference to Virgil's Silenus, the prophet-poet of *Ecl.* 6, and to Pan, who appears in the invocation of the *Georgics* (*Pan...o Tegeaee..., Geo.* 1.17–18).

[4] Prop. 3.1.1–6 makes absolutely certain that *deduxisse* (*Odes* 3.30.14) carries the special sense we have seen in it.

Olympian; the Greek word *heroa* (transliterated, in fact, from Pindar) stands before the caesura after the sixth syllable, a suggestion of the Greek practice in Sapphics. But (as is noted by Nisbet and Hubbard in their excellent commentary on the ode) echoes of Pindar are rare after this first stanza, nor will the Hellenistic versions cited by Nisbet and Hubbard of Pindar's invocation serve as an adequate guide through the next two stanzas.

The 'shady shores of Helicon' must carry definite associations (which are to be confirmed a few lines later): these shores in the area of Helicon must include the poetic springs (Hippocrene and Aganippe) and the river (Permessus); 'shady' may suggest (and with the following context must have been intended to suggest) the pastoral shade we are familiar with from the *Eclogues*. The next geographical feature is Mt Pindus, which (unless its occurrence here is completely gratuitous) can only come from the opening of the Tenth Eclogue, where we have seen it as the sole link with the Theocritean model, standing now in the company of Parnassus and Helicon (*Aonie Aganippe*) as a newly recruited poetic mountain.[1] Mt Haemus in Thrace, with its epithet *gelido*, leads us directly on to Orpheus and the woods which follow as he sings *arte materna*: again, the reference to his mother Calliope might seem gratuitous, but in the context of other suggestions of the *Eclogues* we may be sure that Horace's first readers took these two stanzas as a profession of Gallan-Virgilian poetics. The Pindaric invocation of the first stanza has given way to the art of Horace's immediate Roman precedents, summarized by the magic 'pipes' of Orpheus (here *fidibus*) which had been passed on to Gallus.

At the beginning of the fourth stanza, however, with the introduction of Jupiter in answer to the third question *Quem deum. . . ?*, the ode not only begins its final movement, but the acknowledgement of Gallan-Virgilian poetics is forgotten (it would seem) as completely as is the reference to Pindar in the first stanza. Yet 'forgotten' is not quite the right word: the progression of gods, heroes, and mortals owes much to the spirit of early Greek verse,[2] and, as we will see in greater detail, Horace takes one stage further but does not deny – much less refute – the elaborate structure of inspiration and traditions erected by Gallus and Virgil which served to lend authority to the pronouncements of the initiated

---

[1] We need not share the hesitation with which some commentators (Kiessling–Heinze, Nisbet–Hubbard) have suggested *Ecl.* 10.11–12 as the source of Horace's Pindus: here too the whole context offers confirmation.

[2] For the various difficulties (all of which we may sidestep here) in these lines, see Nisbet–Hubbard, and the thorough recent discussion by H. D. Jocelyn, 'Horace, *Odes* i 12.33–6', *Antichthon* 5 (1971), 68–76.

poet. The ode is in fact a carefully plotted paradigm of Horace's profession in 3.30.13–14: 'Aeolic' song, finely spun according to the purpose and practice of the Roman Callimacheans, now turns itself *ad Italos modos*. The gods (Jupiter, Minerva, Liber, Diana, Apollo) and heroes (Hercules and the Dioscuri, at least) are all those with special Roman associations and importance;[1] and the list of the illustrious mortals of Roman history, to be made famous in Roman song, concludes with Marcellus and Augustus.[2] The ode in its entirety stands as a superb example of what Horace conceived as the ultimate contribution his *Odes* made to Latin poetry. We can understand his conception more fully by looking at what he says of his poetry in that group of odes he must have considered his supreme achievement.

Horace's Roman Odes (3.1–6) are not simply a series of poems related by common themes, but a remarkable unity, a single movement: each poem is related to the ones preceding and following so that the sense of a natural progression from theme to theme is never lost or obscured.[3] 3.1, for instance, ends with the rejection of *divitias operosiores*, and 3.2 begins with its opposite, *angustam pauperiem*, before passing quickly to its real theme, *virtus*; it in turn ends with the unjust man (*scelestum*), anticipating his opposite in the first line of 3.3 (*Iustum et tenacem propositi virum*).[4] Only at one point is the transition from one ode to another handled in such a way that the reader might suspect that the last and first stanzas had been composed for just this purpose (as, for instance, the first stanza of the first ode has often been regarded as a general introduction, 'tacked on', to the whole series): at the end of 3.3 and the beginning of 3.4 the

---

[1] The names *Pallas* (20) and *Phoebe* (24) should not distract us from their importance as Roman deities: these Greek titles elegantly frame the two Latin titles *Liber* and *Virgo* (22). Hercules is similarly identified by his Greek patronymic (*Alciden*, 25), but his recent special significance would not have escaped Augustan readers. Whether the list of heroes should include, besides Romulus and Numa, a Tarquin and Cato, cannot be decided with certainty.

[2] The ode should probably be dated before the death of Marcellus in September, 23 B.C., though not as certainly as (e.g.) Nisbet–Hubbard would have it (the terms of the mention of Marcellus would be both appropriate and moving after his death): but its close relation with 3.30 in itself would indicate a late date.

[3] I can agree with R. Heinze ('Der Zyklus der Römeroden', *Vom Geist des Römertums* (Stuttgart, 1960), 190–204) to a great extent: 6, 4, and 3 probably were conceived and written in some form without any clear idea of a cycle, but I do think that even these poems must have been re-written after the cycle took shape. I cannot, however, discuss the question of unity here.

[4] Heinze saw and admitted the connection between the end of 3.1 and the beginning of 3.2, but 'Hier, und nur hier, meine ich, knüpft der Gedanke an die vorangehende Ode an, die vom Wert der *pauperies* handelt' (p. 199): Heinze's insistence that Horace repeat himself from ode to ode does not allow the poet to have constructed a *unified progression* of ideas from ode to ode.

Muse is addressed by Horace for the only time in these six poems.[1] But these two stanzas are far from being the product of the poet's final attempt to arrange separate poems in a meaningful sequence: the first stanza of 3.4 is a most necessary part of the coherent logic of the ode; the two stanzas serve to mark the conclusion of the first half and the beginning of the second half of the whole series; and their reference to Horace's poetic purpose is an essential indication of how the Roman reader was intended to read and understand not only these six related odes, but the entire collection.

The final stanza of 3.3 follows directly the last words of Juno's long speech at the council of the gods:

> non hoc iocosae conveniet lyrae:
> quo, Musa, tendis? desine pervicax
> referre sermones deorum et
> magna modis tenuare parvis.
> (3.3.69–72)

Horace's lyre is nôt a fitting instrument on which to accompany poems relating epic themes, the *sermones deorum*. This, in essence, is a variation of the *recusatio*: Horace has just done (as so often) precisely what he is claiming to be beyond his poetic competence and powers, but transfers the blame for his lack of decorum to the Muse. The last line of the stanza introduces the important poetic reason for Horace's diffidence: the poet refers his inability to handle grand themes to the Callimachean precedent (*tenuare* is equivalent to *deducere*, the Callimachean ideal of λεπτότης). Yet it is not enough simply to recognize the *recusatio* here. Why does Horace conclude the first half of his group of national odes with such a disavowal of what he is so consciously and so proudly engaged upon? Why does the clearly Callimachean final line of the first half of these poems so intentionally look back to the first line, *Odi profanum vulgus et arceo?*[2]

An answer to these questions has already been advanced. We have seen that Propertius, undoubtedly following Horace's precedent in *Odes* I–III, states his role as a Callimachean poet more explicitly and at greater length precisely in proportion to the increase of his concern to treat national themes: Book III opens with three blatantly Callimachean programmatic statements,[3] and in this Book (and especially in these introductory poems) Propertius has carefully avoided any suggestion of

---

[1] The Camenae are addressed, of course, later in 3.4, in lines closely related to 3.3.69–72 and 3.4.1–4, as we will discuss.

[2] 3.1.1, the translation (again) of Callimachus' σικχαίνω πάντα τὰ δημόσια.

[3] Including (it is worth pointing out again) the paraphrase of *Odes* 3.30 in 3.2.17–26.

his old role of poet-lover, the role on which previously he has based his claim to Callimachean poetry. Propertius, we suggested, had involved himself in certain special difficulties, and his attempts at untying his own proper knots as his interests changed during these crucial years led him to proclamations applicable often only to his own case. But we can often see clearly that he called upon Horace's precedent for help, and we can discern the general principle which guided him out of his poetic labyrinth and apply it in turn to understanding its author.

The 'long and continuous epic' (ἐν ἄεισμα διηνεκές, *Aetia* fr. 1.3) had been anathema for Callimachus; at Rome too it became a useful straw-man for Catullus and for the next generation of Callimachean poets: Virgil, of course, begins his Callimachean *recusatio* in just these terms, *cum canerem reges et proelia*... Volusius was not the only poet at whom a finger of scorn could conveniently be pointed had a literal-minded observer asked for a specific example of what was properly intended as a general poetic principle. But poetry 'on kings and battles' became, by the first years of the decade between 30 and 20 B.C., precisely what had to be written (not, I should add again, because of any external constraints put upon the poets, but because of internal necessities). The danger was clearly that the acceptance of important themes – the themes of Rome, the emergence and realization of her destiny with its concomitant negative aspects – might appear to be a betrayal or disavowal of Callimachean poetics, which had become, in the minds of Gallus and Virgil, a far grander creed than it was a collection of *dicta* on stylistic technique.

Propertius was to follow Horace in loudly proclaiming his Callimachean inheritance just when it might have seemed on the surface at least that he was turning away from it. Horace is more subtle, in this as in every respect. The first half of his Roman Odes is framed with two Callimachean lines, a clear statement of position and purpose to be extended and developed in 3.4. The final stanza of 3.3 has a close parallel in the final stanza of the first poem of the second book of *Odes*:

> sed ne relictis, Musa procax, iocis
> Ceae retractes munera neniae,
> mecum Dionaeo sub antro
> quaere modos leviore plectro.
> (2.1.37–40)

This ode, 'the τηλαυγὲς πρόσωπον of the second book', has been admirably discussed by Fraenkel.[1] It begins in such a way that the reader is not aware

---

1 *Horace* 234–9; Fraenkel, however, is content with a passing reference to the often noted similarities of the final stanzas of 2.1 and 3.3 (p. 239 n. 3).

until line 7 (*tractas*) that its subject, civil war, is in fact a statement of the theme of Pollio's *Historiae*, not (ostensibly) of the ode itself: this device allows Horace to write of the *motum ex Metello consule civicum* at second hand, as it were, and finally to conclude with his admonition to the *Musa procax* who had almost induced him, *iocis relictis*,[1] to this poetic impropriety. But one significant difference between these two final stanzas should be noted. In 2.1.37–40 there is no suggestion that the Muse is Callimachean: she is, if anything, associated only with the lyre of Aeolic poetry.[2] The parallelism between these two stanzas, then, serves to emphasize the added element in 3.3.72.

The *recusatio* at the end of 3.3 is generally taken by scholars at face value; the impression is given that Horace excuses himself for his intrusion into subjects not appropriate to his chosen genre;[3] and on the surface this is, of course, his pretense. We are then asked to accept his profession and are expected, as accomplices, to make genial allowance for the profession of such themes, not only in the Roman Odes, but throughout the collection. But the primary purpose of the *recusatio* was very different – a positive statement, not a negative (and basically rather empty) excuse: the poet, when first turning to themes that appear to violate Callimachean poetics, must make it clear that he does so still in the tradition and with the voice of that summary exemplar. The *recusatio*, from its inception, was a clear signal that new concerns and new interests had forced themselves upon the poet, and that the poet was accepting the challenge of giving, through his art and by means of his position ultimately divine in its origin, universal and timeless significance to events of great moment.

Horace's profession of his Callimachean position has not been adequately recognized, a failure due largely, as we have noted just above, to his reformation of Callimachean principles. Each generation of Latin poets, from Catullus and the neoterics on through Virgil and Gallus, through (the later) Virgil and Horace, through Ovid, and on even

---

[1] Cf. the *pervicax Musa* and her *iocosa lyra* in 3.3.69–72.

[2] We may conveniently note here how Horace has sought a different means to justify the use of the *iocosa lyra* for themes involving *reges et proelia*: he can assume the precedent of Alcaeus. In 2.13 he recounts how closely he had escaped a premature visit to the underworld, where he would have heard Sappho and Alcaeus singing to an enthralled audience, who listen to both *sacro silentio*, but with the greater interest to Alcaeus – *sed magis | pugnas et exactos tyrannos | densum umeris bibit aure vulgus*, 2.13.30–2. (Might this *vulgus* be intended to call to mind Callimachus? Cf. *vulgus* at 2.16.39–40 and 3.1.1.)

[3] For example, Commager (*The Odes of Horace*, 110–11), 'The Ode's final stanza gently banishes Juno's oracular rhythms together with the whole council of the gods... The lines...seem intended, more generally, as a pledge that Horace's abandonment of his usual lighter role is only temporary.' Commager even asks (p. 223 n. 124), 'Might the last stanza of *C.* 3.3 signal Horace's withdrawal from such grand national themes in favor of Vergil?'

through the Silver poets until Statius, was to create a different image of Callimachus according to the needs of their own verse, an image which often has little resemblance to the original; and in the process the creation received from the poets directly preceding was qualified and altered to produce something new and sometimes not immediately recognizable. In 3.4, intended to be read after only slight pause for breath following the final line of 3.3, we can see Horace altering the image of Callimachus he had received from Virgil and Gallus, and we can see how, and why, he does it.

> Descende caelo et dic age tibia
> regina longum Calliope melos,
> seu voce nunc mavis acuta
> seu fidibus citharave Phoebi.
>
> (3.4.1–4)

The first line of the fourth Roman Ode would be taken as a continuation of the preceding address to the Muse, another imperative asking her to give up such themes as the council of the gods in heaven, and we have just been told why: it is not the function of the Callimachean poet *'magna modis tenuare parvis'*. But the next three lines of the stanza would have come as something of a surprise. Only here in all of Horace's poetry is Calliope singled out from the number of the Muses, and, what is crucial and telling, she appears in company with Apollo.[1] What we have observed above about the function of Calliope and Apollo can leave no doubt that here Horace is making a pointed reference to the source of poetic inspiration of Gallus and Virgil, just as Propertius had done in the *Monobiblos* and was to do again in subsequent writings.[2] The clear reference to Callimachean poetics with which the previous ode had concluded has now been further qualified by the invocation of the ultimate divinities of Gallus' and Virgil's poetic genealogy. For the moment Horace claims a position in the line, established by Apollo and Calliope, of Orpheus and Linus, Hesiod, the select Alexandrians, and their Roman successors.

This favored position had to be conferred and confirmed by initiation

---

[1] The singular appearance of Calliope here is notable in that Horace was able to invoke a number of individual Muses (see the *Indices* for Clio, Euterpe, Melpomene, Piplea (-eis?), Polyhymnia, Thalia, and the adjectival Pieris, as well as the collective Musae and Camenae); Melpomene (*Odes* 1.24.3, 3.30.16, 4.3.1), it should be noted, is metrically equivalent to Calliope. It is true that individual Muses had not yet been assigned their separate spheres of influence when Horace wrote (and what Fraenkel says (*Horace*, 281 n. 1) about a single Muse representing them all is also generally valid): but Calliope had clear associations for Horace, as did the Camenae.

[2] See my Index, s.v. *Calliope*.

or reception: the Muses had actually spoken to the shepherd Hesiod, and to Callimachus they had appeared in a dream.

> auditis? an me ludit amabilis
> insania? audire et videor pios
> errare per lucos, amoenae
> quos et aquae subeunt et aurae.
>
> (3.4.5–8)

videor is the key word here: Horace's variation includes the participation of an undefined audience (*auditis?*) and a state of mind neither awake nor asleep; the Muses here do not actually appear to him, though their presence can be felt, but the scene in which he seems to wander (*errare* – a suggestion of a specific state of poetic inspiration, cf. *errantem Permessi ad flumina Gallum?*) is unmistakably the landscape now associated with poetic initiation, the grove, its waters and breezes.

A constant principle of Horace's art in the *Odes* is the creation of expectation in the first stanzas of an ode. The reader begins with the comforting feeling of being on sure ground, of having before him, for instance, simply a new version of Alcaeus or an easily digestible philosophical cliché; but suddenly what was familiar becomes, in various ways that go to the heart of Horace's art, something new and different, the version of the Greek poem becomes strikingly Roman and therefore paradoxical, the philosophical cliché takes on an unfamiliar shape as the kaleidoscope is given a slight turn. The Roman reader of the first eight lines of 3.4 would be expecting several developments: the Muses, or one of their surrogates, certainly, would materialize at any moment to instruct the poet in the proper use of his chosen instrument or to suggest a drink; the haunting unreality of the scene would be confirmed by the poet's admission of having dreamed it all. But what follows in the next three stanzas is characteristically Horatian in several respects. Horace's confirmation as a poet does not take place in the groves he has just conjured up nor in the poetic present he has just arranged: it had been granted him long before this, and, what is more, in a landscape strikingly real. We are again in the land of the legendary Daunus, but where the real Aufidus flows. For a Roman, perhaps, or for a native of northern Italy, the place names Horace recites here (Vultur, Acherontia, Bantia, Forentum) might seem somewhat romantic, but they were nothing of the sort for Horace and his countrymen from Apulia;[1] yet the result of Horace's

---

[1] Fraenkel's remark (*Horace*, 275) about the modern romantic reaction to these lines is worth quoting, for it might, I think, be applied as well to Roman readers at the time still conditioned to having such a scene set in the unreal landscape of Parnassus or Arcadia: 'The manner in which the fabulous happenings are worked out compels us to view them

catalogue, with its epithets that evoke and suggest Greek poetry without ever descending to forgery,[1] is a remarkable fusion of the real and the fantastic, the present and the legendary, the mundane and the purest poetry. The reader, prepared for the poet's transport to the Aganippe or the Aonian mountains, not only finds that the poet long ago, as an infant, had received signs of the Muses' favor in southern Italy, but that his expectations as to the nature of the signs have been crossed. Here we have no legendary pipes, no drink from a proper fountain, no words of instruction; instead, the tokens received are those well known from the stories associated with the infancy of the early Greek poets, Pindar, Stesichorus, or Aeschylus.[2] Horace begins the ode with the clear suggestion of the Callimachean tradition as revised and extended by Gallus and Virgil, but by the end of the fifth stanza has introduced, equally clearly, his own role in a novel tradition.[3]

The beginning of the sixth stanza gives the ode a new movement, reveals its purpose and direction, but at the same time clarifies and qualifies Horace's poetic credentials:[4]

against a real background and under a glaring sunshine while we, brought up in conventions of romantic poetry, might prefer such miracles to take place in the twilight between the land of fairy-story and the world of every-day life.'

[1] These lines are a splendid example of Horace's careful avoidance of epic vocabulary in the *Odes* while achieving a diction somehow equally grand (an aspect of Horatian art that would repay careful study). *Celsae* (*Acherontiae*), for example, is epic in tone and function, but the genitive depends on the homely *nidum*; *arvum pingue* (*Forenti*) suggests immediately its Homeric models, but at the same time is simple and direct Latin. (I should add here that I see no poetic purpose in the appearance of Horace's nurse Pullia in line 10, nor what her *limina* could possibly be – *limina* could hardly mean anything like 'play pen' in a geographical context; Horace must have written something similar to *limina Dauniae*.)

[2] See e.g. Kiessling–Heinze *ad loc.*

[3] The parallel with 3.30.10–14 should be obvious and should be kept in mind in what follows: there, too, Horace presents the sources and tradition, *Aeolium carmen, deducere, ad Italos modos,* and does so against the background of his native Apulia. 3.4.9–20 must also, of course, be read with 1.22.9–16, where a sign of divine protection for the poet (*dum meam canto Lalagen*), received *in silva Sabina,* will guard him even in 'fabulous' foreign lands; or with 1.17, where Lycean Faunus' protection of Horace's own farm is associated with song (*di me tuentur, dis pietas mea | et musa cordi est,* 13–14). The close similarity in ideas and presentation between 3.4 and 1.12 will be discussed below.

[4] Stanzas 6–11 (concluding the first 'half' of the poem) are obviously paired: *vester...* (21) *vestris...* (25) and *vos...* (37) *vos...* (41) formally support the unity of content in stanzas 6–7 and 10–11; the coherent content of stanzas 8–9 is supported by the future verbs. Stanza 11, however, is transitional (Horace avoids the mechanical division of the ode into two exact halves); *scimus ut impios...* (42) introduces the *exempla* which continue through line 64. The Ode then concludes with a *gnome* (*vis consili expers mole ruit sua...,* 65) and further *exempla* (*testis mearum centimanus Gyas | sententiarum...,* 69–70). The crucial point in the structure of the ode is the transition from Horace's presentation and explanation of his poetic authority to the application of that authority: stanzas 6–11 in effect take the poet, privately initiated or recognized, from the seclusion of the *pios lucos* to the real world of Caesar and the use and misuse of power.

vester, Camenae, vester in arduos
tollor Sabinos, seu mihi frigidum
Praeneste seu Tibur supinum
seu liquidae placuere Baiae.

vestris amicum fontibus et choris
non me Philippis versa acies retro,
devota non exstinxit arbos,
nec Sicula Palinurus unda.

(3.4.21–8)

Here again, I think, modern readers have lost the key to Horace's purpose. It is clear that the Camenae are made particularly prominent (*vester, Camenae, vester...*, followed in the next stanza by *vestris amicum*...) and, unless we are content to see this simply as an empty rhetorical effect, we may well ask just why Horace puts such emphasis on his claim, 'I am *yours*, Camenae, *yours*...'[1] We have observed that there is a significant progression in Horace's addresses to the 'Muse' thus far: in the final stanza of the preceding ode he had invoked the *Musa* of Greek lyric (*iocosae lyrae*), who then in the last line of the stanza had taken on Callimachean attributes; and in the first two stanzas of 3.4 Calliope, with Apollo, appeared unmistakably as the inspiration of Gallus and Virgil. Are the Camenae here simply a pointless variation, or is Horace further qualifying the 'Muse' and introducing a new embodiment of a different sort of poetry?

We are fortunately well enough informed about the early history of the Camenae in Latin poetry, and Horace gives us every indication necessary to understand precisely what he intended. The Camenae, originally water-nymphs, had become the first, and only, equivalent of the Greek Muses:[2] Livius Andronicus, for instance, begins his translation of the *Odyssey* by invoking one of them (*Virum mihi, Camena, insece versutum*), and they appear in Naevius' epitaph (*Immortales mortales si*

---

[1] Commentators and critics are of no help in answering this question: e.g. Fraenkel (*Horace*, 281 n. 1, referred to above, and cf. also 306 n. 2) sees no difference between Calliope and the Camenae ('The one Muse, Calliope, represents them all, so that the invocation in the plural, *Camenae*, which dominates the whole section from 21–42, attaches smoothly to the beginning of the ode'). We should not look for spheres of influence not yet assigned to individual Muses (Clio, Euterpe, Polyhymnia, or Thalia have no recognized characters in the *Odes*, and may well be introduced simply as a somewhat more elegant equivalent to 'Muse'); but we should be ready to see the function of those proper names that have taken on special significance.

[2] See *ThLL*, Onomasticon II, coll. 116.59–118.18 (which refers, for their religious history, to G. Wissowa, Roscher I, 846–8, and E. Aust, *RE* III, 1427–8). Etymology had a lot to do with their assumption of the position of Roman Muses: cf. Varro, *LL* 7.26–7; Paulus-Festus p. 38 Lindsay (CAMENAE *Musae a carminibus sunt dictae*...).

foret fas flere, | *flerent divae Camenae Naevium poetam, FPL,* p. 28, Morel).
Ennius, however, banishes them rudely: with the introduction of the
Greek hexameter and his replacement of *carmina* with *poemata* come the
Greek Μοῦσαι, *Musae quae pedibus magnum pulsatis Olympum* (*Ann.* 1),
deities so foreign and strange that they must introduce themselves,
Musas quas memorant, nosce nos esse Camenas (*Ann.* 2).[1] The exile of the
Camenae, along with other quaint and rustic figures of that rude and
innocent age, seemed permanent.[2]

Suddenly, however, they returned. For some reason no longer entirely
clear to us Virgil has Palaemon, who is to act as judge in the singing con-
test in the Third Eclogue, introduce the main event with the words,
'*incipe, Damoeta; tu deinde sequere, Menalca.* | *alternis dicetis; amant alterna
Camenae*' (58–9). It may be that Virgil thought the Camenae appropriate
for the rustic, and somewhat rude, exchange of this particular Eclogue,
but he never mentions or invokes them again. Horace is perhaps pointing
to this passage at *Sat.* 1.10.44–5, *molle atque facetum* | *Vergilio adnuerunt
gaudentes rure Camenae,* but it was Horace himself who was responsible for
restoring them to the position of their former dignity. After their appearance in the nod to Virgil in the first book of his *Satires* (published in
35 B.C.), they are absent again from the two collections published in
30 B.C., *Satires* II and *Epodes,* but in *Odes* I–III they appear significantly
three times, once in each book.[3]

When in *Odes* 1.12 Horace answers the question *Quem virum. . . ?*,
he manages to include a reference to 'the Camena who confers renown':[4]

> Regulum et Scauros animaeque magnae
> prodigum Paulum superante Poeno
> gratus insigni referam Camena
> Fabriciumque.

> (1.12.37–40)

---

[1] On the significance of Ennius' innovation, see O. Skutsch, *Studia Enniana,* 3–5, 18–22.
(It is Skutsch's 'fanciful suggestion' that the Camenae actually speak *Ann.* 2; he removes
the line, however, to the fifteenth book of the *Annals,* referring it to the foundation of the
temple of the Muses by M. Fulvius Nobilior after the Aetolian War.)

[2] Ennius successfully drove out as well the *Fauni vatesque.* Only Lucilius (1028, Marx)
mentions the Camenae between Ennius and Virgil.

[3] *Odes* 1.12.39, 2.16.38, 3.4.21; in *Odes* IV at 4.6.27, 9.8, both very significant contexts;
elsewhere *Epist.* 1.1.1, 18.47, 19.5; *AP* 275; *Carm. Saec.* 62. It is worth noting that in
Propertius the Camenae only appear once – in the 'Horatian' book, 3.10.1, where they
have none of the significance Horace gave them: Propertius had not had time to digest
the importance of Horace's innovation. Newman somehow never associates Horace's
discovery of the Camenae with his extension of the '*vates*-concept'. The *vates* had been
banished likewise by Ennius, and likewise returns in the *Eclogues* (perhaps from Virgil's
reading of Varro – and would he also then have been reminded of the Camenae by
Varro?).

[4] So Kiessling–Heinze *ad loc.,* who paraphrase *insigni Camena,* '*camena quae insignes reddit*';
but *Camena* here (though not at *Epist.* 1.1.1) is not 'song' and should be capitalized.

The Roman Muse has been restored as the patron deity of the poet who will sing the deeds of famous Romans: perhaps we are to think momentarily of Naevius' historical epic. The occurrence of the Camena (again singular) in the last stanza of 2.16 is more significant; here, at the end of a poem praising *otium* and simplicity (*vivitur parvo bene, cui paternum | splendet in mensa tenui salinum*, 13–14) comes a profession of Callimachean poetics – employing, of course, the same terms as had been applied to the ideal life in the preceding stanzas:

> mihi parva rura et
> spiritum Graiae tenuem Camenae
> Parca non mendax dedit et malignum
> spernere vulgus.
>
> (2.16.37–40)

The 'Greek Camena' will find a reverse echo later in the fourth book of the *Odes*, where Horace refers to Ennius' Muses as the *Calabrae Pierides* (4.8.20); but it is impossible to say here whether the old Roman 'Muse' has become Hellenized, or whether the Callimachean *tenuem spiritum* has become Italian.[1] In the fourth book of *Odes* Horace continued to refer to the special significance he had given his Camena: 4.6, proudly anticipating the performance of the *Carmen Saeculare*, includes this invocation of Apollo:

> doctor argutae fidicen Thaliae,
> Phoebe, qui Xantho lavis amne crines,
> Dauniae defende decus Camenae,
>   levis Agyieu.
>
> spiritum Phoebus mihi, Phoebus artem
> carminis nomenque dedit poetae.
>
> (4.6.25–30)

The Greek Apollo is called on to support the Daunian Camena: once again Greek and Roman poetry are fused in Horace's own description of his art.[2] Finally, in another context dealing with the power of poetry, Horace, 'born by the far-sounding Aufidus', claims immortality for his new art, citing as precedents Homer, Pindar, Simonides, Alcaeus, and Stesichorus, then Anacreon and Sappho:

---

[1] For the metaphor of *tenuem spiritum*, cf. Prop. 2.34.32, *et non inflati somnia Callimachi*.

[2] Apollo, who washes his hair in the Xanthus, is given the unusual Greek epithet *Agyieu* ('Ἀγυιεύς): Wickham is right in remarking (*ad loc.*) that 'The associations of the name were...purely literary.' The *Daunia Camena* looks back, not only to 3.30.10–14, but as well to 3.4.9–20: see Fraenkel (*Horace*, 402), who perceptively points to the anaphora 'reserved for thoughts of special dignity' in these passages about divine patronage. (We may note in passing that only here in the *Odes* does Horace mention himself by name – though not *in propria persona* – in the final line and with the title *vates*.)

Ne forte credas interitura, quae
longe sonantem natus ad Aufidum
non ante vulgatas per artis
verba loquor socianda chordis:

non, si priores Maeonius tenet
sedes Homerus, Pindaricae latent
Ceaeque et Alcaei minaces
Stesichorive graves Camenae.

(4.9.1–8)

Here again is the *Graia Camena*, who conferred immortality on the Greek heroes (*vixere fortes ante Agamemnona | multi...*, 25–6), just as she will on Romans (*insigni referam Camena...*, 1.12.39).

The Camenae, then, made their triumphant return to Rome precisely because they alone could represent for Horace the confluence of the various sources and purposes of his poetry. They are natively Italian and go back to the beginnings of Latin poetry, when they celebrated the deeds of the great figures of Roman history; they could, as well, represent the Hellenization of the old Roman traditions by the simple assumption of a slight change of costume – or (what is almost but not quite the same thing) they could represent the Hellenistic tradition made Italian. No other figure of poetic inspiration, however, could have stood for what Horace achieved with his *Odes*, the fusion of early Greek poetry, Callimachean principles, and Roman content and purpose – that new movement in Latin poetry in which Virgil in the *Georgics* was a co-worker and which attracted the attention of a somewhat perplexed Propertius, when, at the beginning of the third book of his elegies, he stated that he too wished *Itala per Graios orgia ferre choros* (3.1.4).

To return now to the sixth stanza of Odes 3.4,

vester, Camenae, vester in arduos
tollor Sabinos, seu mihi frigidum
Praeneste seu Tibur supinum
seu liquidae placuere Baiae.

The patronage of the Camenae is obviously the climax of what has preceded: they are not to be regarded as equivalent to the *Musa* of 3.3.70, nor is Calliope merely one of their number, but rather they represent a significant new stage, the final stage, in the process of poetic development here described. It has long been recognized that the beginning of this ode takes the form of a hymn or prayer: in the sixth stanza the anaphora *seu...seu...seu...*resumes the hymnic form that has been somewhat obscured since the first stanza, a particular anaphora made much of by Catullus, for instance, both in proper prayers and hymns and in the (related) geographical excursus.[1] What is notable here, however, is the highly solemn substitution of Italian sites – the Sabine district, Praeneste, Tibur, and Baiae – for the list of Greek sites that would have been expected:[2] but the calculated reaction of surprise is made perfectly understandable following the local geography in which the *non sine dis animosus infans* received the early signs of the Muses' favor, and on many occasions previously in the collection of *Odes* Horace has given poetic prominence to Italian sites by the use of what can be regarded as a neoteric discovery, the formal geographical excursus. Virgil, at the same time and in similar ways, was also ennobling the Italian landscape and specific places in the *Georgics*. However, the controlling word of this stanza, *tollor*, has not to my knowledge been properly defined: in what sense has the poet been 'raised'?[3] Horace here returns to fulfill the expectations he had aroused, and frustrated, in the first two stanzas of the ode, when he had suggested the initiation or reception of the Callimachean poet. Most of what we know about Callimachus' famous dream (related in a passage now lost at the beginning of the *Aetia*) comes from a late anonymous epigram (*Anth. Pal.* 7.42), which salutes the μέγα περίπυστον ὄνειαρ which transported Callimachus to his reception on Helicon by the Muses.

εὖτέ μιν ἐκ Λιβύης ἀναείρας εἰς Ἑλικῶνα
ἤγαγες ἐν μέσσαις Πιερίδεσσι φέρων.

We cannot be sure, of course, that Callimachus had a comparable form of the verb ἀναείρας used by the epigrammatist here for 'you transported Callimachus from Libya to Helicon', but I suspect that with *tollor* Horace is reproducing the sense necessary to whatever verb actually appeared in Callimachus' passage,[4] that the use of *tollor* is quite specific,

---

[1] *Style and Tradition in Catullus*, 96–100.

[2] Catullus, for instance, often upset such expectations (e.g. in the list of possibilities for Egnatius' origin, 39.10–13), but only for the obviously parodic effect gained by the contrast of form and content; and we have seen Propertius in 1.20 (esp. lines 7–10 dealing, as here, with Baiae and the resort towns around Naples) writing of local geography with exaggerated poetic loftiness, but again only as an amusing, and somewhat outrageous, *tour de force*. Commentators have pointed to, but have not explained, the unusual effect that Horace's stanza has upon the reader; Fraenkel (*Horace*, 275), for instance: 'Nor is the strain on our imagination very much eased in the following stanza (21–24)...from what we know about life at Baiae during the Augustan period we may be mildly surprised to learn that the Muses, wanting to pay a visit to their old friend, should have chosen the time when he was staying at that fashionable seaside resort.'

[3] Kiessling–Heinze (*ad loc.*) gloss *tollor* with 'medial, ἀείρομαι', but the rest of their comment comes no nearer the truth than other commentators.

[4] For this epigram and related testimonia, see Pfeiffer's commentary to the Schol. Flor., *Callimachus*, vol. 1, p. 11.

and that by the reference Horace has completely united, in a single stanza, the various strands of reference he has previously been following: 'It is as your own poet, Camenae, that I have been transported to my reception, held not on the Helicon of the Μοῦσαι, not *Aonas in montis*, but appropriately on the Sabine hills.'

The Muses' protection is again the subject of the next three stanzas, first in personal terms with which the reader is familiar (that the poet had been saved from death at Philippi, again from the falling of the *devota arbos* on his own farm, and again – though the occasion in this case is otherwise unknown – from drowning), then (29–36) in distant places more conventional (though here, too, certain of these names would have had an immediate reality for Roman readers).

Finally, in the tenth stanza (of twenty), the relevance of Horace's position as a divinely protected poet and the significance of the patronage of the Camenae are made clear:

> vos Caesarem altum, militia simul
> fessas cohortis abdidit oppidis,
>   finire quaerentem labores
>   Pierio recreatis antro.
>
> vos lene consilium et datis et dato
> gaudetis almae. scimus ut impios . . .
> (3.4.37–42)

A number of scholars have written at length on these lines, and on what follows;[1] we need here only summarize briefly in the light of the above what Horace intended. Early in the summer of 29 B.C. Octavian, with his legions, had returned to Italy from Egypt; before entering Rome to stage the triple triumph (in mid-August, for his victories in Illyricum, Actium, and Egypt), he stopped at Atella in Campania, where Virgil and Maecenas read the *Georgics* to him. The hope for peace must have been foremost in everyone's mind as Rome awaited his return, hope which historical precedents did not encourage; and in addition there was the question of the settlement of the tired legions. At this moment, then, the message of the *Georgics* must have appeared crucial to Horace, and the very fact that this message could have been directly conveyed to Octavian by the poet must have seemed extraordinary. The fourth Roman Ode, in fact as well as in form, is centered around this stop at Atella, the *Pierio antro* where Octavian received the *lene consilium*: Horace's poem

---

[1] We may single out Heinze, 'Römeroden', 196–8; Fraenkel's entire discussion, *Horace*, 273–88; and Commager, *The Odes of Horace*, 194–209.

is his own contribution on the subject of the misuse of power by the mighty.

Fraenkel's important contribution to the understanding of this ode – the elucidation of the Pindaric background against which Horace writes – goes a long way toward explaining how a mere poet could address words of advice to the most powerful figure in the Roman state: the poet's position as intermediary between things divine and human (a reality, more or less, for Pindar) is a convenient fiction for Horace, and was, in this poem, one of the reasons for relating his protection as an infant by signs similar to those granted Pindar, Stesichorus, and Aeschylus. We should not, however, let the detail in which we now understand the Pindaric elements of 3.4 obscure for us the similar position of the poet elaborated by Gallus and Virgil: the poet who had been received and ritually instructed by Apollo and the Muses possessed knowledge and understanding, like Orpheus, of the universe and had the ability, or the magic, to control the universe – to the extent, at least, that he could control the limitations of his own humanity. Horace, by associating himself with this initiation and instruction, claims a second right to address Caesar. Moreover, his Camenae, the Italian Muses, are a particularly appropriate source of ultimate authority for the poet who addresses words of caution and advice to the one man who had finally emerged as the ruler of the Roman world.

The *Odes* of Horace are the distilled essence of Augustan poetry: they reach naturally to the past, both the Greek literary past and the national past of Rome itself; they owe their depth and variety of expression, their power to move the reader either by simplicity or by the Pindaric torrent, to the poetic activity of what may well be the most sudden and fruitful literary maturation any society has experienced; and they are concerned, finally, with the experience of their own time, transforming it, in turn, through the timely maturity of poetic expression and theory, into a comprehensible vision of past and future. V. Pöschl has recently expressed it well:

The poetry of Horace stems from the deep experience of a dreadful catastrophe: the collapse of the order of state and life at the end of the Roman republic. This collapse occurred in a relentless sequence of murderous civil wars. The works of Augustan poetry are real *fleurs du mal*, blossoms that grow out of evil. They are the answer of the Roman mind to this challenge, the result of the meeting of subtle sensibility and fearsome threat.[1]

[1] 'Poetry and Philosophy in Horace', in *The Poetic Tradition*, edited by D. C. Allen and H. T. Rowell (Baltimore, 1968), 47.

Horace gives us our best introduction to Tibullus, not just to the man,[1] but, more important, to his poetry: it is against such a setting as the one we have just drawn that Tibullus must be read. He shares with Horace the misfortune of being taken literally or out of context, a lover of the country and its simplicities: homely clichés, though nicely turned, are all (it would seem) he has to offer. In addition, as a result of the fascination Propertius exercises upon us, he is read primarily as a love poet, though without the depth of passion the modern reader feels instinctively in his contemporary in elegy. The lucid transparency and charm of his verse are continually praised, perhaps because it is so difficult to see beneath this surface. We forget that Tibullus was, after all, an Augustan poet: it is easy to conclude that Messalla's poet should have little or nothing to do with the concerns of the regime – particularly easy if we imagine Virgil, Horace, and Propertius writing purely on demand.[2] But if their needs to express the hopes and doubts involved in the *pax Augusta* were genuine, then any real poet, even Tibullus, may be assumed to have felt the same necessity to give form and meaning to 'the deep experience of a dreadful catastrophe'.

In these concluding pages we will consider primarily one elegy of Tibullus, 2.5, a poem either neglected or regarded as highly unusual.[3] The fact that it was written for an occasion (the election of Messalla's son to the college of the *quindecimviri sacris faciundis*, who had charge of the Sibylline Books now kept in the Temple of Apollo on the Palatine) should not lead to the assumption that it is therefore an empty rhetorical exercise, different in nature from the rest of Tibullus' elegies. In much the same way that Horace's Roman Odes represent the culmination of his achievement, so in 2.5 much of what had been previously important for Tibullus, in both content and presentation, is unified and made more explicit.

[1] In his vivid and warm sketches of his friend, *Odes* 1.33 and *Epist.* 1.4.

[2] The most illuminating and suggestive study of Tibullus is the first part of the article by F. Solmsen, 'Tibullus as an Augustan Poet', *Hermes* 90 (1962), 295–325. I suspect that we make too much of Tibullus' membership in Messalla's circle, as if that (or Maecenas') was an exclusive club. Tibullus' intimacy with Horace should not be forgotten – there is no reason to consider him an 'outsider'.

[3] For instance: G. Luck has very little to say about it in *The Latin Love Elegy* (New York, 1960), and refers to it as a '*pièce d'apparat*' (p. 116); J. P. Elder ('Tibullus: *Tersus Atque Elegans*', in *Critical Essays on Roman Literature: Elegy and Lyric*, ed. J. P. Sullivan (Cambridge, Mass., 1962), 65–105) mentions 2.5 only once (p. 104 n. 10); Solmsen dismisses this most characteristically Augustan poem in a single paragraph, 'In a study of Tibullus as an Augustan poet the patriotic topics of 2,5 cannot be treated as typical' (p. 300), though he returns to it later to discuss *amor* (pp. 309–10). K. F. Smith in his standard commentary (*The Elegies of Albius Tibullus* (New York, 1913), 443) notes that 'This is the longest of Tibullus' poems, and the only one of a national character.'

The structure of the poem is simpler and more formal than that of any other Tibullan elegy:[1]

Opening address to Apollo, 1–22
    I Ancient Rome, 23–70
      (a) Pastoral peace before Aeneas, 23–38
      (b) Aeneas and war, 39–70
    II Modern Rome, 71–104
      (a) War (before Augustus), 71–8
      (b) Rural peace (under Augustus), 79–104
Closing address to Apollo, 105–22

The opening lines of the poem are remarkable: *Phoebe, fave: novus ingreditur tua templa sacerdos*... Any reader familiar not only with Horace's position as *Musarum sacerdos* (*Odes* 3.1.1–4), but with the development and significance of the role of poet-priest in contemporary Latin poetry, would have been immediately struck by Tibullus' assumption of the role, so unexpected from all his previous poetry.[2] But that characteristic diffidence combined with light wit reasserts itself at line 17, *Phoebe, sacras Messalinum sine tangere chartas...*, when (with the second vocative *Phoebe*) it becomes suddenly clear that the poet-priest is in fact not a role Tibullus is claiming for himself, but rather that the *sacerdos* is Messalinus: Tibullus' favorite gambit, whether he is playing the lover or a pretender to inspired knowledge, is to undercut an assumed position. But a further convolution occurs in the closing lines (113–15), when Tibullus *does* (for the only time in his elegies) accept the position of the *sacer vates*. It is only in this poem that Tibullus makes any clear statement about his poetic role, and only here that his private voice becomes public and prophetic; but we should not conclude that the unusual quality of the poem is due simply to the occasion for which it was composed,[3] or that Tibullus is addressing himself to national, or Augustan, topics for the first time.

The final lines of this introduction lead up to the first major section of the poem, an account of the founding of the *aeterna urbs*, but before the Sibyl has a chance to speak, there is a long parenthesis devoted to the

---

[1] The transition (lines 19–22) from the opening address to Apollo to the first major section on Ancient Rome is completely natural and smooth as is the transition in lines 67–70: the arbitrarily sharp divisions given here should not be an encouragement to numerologists. (There does not, in any case, seem to be any observable balance or numerical relationship between sections.)

[2] See Newman, *Augustus and the New Poetry*, 178–81, for this poem (and further, 383–93, for an excellent appreciation of Tibullus as a Callimachean poet).

[3] The occasion of 1.7, for instance, might have evoked a similar approach, had Tibullus so wished.

pastoral origins of the site,[1] the first two couplets of which make it clear that a distinction is to be understood between the pastoral prehistory (23–38) and the wars and strife after Aeneas' arrival (39–70):

> Romulus aeternae *nondum* formaverat urbis
> moenia, consorti non habitanda Remo;
> *sed tunc* pascebant herbosa Palatia vaccae
> et stabant humiles in Iovis arce casae.
>
> (2.5.23–6)

The strife of Romulus and Remus, culminating in fratricide, had become for the Augustans a sort of curse on the house of Atreus, an embarrassing original explanation of later civil war;[2] the state of pastoral peace which Aeneas found in Evander's Rome had also become an Augustan topic, already a subject for popular reflection:[3] the contrast Tibullus draws here was nothing new.

The pastoral origins of Rome are emphasized by Tibullus in a manner eminently Callimachean, with an elaborate etymological *aetion*:

> sed tunc *pascebant herbosa Palatia* vaccae
> et stabant humiles in Iovis arce casae.
> lacte madens illic suberat *Pan* ilicis umbrae
> et facta agresti lignea falce *Pales*,
> pendebatque vagi *pastoris* in arbore votum,
> garrula silvestri fistula sacra deo,
>
> (25–30)

The words italicized are all intended to be derived from the same root (as from the Greek *$\pi\alpha$-, as in $\pi\alpha\tau\acute{\epsilon}o\mu\alpha\iota$). Varro gives us an etymology (with a literary precedent) that allowed Tibullus to connect the *Palatia* with *pasco*/*pastor*: ...*eundem hunc locum a pecore dictum putant quidam; itaque Naevius Balatium appellat* (*LL* 5.53). Livy (1.5.1–2) also helps us see the Roman antiquarian mind at work on the question: Evander brought the Lupercalia, rites connected with Pan, to the Palatine from Arcadia.[4] Pales naturally finds a place. Tibullus then adds a final touch in giving *Palatia* an epithet (*herbosa*) to explain its etymology: Propertius was

[1] Aptly punctuated as such by Postgate in the O.C.T., and set off by dashes by Ponchont in his Budé text.

[2] See R. M. Ogilvie, *A Commentary on Livy Books 1–5* (Oxford, 1965), 54 and 60 (on 1.7.9), with refs.

[3] Cf. Varro, *RR* 2.1.9, *Romanorum vero populum a pastoribus esse ortum quis non dicit?*... Cf. also the numerous passages in the Augustan poets portraying early Rome as Tibullus does here (see Smith on 2.5.25–6), e.g. Vir. *Aen.* 8.360–1, ...*passimque armenta videbant* | *Romanoque foro et lautis mugire Carinis* (with lines 314–36); Prop. 4.1.3–4, *atque ubi Navali stant sacra Palatia Phoebo,* | *Euandri profugae procubuere boves.*

[4] Livy's etymology for the Palatine is different from Naevius' (see Ogilvie *ad loc.*), but the old connection with Pan must have been in Tibullus' mind.

perhaps referring to these lines at the beginning of 4.9 (*venit ad invictos pecorosa Palatia montis*, 3) when he too glossed *Palatia* with an etymological epithet and then, in addition, added a neoteric appositive which also included an *aetion* (*invictos* [*montis*] = [*Hercules*] *Invictus*, the aetiological subject of the poem).[1] We should note one further *aetion* in these lines of Tibullus: the ancient Velabrum (*at qua Velabri regio patet...*, 33) was once under water, accessible only by small boats (*...ire solebat | exiguus ...linter*, 33–4), where on festal days a girl rowed to her lover (*...ad iuvenem festa est vecta puella die*, 36); Varro again supplies the key, *...quod ibi vehebantur lintribus, velabrum* (*LL* 5.156). This is the poetry of Augustan learning.[2]

From this scene of pastoral peace, reflected in the very names connected with Rome's origins, we are presented in the next section (the Sibyl's speech, 39–64) with war, slaughter, and religion abandoned, all of which, dating from Aeneas' arrival, preceded the actual foundation of the City: Victory is the *superba diva* (46), bringing fire (*incendia*) to the Rutulians, and to Turnus death: *iam tibi praedico, barbare Turne, necem* (48). Ilia, having deserted Vesta's fire (*...Vestales deseruisse focos*, 52), lies secretly with Mars (*...concubitusque tuos furtim,...cupidi dei...*, 53–4).[3] At this point in her speech there is a sudden break:

> carpite nunc, tauri, de septem montibus herbas
> dum licet: hic magnae iam locus urbis erit.
>
> (55–6)

If we want to know what the second half of the *Aeneid* is about, this section of 2.5 makes an excellent beginning, offering, as it must, an informed reading by a contemporary.

[1] See H. E. Pillinger, *HSCP* 73 (1969), 184 (on the 'neoteric appositive' collocation, see O. Skutsch, *RhM* 99 (1956), 198–9, who attributes it to Gallus and names it the *schema Cornelianum*). On what I think is the first such aetiological gloss in Latin poetry, see my note '*Urioque apertos*: A Catullan Gloss', *Mnem.* 26 (1973), 60–2.

[2] That Propertius did have this passage of Tibullus in mind in the first lines of 4.9 seems more certain from his mention of the Velabrum immediately after *pecorosa Palatia*: *qua Velabra suo stagnabant flumine quoque | nauta per urbanas velificabat aquas* (4.9.5–6); I am somewhat hesitant about suggesting that he gives his own etymology here, VEL-ABRA from VEL-*ificabat* URBA-*nas aquas*.

[3] Justice is not being done to Tibullus here by stating so positively what he conveys so quietly, but his restrained understatement is due more to his poetic temperament than to any deference toward Augustus' sensibilities. Many literary critics (especially of the *Aeneid*), though few historians, still seem to feel that Augustus would not have appreciated as ancestors a less than noble Aeneas or a somewhat imperfect Julius; but by 19 B.C. (and generally even as early as Actium) Augustus could present himself not as the successor to Julius, but (in distinction) as the bringer of peace and order. Virgil and Tibullus knew, or supposed, that Augustus inherited Aeneas' city, but restored to it Evander's peace.

Having suggested the founders not only of Rome but of the Julian line (Aeneas, Ascanius, Ilia, Mars, and Romulus), Tibullus, again through the dramatic agency of the Sibyls (67–70), turns to the immediate ancestry of Augustus[1] and contemporary history: the omens of civil war (71–8). But all this passed with Actium:[2]

> haec fuerant *olim*: *sed* tu *iam* mitis, Apollo,
> prodigia indomitis merge sub aequoribus.
> (79–80)

What follows in the final section (79–104) needs little comment. Rural peace (*gaudete, coloni*, 83) is celebrated in terms familiar to a reader of Tibullus, in a countryside which intentionally reflects the golden age of Saturn's Latium – Ceres is bountiful, wine flows, and the wolves presumably do stay away from the sheep folds (83–8). We should not miss one touch that completes the circle:

> ac madidus baccho sua festa *Palilia pastor*
> concinet: a stabulis tunc procul este lupi.
> (87–8)

Tibullus again plays with the same etymological aetiology.[3] With the completion of Apollo's new temple on the Palatine, Rome has returned to the ways of Evander's site: for this reason the Apollo invoked at the beginning of the poem was asked to appear as he was at that critical juncture of prehistory when Saturn took refuge in Latium (...*qualem te memorant Saturno rege fugato* | *victori laudes concinuisse Iovi*, 9–10).[4]

2.5, then, is a tightly integrated design uniting past and present, legend and fact, in manner and matter thoroughly Augustan. It was Virgil and Horace (particularly in the *Georgics* and in *Epodes* 7 and 16) who first found a way to write about the national experience. At a time when the future of Rome was still a matter of doubt and fear, political chaos could be understood against a background of the legendary past created by the poetic imagination. History contained scenes and figures that could be fitted into an existing poetical pattern: the initiated poet of the *Eclogues*

---

1 Through the *cometen*, the *sidus Iulii*, which appeared in the summer of 43 B.C.
2 Note the emphatic temporal adverbs *olim* | *sed iam*, similar in structural purpose to *nondum* | *sed tunc* in 23–6. The Actian Apollo is made prominent by the occasion of the poem.
3 Pan Lycaeus and the Lupercal (see Ogilvie on Livy 1.5.1–2) are part of the associations suggested by...*tunc procul este lupi*.
4 Cf. the etymological *aetion* at the beginning of Evander's speech to Aeneas on the origins of Latium: *Saturnus*... | *arma Iovis fugiens et regnis exul ademptis* | ...*Latiumque vocari* | *maluit, his quoniam* latuisset *tutus in oris* (*Aen*. 8.319–23).

could then find in Saturn's Latium a recognizable order, still imaginary, but one step closer to reality than Arcadia had been. As the *pax Augusta* became an established fact during the first years of the decade of the twenties, Horace's *arva beata... divites et insulas* (*Epod.* 16.41–2) and the return of the *magnus ordo* in Virgil's Fourth Eclogue must have seemed strangely archaic in conception: the Roman Odes and the *Georgics* could consider the possibility (it was still no more than a possibility) of order and peace in a real landscape, and since the setting was real, could present actual storm clouds still threatening the land. Tibullus must have written 2.5 very near the end of that decade: the unity he is able to see in the national experience represents the culmination, much as does the *Aeneid*, of the Augustan vision, but it was not a realization he came to suddenly or had taken over already formed by others.[1] Tibullus' conception of the pastoral peace that existed before Aeneas' arrival and the rural peace that returned to the Roman world after Actium was very much the result of his poetic thought during the first years of the twenties.

A head-on disagreement between two eminent scholars often provides a useful focus on a problem. In 1962 Elder took for granted the existence of a 'pastoral world' in Tibullus,[2] and in the same year Solmsen (independently) denied that such a world was to be found. The latter noted the absence of specific pastoral elements one might expect,[3] and found only one possible suggestion of the bucolic.[4] But, on the other hand, if we assume that the opposite of the pastoral might be found in the realism of the *Georgics*, a further question is raised by Solmsen's

[1] Solmsen in his otherwise extremely perceptive article (*Hermes* 1962) seems to misunderstand the nature of 2.5: 'Integration has been achieved for the rural and the erotic topic, but the connection between the *rura* and the national themes is "literary" rather than intrinsic... In a study of Tibullus as an Augustan poet the patriotic topics of 2, 5 cannot be treated as typical' (p. 300).

[2] *Critical Essays*, p. 80, for instance, 'But what of Tibullus' pastoral world? Unlike Virgil, Tibullus, as we have noted, draws his pastoral world and its folk with indistinct lines and misty hues. Generalization and wish mingle with description. We have no clear idea of specific landscape, nor of season, nor of weather, nor of the people – their work and their aspirations.' The mist that Elder sees hanging over this pastoral world should alert us to certain questions about what Tibullus was actually doing: why has he made the pastoral features of his landscape so indistinct?

[3] P. 303: 'There is no Daphnis and no Adonis in Tibullus' elegies...no singing, whether singly or in *amoibaia*...no whispering pine trees or humming bees, no cicadas, no grasshoppers, no lizards, and no ring-doves. We find no baskets of cheese on Tibullus' farm nor do we read of anyone reclining on "couches made of grass" or "strewn with fleabane, celery and asphodel".' Solmsen then notes that the typical characteristics of Tibullus' countryside are conversely not found in bucolic poetry: 'his landscape is the concrete, if idealized, Italian *ager*.'

[4] 1.2.71–2, *ipse boves mea si tecum modo Delia possim | iungere et in solito pascere monte pecus,* lines which 'may indeed be called bucolic. It may have had parallels in Gallus' elegies. But it has no parallel in Tibullus himself' (p. 304). On the other hand, there is no real reason to see even in these lines a purposeful suggestion of a pastoral world.

finding only a general response by Tibullus to Virgil's poem.[1] Obviously we need a clearer understanding of Tibullus' countryside in his first book of elegies.

The first poem of Book I is an 'overture' to the collection.[2] It is intentionally divided into two 'halves' (1 *Divitias alius...* – 40 and 41 *Non ego divitias...* – 78), the first dealing generally with Wealth versus Tibullus' *rura*, the second with Wealth versus Love. In the first 40 lines there is no suggestion of the pastoral whatsoever: this is a real farm, and though we are allowed only carefully selected glimpses, nothing of what we see would have seemed in any way foreign or strange to an Italian gentleman farmer. We are not allowed to see the weeds or the continual struggle of Virgil's farmer, but this should not distract us from the fact that conversely we are not in an Arcadia, but on an Italian farm where abundance is a hope rather than a fictional topic.[3] Our final impression, though, is that something of the pastoral fantasy, with its simple pleasures, certain plenty, and never-ending sun, has been transferred to Italy and has found a place in a recognizable setting. But in the second half of the poem 'indistinct lines and misty hues' do in fact predominate: suddenly the simplicity of country life is interrupted by war (*te bellare decet terra, Messalla, marique...*, 53), love (Delia, mentioned first at line 57), death (59–70) and old age (71–2), in a Horatian succession of associations. The introduction of these themes effectively makes 'literary' what in the first half had been a reality, and we feel for the first time the intrusion of the elegiac poet. Description gives over to imagination, a real setting becomes a stage on which a rapid succession of almost allegorical figures confront, and yield place to, one another.

The third poem finds Tibullus sick and close to death, far from home on a military expedition with Messalla. At line 33 he thinks of home, *at mihi contingat patrios celebrare Penates | reddereque antiquo menstrua tura Lari*; but this thought of his farm leads to reflections (prompted, of course, by the topics of war and travel) on the Saturnian Age (35–48), *quam bene Saturno vivebant rege...!*, complete with the idealized sufficiency of the country then. At line 49 (*Nunc Iove sub domino...*) he returns to the present, to war and his own imminent death, which in turn leads to a highly

---

[1] Pp. 300–2: Solmsen is somewhat equivocal on this question, but the differences he finds between Tibullus' *rura* and that of the *Georgics* are important.

[2] This is Fraenkel's term (*Horace*, 413 and n. 2), a useful distinction to a 'programmatic' poem: 'Like the overture of many a classical opera it introduces the main themes of the subsequent work and merges them into an organic whole.'

[3] We may compare the optative *nec Spes destituat sed frugum semper acervos | praebeat et pleno pinguia musta lacu* (1.1.9–10) with the vivid future of *distendet spicis horrea plena Ceres, | oblitus et musto feriet pede rusticus uvas, | dolia dum magni deficiantque lacus*(2.5.84–6).

unusual conception of the Underworld that awaits him (57–66), where
Venus will lead him to the Elysian Fields:

> hic choreae cantusque vigent, passimque vagantes
> dulce sonant tenui gutture carmen aves;
> fert casiam non culta seges, totosque per agros
> floret odoratis terra benigna rosis.
>
> (1.3.59–62)

The Saturnian Age, when all things grew unattended, has been transferred to the Underworld, where love and song thrive as well. It is
notable here that the dramatic occasion of the poem (war and death)
has led to two thoughts of happiness in the country, neither of which are
intended to be taken as more than dreams immediately dismissed, both
equally impossible. The fifth poem is again a lament by the unhappy
lover, whose magic has failed, in which occurs the well-known passage
(19–36) of Tibullus' vision of love in the country: *at mihi felicem vitam. . .
fingebam demens* (19–20). Delia is to superintend the farm, delighting
(presumably) in her simple tasks, and there too Messalla will come, for
whom, with the utmost respect, Delia will select the finest apples from
the trees. The scene unites war and the real world (in the figure of Messalla) and love in a perfect resolution – perfect as long as Tibullus can let
his imagination rule: *haec mihi fingebam, quae nunc Eurusque Notusque |
iactat odoratos vota per Armenios* (35–6). This is the same dream of love in
the country (though expanded to include Messalla in its vision of har-
mony) as had been dismissed in a similar situation in the second poem:

> ipse boves mea si tecum modo Delia possim
> iungere et in solito pascere monte pecus,
> et te dum liceat teneris retinere lacertis,
> mollis et inculta sit mihi somnus humo.
>
> (1.2.71–4)

Each of these three poems may be seen as a demonstration of the in-
effectiveness of the various resources at the disposal of the elegiac poet,
abandoned one after the other.[1] We should, I think, be reminded of
Gallus in the Tenth Eclogue in order to appreciate what Tibullus is

---

[1] We have here concentrated on only one topic, Tibullus' visions of the *rura*, and on that
only in outline. The inadequacy of other elegiac positions can be shown to have been
Tibullus' purpose in most other poems in the first book, and lies behind the fact that
Tibullus, 'with conscious self-irony, at times "undercuts" the emotional effect he has
been creating' (Newman, *Augustus and the New Poetry*, 387, referring to an observation
by Elder). For instance, the amatory instruction offered by Priapus with full-blown poetic
pomposity in 1.4 is shown to be impossible in at least three convolutions in six couplets
at the end of the poem.

doing here: it seems likely that rural, or even pastoral, love had been a topic of some importance in Gallus' *Amores*.[1]

The last poem of the book serves a purpose similar to the 'overture': important themes are resumed and given their final significance. The poem opens with a variation on the *primus inventor* topic, suggesting the end of the Saturnian Age and resultant wealth, war, and death (1–10). Again in this poem temporal particles (*tunc...nunc...*, 11 and 13) emphasize the contrast between the pastoral past and present war and introduce Tibullus himself, about to go off to war and possible death (*nunc ad bella trahor...*, 13). As in 1.3, the thought of death brings to mind the *patrii Lares* (15–18), and the next lines present rural simplicity and religion (19–28). Thus far there has been nothing unusual or unexpected in Tibullus' development of these associations, but following the reintroduction of war and death at lines 33–4, he explicitly denies a previous conception of the Underworld: *non seges est infra, non vinea culta...* (35). A similar situation in the third poem had produced the fantasy of a unique Underworld (*fert casiam non culta seges...*, 1.3.61) in which Saturnian peace in a self-sufficient countryside was to be the final reward for the elegiac poet. The explicit denial of that fantasy leads in the last half of the tenth poem to the resolution of an entire sequence of similar elegiac fantasies: *quin potius laudandus hic est quem prole parata | occupat in parva pigra senecta casa* (39–40). In the following lines (41–50) the description of the *rura* is identical in spirit to the first half of the first poem: again this is no Arcadia, but rather a real Italian farm with its animals, ploughing, wine-making, and tools; there is a reality in these scenes, too, that contrasts sharply both with such visions as that of Delia and Messalla in the country (1.5.19–36) or with Saturnian rural peace. All is dependent upon peace (*interea pax arva colat. pax candida primum | duxit araturos sub iuga curva boves...*, 45–6), a peace which may or may not exist: the only wars are to be those of Venus (53–66), and from these Tibullus may be disassociating himself in the final couplet: *at nobis, Pax alma, veni spicamque teneto | profluat et pomis candidus ante sinus*.[2]

---

[1] We can catch a glimpse of the pastoral setting of Gallus' treatment of the Acontius and Cydippe story and of the landscape of Milanion's labors of love, though we may suspect that much more was made of the country in his elegies. But in the Tenth Eclogue we cannot really distinguish pastoral touches appropriately Virgilian from those which may have pointed to Gallan elegy. Bréguet (*REL* 26 (1948), 212) sums up an old hypothesis: 'je croirais volontiers que, si Virgile mêle à la plainte de Gallus quelques motifs bucoliques, cela n'est pas seulement pour conserver l'harmonie de son poème, mais parce que ce n'est pas en contradiction avec les élégies de Gallus; comme Tibulle qui fut son "successeur", nous dit Ovide, Gallus peut avoir fait place dans ses vers à des motifs de la poésie bucolique.'

[2] On *Pax* in this poem Solmsen (*Hermes* 90 (1962), 297–9) should be consulted; he notes,

The last half of the tenth poem thus completes a full circle. The book had begun with a description of rural life which then in the second half of the poem was subjected to distortion with the entry both of elegiac topics and of such themes as war and death. The following poems then develop topics and themes which increase the tension without offering any solution: the elegiac poet can find no satisfactory resolution to the problems caused by love, nor can he deal with other issues within the terms demanded by his conventions.[1] Conflicts and tensions are finally resolved by the return to Tibullus' farm, a setting no longer Arcadian or existing only in an imagined prehistory, but a real possibility if only peace were assured.

The book is the product of its time, both poetically and in matter, and contains in its resolution all the elements Tibullus combined later in 2.5, when peace had come to seem no longer a hope but a reality. Tibullus is very much an Augustan poet and played an important part in the transformation of poetic expression. He offers us the means of correcting a view that is still, owing to our reaction against the nineteenth- and early twentieth-century outlook, prevalent, that Maecenas' poets were somehow coerced into writing propaganda for the new regime. Tibullus was subjected to no such pressure,[2] yet his work reflects the same doubts and concerns that occupied Virgil, Horace, and Propertius. If what can be called 'national themes' are much less obtrusive in Tibullus, the reason is simply that in every way he is so unobtrusive. J. W. Mackail called him 'a Virgil without the genius',[3] with more truth than he was ready to admit.

among other valuable observations, that 'Tibullus is for our knowledge the first of the Augustan poets, and may well be the first of all Roman poets, who gave the idea of *pax* a place in poetry.'

[1] A great deal, of course, has been left unsaid in this outline of Tibullan elegy, but I hope that this sketch of the poet will allow details to be supplied.

[2] It is perhaps for this reason that scholars have been reluctant to see any 'political' significance in his poetry, to the extent of ignoring 2.5.

[3] *Latin Literature* (New York, 1895), 130.

8

Conclusions

Our subject has been 'Augustan poetry as a natural growth in the soil prepared by Catullus'. We may summarize here certain observations and conclusions that have recurred in detached contexts and changing perspectives in the preceding pages.

Perhaps our most important theme has been the process whereby Augustan poetry finally became fully Roman. Old Italic verse at Rome did not survive the arrival of literature. We know next to nothing, for instance, of Atellan farce or the *versus Fescennini*; even Cicero appears ignorant of the old songs celebrating the *laudes clarorum virorum* Cato had known about; and the *versus quadratus* and the Saturnian measure had only a brief and fundamentally altered existence after the new literary awareness that came as a by-product of Rome's struggle with Carthage.[1] Ennius' introduction of the Muses, the *poeta*, and the Homeric hexameter necessarily expelled the *Camenae*, the *vates*, and native verse forms: it also meant that the goal of Latin poetry from its beginning as literature was to be artificiality. For almost a century and a half Latin poets (far more so than, for instance, the dramatists) were to be occupied with the perfection of artificiality; the higher the genre, the more essential it was that the manner and matter of Greek verse be made to prevail, whatever the cost.

To regard the Alexandrianism of the neoterics as the discovery or exploitation of artificiality is a serious misconception that obscures the very different contribution Catullus and his associates actually made: theirs was the first step in restoring to poetry what was Roman. Callimachus did not provide them simply with yet another territory to be conquered which in turn, as Horace saw, would take captive the victor;[2] had this been so, there would have been far more of Callimachus obvious

---

[1] As Licinus somewhat inaccurately, but revealingly, saw it, *Poenico bello secundo Musa pinnato gradu | intulit se bellicosam in Romuli gentem feram* (FPL p. 44 Morel). On Atellan farce and Fescennine verse, the *locus classicus* is Livy 7.2; and on the *laudes clarorum virorum*, Cic. *Brut.* 19.75, *Tusc.* 1.2.3, 4.2.3, Varro quoted by Nonius (s.v. *assa voce*, pp. 107–8 Lindsay). On the *versus quadratus* see E. Fraenkel, 'Die Vorgeschichte der versus quadratus', *Hermes* 62 (1927), 357–70 (=*Kleine Beiträge*, vol. 2, 11–24); and on the Saturnian, most recently, A. T. Cole, 'The Saturnian Verse', *YCS* 21 (1969), 3–73.

[2] *Graecia capta ferum victorem cepit...*, *Epist.* 2.1.156.

and prominent in Catullus' poetry than there is. What the Alexandrians did offer was principle and example. At the beginning of the third century B.C. Greek poetry had been subjugated to an overwhelming literary past: the freedom won by Callimachus was necessarily brief, but how he had achieved it was as clear from his technique as from the poetic principles he proclaimed. The individuality of the Alexandrian scholar-poet showed the neoterics how Latin poetry could likewise overcome its subjection to Greek precedent. As we saw in the first chapter, the neoterics discovered the poet's place both in his own poetry and in a literary tradition: for the first time Latin poetry had become Roman and a living part of the literary past, both personal and traditional.

If we think for a moment of the transformation of the pastoral landscape in the poetry of the period, we can see clearly what was involved. Gallus had taken the pastoral setting for his Acontius and Linus directly from Callimachus and (as we can understand from certain correspondences in the *Eclogues*, Propertius, and Tibullus) had made free use of other pastoral suggestions. We have inferred that such scenes presented landscape in sympathy with the unhappy lover, literally responsive to his laments, warm and receptive, and that Linus came to be the divine archetypal poet of the pastoral world. In the *Eclogues* Virgil recognizes the power of the pastoral mode of thought to transform reality: his Corydon, for instance, leaving shade and somnolence to sing his lament alone in the heat of mid-day, finally returns to its peace and another lover. What pastoral poetry offers is a means of transforming reality into something receptive and comforting, but precisely because it is imagination rather than understanding its failure is inevitable, as the last two poems of the Eclogue Book make clear.

Virgil was not content, as perhaps Gallus had been, to concern himself with literary abstractions. The Fourth Eclogue, like Horace's Sixteenth Epode, finds an order in the projection of an unreal future, a Never Never Land open to a pastoral poet but basically as unsatisfactory as Corydon's shade or Tityrus' beech tree. There could be hope, but there was little chance of its realization. After Antony's departure from Italy, however, and especially shortly after Actium, what had been hope became expectation, and the landscape of the pastoral imagination became the countryside of Italy. It was possible now to accept the real world on its own terms: the *Georgics* deals with violence and peace, struggle and contentment, as they actually exist. The farmer's labors may be swept away by natural disaster, and the struggle may be continual, but the possibility of peace is at least apparent, if not obtainable. In the *Georgics* too is a new understanding of the past, not original with Virgil, but to which he gave new shape and purpose: the pastoral landscape became a golden age, the first stage in an historical evolution. What is most significant about this innovation is that the land of peace and natural order is an historical reality and had once existed in Italy itself: no longer need it be a literary topic (as in Catullus 64), nor an imaginative projection into an impossibly distant future such as the Blessed Isles far across a sea never to be sailed upon.

In the last chapter we discussed the final stage in the transformation of the pastoral landscape. Whether it is to be found or not in Tibullus' poetry is a question due precisely to the new form it had taken. In the few years following Octavian's return to Italy after Actium peace had become a reality in which even the struggle inherent in the *Georgics* no longer existed: Tibullus' landscape is as real as Virgil's, but is without Virgil's *labor*; yet in Tibullus' first book it is still a somewhat tentative projection, and only in the last poem of the book does it seem to have been pruned of literary qualifications. In the *Aeneid* and in Tibullus 2.5 the historical realization of the pastoral world found its final expression. The kingdoms of Latinus and Evander are presented by Virgil with many, often rather strange and incongruous, evocations of the pastoral world, and in the Latium of their day vestiges of Saturnus' rule are still to be found.[1] Strife and chaos begin with Aeneas – and will end with Julius Caesar. Tibullus in 2.5 takes this historical outline of the *Aeneid* one step further in making explicit what in Virgil had been implicit, though often a firm suggestion: that the peace existing before Aeneas' arrival had actually returned to Italy.

We have viewed the development of elegy as a similar, parallel process. Catullus 68 is the one poem most like Augustan elegy, but in it the central focus is provided by myth rather than by the personality of the poet himself: it can thus be termed objective rather than subjective and is thus more like 64 than like the polymetrics. Its objectivity, however, provides a capacity for that abstract expression through which the individuality of the poet and his Roman world can be most deeply and truly reflected. From what we know of the subjects treated by Gallus in what almost certainly was elegy, and from what we can gather (from Propertius 1.20 and passages in other poems) of Gallus' style and manner, it seems likely that such objectivity and abstract expression were retained and exploited in his first elegies, and it was for this character that

---

[1] Incongruity was inevitable: in these same people Virgil had to find and create military valor and Homeric exploits worthy of opposing the Trojans.

his elegy was subsequently noted. It also seems likely, however, that he began to change the fundamental nature of his elegy. The hero or heroine typical of Alexandrian mythological narrative, given to long speeches of self-examination, yielded place to the poet himself, just as in the Tenth Eclogue Gallus becomes his Milanion and Acontius: the monologue of the mythological lover becomes the elegy of the poet. The poet, then, 'yields to Love'.

This was the process Virgil represented in the Tenth Eclogue as the futility of both knowledge and imagination before human passion, taking the poet Gallus as his *exemplum* of this failure. It was here that Propertius began: his *Monobiblos* was the first book of subjective love-elegy, though we must remember that subjectivity is properly a manner of writing, not a mirror reflecting the poet's own experience. Propertius assumed the role of the poet-lover and set himself at the center of his stage, appropriately modifying his diction as well as his presentation. The limitations of his assumed role, however, soon became too restricting: not only were the possibilities of personal amatory situations soon exhausted, but it is also clear that his role becomes most oppressive precisely during those years when the necessity to speak for Augustan Rome was most deeply felt. To put aside his position as poet-lover was to abandon his claim to originality as an elegist and at the same time to appear to deny his pretense as a Callimachean poet: it was thus only with some difficulty that he finally emerged as the *Romanus Callimachus*.

Propertius' last book should be regarded as a reversion to type, not as an uncharacteristic innovation in the development of Latin elegy. Its manner and presentation is thoroughly objective in the same way Gallan elegy had been, at least at first: the difference lies in its Augustan subject matter. Tibullus' poetry, too, makes it seem likely that the amatory element in Latin elegy was a secondary characteristic to which we have given undue attention. Erotic psychology was not an end in itself in Catullus' presentation of Ariadne, and even his Lesbia serves as a focus for more than personal amatory experience; in Gallus' elegy we may assume that erotic narrative was a proper convention appropriate to the genre but did not limit the range of human experiences he intended to express. Throughout his first book Tibullus played with and discarded in turn the conventions and manners of the elegist until he arrived in the last elegy of the book at a strikingly contemporary position, tentatively accepting the possibility of peace in the Italian countryside; in 2.5 the process is complete. Catullus' epyllion was the first fusion of the perfection of literary artificiality with the Roman world, intellectual and spiritual, but it was the Augustan achievement that provided the opportunity and necessity for its supreme realization.

We have followed too the parallel transformation of the position of the poet. Gallus' reception by the Muses had been purely literary, its purpose to establish the poet in a genealogy reaching back to the Callimachean Apollo: it expressed a new position, but in a manner essentially Greek. It was Horace who saw how the terms expressing the poet's position could be altered to reflect the spirit and purpose of Augustan poetry after Augustus' final victory. The scene of the poet's reception becomes Italian, his Apollo is the god of Actium, and his Muses are the old Camenae. As poetry became more Roman in content and spirit, its forms remained the same. The *Aeneid* is very much an Alexandrian poem; Horace, as much as Propertius, never intended to disavow his Callimachean or neoteric inheritance. The initiated or received poet, enjoying the favors of the Muses and Apollo and the tokens of divine protection, became finally not only the voice of the new order but the Pindaric adviser.

The culmination of this process lasted only a brief moment. The sudden loss of vigor and power in Augustan poetry coincides, almost, with the death of Virgil and Tibullus. The desiccation that followed was not due to the stultifying effects of the developed style. Ovid was not restricted in expression by the necessity of ending his pentameters with an iambic word or by the need he felt to structure his couplets with artful patterns of anaphora. The Silver epic poets did not write drily simply because of the utter domination of Virgil's precedent, nor was Statius in his *Silvae* led so often to the ridiculous or vapid simply by his tasteless obedience to the demands of the learned Muse. As we have seen, it was the discovery of a new style that enabled the neoterics to speak for themselves, and it was through the same principles of style, developed and exploited, that the Augustans were able to express such a range of experience. That poets afterwards continued to express themselves and to state their position in a similar manner was inevitable, given what had been achieved in such a short time: as we noted much earlier, after Gallus and Virgil began to write, there was only one course left for subsequent poets to follow.

What caused the abrupt and continuing barrenness was simply the sudden loss of purpose. Virgil and Horace had grown up and reached maturity during the years when the final stage of civil war had been at its fiercest, and the youth of Propertius and Tibullus had been passed in this same period. Ovid, however, born in 43 B.C., was still a boy in the year Actium was fought: his years of intellectual maturity thus fall within the time when peace had become a reality, and having experienced nothing else, he can hardly be expected to have reacted with the relief and gratitude towards the new regime felt by the older poets. They were ready to imagine (at least) the restoration of a golden age and to forgive or overlook the shortcomings or excesses of Augustus' politics.[1] Ovid was not, and may in fact have been more perceptive and realistic. A superb versifier, with more native ability and a surer poetic instinct than either Propertius or Tibullus, he nevertheless could not reach the intensity which the times granted them. A note of irony is inevitably heard when he deals with Augustan themes or with the Italian past, and for him the role of *vates* can only be a source of deprecating amusement. It is noteworthy, though, that at the same time his poetry is otherwise eminently Alexandrian, in his subjects, in the forms he writes in, and in expression.

The achievement of the Augustan poets is due to the discovery and development of a means of expression at a time when events demanded the poet's understanding. For a few relatively short years experience and art coincided, and the increasing intensity of the one was met and reflected by the sudden maturity and developing complexity of the other.

[1] But in Book IV of the *Odes*, and especially in the *Carmen Saeculare*, there is likewise a detectable note of weariness, a somewhat mechanical manipulation of themes and ideas that had only a few years before been spontaneous and alive.

List of works cited

Abbreviations

AJP	*American Journal of Philology*
ALL	*Archiv für lateinische Lexikographie und Grammatik*
AUMLA	*Journal of the Australasian Universities Language and Literature Association*
BICS	*Bulletin of the Institute of Classical Studies, University of London*
CJ	*Classical Journal*
CP	*Classical Philology*
CQ	*Classical Quarterly*
CR	*Classical Review*
FGH	*Die Fragmente der griechischen Historiker*, ed. F. Jacoby
FPL	*Fragmenta Poetarum Latinorum*, ed. W. Morel
GRBS	*Greek, Roman and Byzantine Studies*
HSCP	*Harvard Studies in Classical Philology*
JP	*Journal of Philology*
Mnem.	*Mnemosyne*
Mus. Helv.	*Museum Helveticum*
PCPhS	*Proceedings of the Cambridge Philological Society*
Philol.	*Philologus*
RE	Pauly–Wissowa–Kroll, *Real-Encyclopädie der classischen Altertumswissenschaft*
REA	*Revue des études anciennes*
REL	*Revue des études latines*
RhM	*Rheinisches Museum*
Riv. di Fil.	*Rivista di Filologia e di Istruzione Classica*
Roscher	*Ausführliches Lexicon der griechischen und römischen Mythologie*, ed. W. H. Roscher
SIFC	*Studi Italiani di Filologia Classica*
ThLL	*Thesaurus Linguae Latinae*
YCS	*Yale Classical Studies*

Alfonsi, L. 'L'elegia di Gallo', *Riv. di Fil.* 21 (1943), 46–56.
  'Euforione e l'elegia', *Miscellanea di Studi Alessandrini* (Turin, 1963), 455–68.
Allen, A. W. '"Sincerity" and the Roman Elegists', *CP* 45 (1950), 145–60.
  'Sunt qui Propertium Malint', *Critical Essays on Roman Literature: Elegy and Lyric*, ed. J. P. Sullivan (Cambridge, Mass., 1962), 107–48.
Baker, R. J. 'Propertius III 1, 1–6 Again. Intimations of Immortality?', *Mnem.* 21 (1968), 35–9.
Bardon, H. 'Les Élégies de Cornélius Gallus', *Latomus* 8 (1949), 217–28.
  La littérature latine inconnue, vol. 2 (Paris, 1956).

Barigazzi, A. 'Euforione e Cornelio Gallo', *Maia* 3 (1950), 16–25.

Becker, C. 'Virgils Eklogenbuch', *Hermes* 83 (1955), 314–49.

Boucher, J.-P. *Caius Cornélius Gallus*, Bibliothèque de la Faculté des Lettres de Lyon, XI (Paris, 1966).

Bowersock, G. W. 'A Date in the *Eighth Eclogue*', *HSCP* 75 (1971), 73–80.

Bréguet, E. 'Les Élégies de Gallus', *REL* 26 (1948), 204–14.

Brown, E. L. *Numeri Vergiliani*, Coll. Latomus 63 (1963).

Büchner, K. 'P. Vergilius Maro', *RE* 8.A.1 (1955), 1021–264.

Bühler, W. *Die Europa des Moschos*, Hermes Einzelschriften 13 (1960).

Butler, H. E. and Barber, E. A. *The Elegies of Propertius* (Oxford, 1933).

Cairns, F. 'Propertius i.18 and Callimachus, *Acontius and Cydippe*', *CR* 19 (1969), 131–4.

Camps, W. A. *Propertius Elegies*, Books I, II, III, IV (Cambridge, 1961, 1967, 1966, 1965).

Clausen, W. V. '*Silva Coniecturarum*', *AJP* 76 (1955), 47–62.

'Callimachus and Latin Poetry', *GRBS* 5 (1964), 181–96.

rev. of P. J. Enk, *Propertii Liber Secundus*, in *AJP* 86 (1965), 95–101.

'On the Date of the *First Eclogue*', *HSCP* 76 (1972), 201–5.

Cole, A. T. 'The Saturnian Verse', *YCS* 21 (1969), 3–73.

Coleman, R. 'Gallus, the Bucolics, and the Ending of the Fourth Georgic', *AJP* 83 (1962), 55–71.

Commager, S. *The Odes of Horace* (New Haven, 1962).

Conington, J. P. *Vergili Maronis Opera*, 5th ed. revised by H. Nettleship, vol. 1 (London, 1898).

Curran, L. C. 'Vision and Reality in Propertius 1.3', *YCS* 19 (1966), 189–207.

Day, A. A. *The Origins of Latin Love-Elegy* (Oxford, 1938).

Della Corte *et al.* 'Euforione e i poeti latini' (discussions by Della Corte, Treves, Barigazzi, Bartoletti, Alfonsi), *Maia* 17 (1965), 158–76.

Duff, J. W. *A Literary History of Rome from the Origins to the Close of the Golden Age*, 3rd ed. (New York, 1953).

Earl, D. C. *The Political Thought of Sallust* (Cambridge, 1961).

Elder, J. P. '*Non iniussa cano*: Virgil's Sixth Eclogue', *HSCP* 65 (1961), 109–25.

'Tibullus: *Tersus atque Elegans*', *Critical Essays on Roman Literature: Elegy and Lyric*, ed. J. P. Sullivan (Cambridge, Mass., 1962), 65–105.

Enk, P. J. 'Lucubrationes Propertianae', *Mnem.* 3 (1936), 149–64.

Sex. Propertii Elegiarum Liber I (*Monobiblos*), 2 vols. (Leiden, 1946).

Fedeli, P. 'Osservazioni sullo stile di Properzio', *SIFC* 41 (1969), 81–94.

Fraenkel, E. 'Die Vorgeschichte des versus quadratus', *Hermes* 62 (1927), 357–70 (= *Kleine Beiträge*, vol. 2, 11–24).

Horace (Oxford, 1957).

Gagé, J. *Apollon Romain* (Paris, 1955).

Granarolo, J. *D'Ennius à Catulle* (Paris, 1971).

Gow, A. S. F. *Theocritus*, 2 vols. (Cambridge, 1965).

Guillemin, A. 'Properce, de Cynthie aux Poèmes Romains', *REL* 28 (1950), 182–93.

Heinze, R. 'Der Zyklus der Römeroden', *Vom Geist des Römertums* (Stuttgart, 1960), 190–204.

Holland, L. A. *Janus and the Bridge* (Rome, 1961).

Housman, A. E. 'Emendationes Propertianae', *JP* 16 (1888), 1–35.

Hubaux, J. *Les Thèmes Bucoliques dans la Poésie Latine* (Brussels, 1930).

Jachmann, G. 'Vergils Sechste Ekloge', *Hermes* 58 (1923), 288–304.

Jacoby, F. 'Zur Entstehung der römischen Elegie', *RhM* 60 (1905), 38–105.

Jacques, J. M. 'Sur un acrostiche d'Aratos', *REA* 62 (1960), 48–61.

Jocelyn, H. D. 'Horace, *Odes* i 12.33–6', *Antichthon* 5 (1971), 68–76.

Jones, C. P. '*Tange Chloen semel arrogantem*', *HSCP* 75 (1971), 81–3.

Kiessling, A. and Heinze, R. Q. *Horatius Flaccus Oden und Epoden*, 12th ed. (Dublin/ Zürich, 1966).

Klingner, F. *Virgil* (Zürich, 1967).

La Penna, A. *Properzio* (Florence, 1951).

Leo, F. 'Vergil und die Ciris', *Hermes* 37 (1902), 14–55.

Lonie, I. M. 'Propertius and the Alexandrians', *AUMLA* 11 (1959), 17–34.

Luck, G. 'The Cave and the Source', *CQ* 7 (1957), 175–9.

   The Latin Love Elegy (New York, 1960).

Lyne, R. O. A. M. 'Propertius and Cynthia: Elegy 1.3', *PCPhS* 16 (1970), 60–78.

Mackail, J. W. *Latin Literature* (New York, 1895).

Mendell, C. W. *Latin Poetry: The New Poets and the Augustans* (New Haven, 1965).

Morel, W. *Fragmenta Poetarum Latinorum* (Leipzig, 1927).

Moritz, L. A. 'Well-matched Lovers (Propertius 1.5)', *CP* 62 (1967), 106–8.

Newman, J. K. *Augustus and the New Poetry*, Coll. Latomus 88 (1967).

   The Concept of Vates in Augustan Poetry, Coll. Latomus 89 (1967).

Nisbet, R. G. M. and Hubbard, M. *A Commentary on Horace: Odes, Book* 1 (Oxford, 1970).

Norden, E. *Ennius und Vergilius* (Leipzig/Berlin, 1915).

   P. Vergilius Maro Aeneis Buch VI, 4th ed. (Stuttgart, 1957).

Ogilvie, R. M. *A Commentary on Livy Books 1–5* (Oxford, 1965).

Otis, B. 'Propertius' Single Book', *HSCP* 70 (1965), 1–44.

Page, T. E. *P. Vergili Maronis Bucolica et Georgica* (London, 1965).

Paratore, E. 'Spunti Lucreziani nelle "Georgiche"', *Atene e Roma* 7 (1939), 177–202.

Pasquali, G. *Orazio Lirico* (Florence, 1920).

Pfeiffer, R. 'Ein Neues Altersgedicht des Kallimachos', *Hermes* 63 (1928), 302–41.

   Callimachus, 2 vols. (Oxford, 1949, 1953).

   History of Classical Scholarship (Oxford, 1968).

Pillinger, H. E. 'Some Callimachean Influences on Propertius, Book 4', *HSCP* 73 (1969), 171–99.

Platnauer, M. *Latin Elegiac Verse* (Cambridge, 1951).

Pöschl, V. 'Poetry and Philosophy in Horace', in *The Poetic Tradition*, ed. D. C. Allen and H. T. Rowell (Baltimore, 1968), 47–61.

   Horazische Lyrik (Heidelberg, 1970).

Putnam, M. C. J. 'The Art of Catullus 64', *HSCP* 65 (1961), 165–205.

   Virgil's Pastoral Art (Princeton, 1970).

Quinn, K. *Latin Explorations* (London, 1963).

Rand, E. K. 'Catullus and the Augustans', *HSCP* 17 (1906), 15–30.

Reitzenstein, E. 'Zur Stiltheorie des Kallimachos', *Festschrift Richard Reitzenstein* (Leipzig/Berlin, 1931), 23–69.

Reitzenstein, R., 'Properz Studien', *Hermes* 31 (1896), 185–220.

Rose, H. J. *The Eclogues of Vergil* (Berkeley, 1942).

Ross, D. O. *Style and Tradition in Catullus* (Cambridge, Mass., 1969).

Rothstein, M. *Propertius Sextus Elegien*, 2 vols. (reprinted, Dublin/Zürich, 1966).

Shackleton Bailey, D. R. *Propertiana* (Cambridge, 1956).

Skutsch, F. *Aus Vergils Frühzeit* (Leipzig, 1901).
  Gallus und Vergil (Leipzig, 1906).

Skutsch, O. 'Zu Vergils Eklogen', *RhM* 99 (1956), 193–201.
  'The Structure of the Propertian Monobiblos', *CP* 58 (1963), 238–9.
  Studia Enniana (London, 1968).
  'Metrical Variations and some Textual Problems in Catullus', *BICS* 16 (1969), 38–43.

Smith, K. F. *The Elegies of Albius Tibullus* (New York, 1913).

Solmsen, F. 'Three Elegies of Propertius' First Book', *CP* 57 (1962), 73–88.
  'Tibullus as an Augustan Poet', *Hermes* 90 (1962), 295– 325.

Spoerri, W. 'Zur Kosmogonie in Vergils 6. Ekloge', *Mus. Helv.* 27 (1970), 144–63.

Stewart, Z. 'The Song of Silenus', *HSCP* 64 (1959), 179–205.

Sullivan, J. P. 'Propertius: A Preliminary Essay', *Arion* 5 (1966).

Swanson, D. C. *The Names in Roman Verse* (Madison, 1967).

Thomson, D. F. S. 'Aspects of Unity in Catullus 64', *CJ* 57 (1961), 49–57.

Tränkle, H. *Die Sprachkunst des Properz und die Tradition der Lateinischer Dichtersprache*, Hermes Einzelschriften 15 (1960).

Traglia, A. *Poetae Novi*, Poetarum Latinorum Reliquiae vol. 8 (Rome, 1962).

Vahlen, J. *Ennianae Poesis Reliquiae*, 2nd ed. (Leipzig, 1928).

Wagenvoort, H. *Studies in Roman Literature, Culture and Religion* (Leiden, 1956).

Watkins, C. 'An Indo-European Construction in Greek and Latin', *HSCP* 71 (1966), 115–19.

West, M. L. *Hesiod Theogony* (Oxford, 1966).

Wickham, E. C. *The Works of Horace*, vol. 1 (Oxford, 1877).

Wilamowitz-Moellendorf, U. von, 'Die griechische Heldensage. II.', *Sitzungsber. der Berl. Akad. der Wiss.* 1925, 214–42.

Wilkinson, L. P. *Horace and his Lyric Poetry* (Cambridge, 1946).
  'The Continuity of Propertius ii.13', *CR* 16 (1966), 141–4.

Williams, G. *Tradition and Originality in Roman Poetry* (Oxford, 1968).

Wimmel, W. *Kallimachos in Rom*, Hermes Einzelschriften 16 (1960).

Wiseman, T. P. *Catullan Questions* (Leicester, 1969).

Zinn, E. *Der Wortakzent in den lyrischen Versen des Horaz* (Munich, 1940).

Indexes

Index rerum notabiliorum

Acontius and Cydippe, *see* Gallus
acrostic signatures, in Aratus and Virgil, 28–9
Aganippe (*fons Permessi*), 33, 97–8, 117–18, 138
ἀγρυπνίη (-ος), 22, 29 n.2
Alexandrianism, Latin, *see* neotericism
amicitia in Catullus, 9–15
antrum, 63, 151
Apollo, 27, 98, 157
Apollo and Calliope: in Virgil, 28; in Propertius, 59–60, 115–16, 121–2; in Horace, 143
Apollonius Rhodius, 25–6, 28
appositional construction, neoteric, 69 n.2, 156
Aratus, 24, 28–9, 30 n.3
archaic–epic diction and usage, 55, 61, 76–7, 78–9

Callimachus: his influence on neoterics, 6–7, 16, 18–19; Linus in, 22–3; his dream, 33, 150–1; terminology of in Propertius, 115, 123
Calliope, 138, 146 n.1; *see also* Apollo and Calliope
Calvus' *Io*, 57; *see also* neoteric poets
Camenae, 140 n.1, 146–9, 163
canon of Latin elegists in antiquity, 44–6, 101
Cato (*grammaticus*), school of?, 3
Catullus: his use of Callimachus, 6; his Lesbia, 8–15; the three groups of his poems characterized, 16–17, 47–8; his influence on later poets, 54–7, 101; *see also* neotericism, neoteric poets
Catulus, Lutatius, 4, 5, 15
Cicero, 3, 4, 13
Cinna's *Zmyrna*, 55; *see also* neoteric poets
cold *vs* heat, 93–6, 105
conflation of two myths, 38, 62
Conon (astronomer), 24, 28
Conon (mythographer), 22, 35
cosmogony, 25–7
cura = amica, 68–9
Cynthia: as Propertius' elegy, 35, 58–9, 70, 117, 122, 125; lessened role of in Bks *III–IV*, 125–6

deducere (*deductum*), 19, 26, 65–6, 134–5, 140
diminutives, 54, 76

elegy, Latin: origins of, 108–13; development of, 165–7
Ennius' *Musae*, 147
epanalepsis, 55
epic *vs* elegy, *see* recusatio
epyllion, 17, 78, 82, 108
Etymological aetiology, 22, 23, 25 n.1, 62, 69 n.1, 77 n.2, 146 n.2, 155–7
Euphorion, 28, 31, 40–3, 102

fagus, 72
Fauni, 24–5
'Filagrius', 42–3
furor, 60, 68, 91, 94, 95 n.2, 96, 111

Gallus: general importance of, 1–2; his Grynean Grove, 21, 31, 45, 79–80, 82, 86–7; his one surviving line, 39; and Euphorion, 40–6; and origins of elegy, 46–50; character of his elegy, 48–50; his Milanion, 61–5, 81, 82, 90–1, 93, 97–8, 100, 111, 166; his poetic style, 64, 79, 82, 101–2; *medicina* (*amoris*) in, 66–8, 91, 116; topic of natural solitude in, 68, 71–4, 77, 95; his Acontius, 72–4, 89, 95, 100, 164, 166; his elegies entitled *Amores*, 73, 89, 99; pastoral elements in, 74, 82, 85–6, 89, 161; his Hylas?, 79–81, 82; named by Propertius, 82–4, 102–3; development of his elegy, 99–106, 109–10, 165–6
geographical excursus, 76, 149–50
gracilis, 26, 34
Grynean Grove, *see* Gallus

Hebrus (river), 93
Hesiod: 'pipes' of, 21, 23; and 'scientific' poetry, 28, 70; his grove and springs, 32–5, 118–20
hymn (prayer) form, 149–50

173

Index locorum potiorum